AROUND MANHATTAN ISLAND

AROUND MANHATTAN ISLAND

AND

OTHER MARITIME TALES

OF NEW YORK

BRIAN J. CUDAHY

FORDHAM UNIVERSITY PRESS

New York

1997

Library of Congress Cataloging-in-Publication Data

Cudahy, Brian J.
    Around Manhattan Island and other maritime tales of New York / by
Brian J. Cudahy.
        p.   cm.
    Includes bibliographical references and index.
    ISBN 0-8232-1760-4 (hardcover).—ISBN 0-8232-1761-2 (pbk.)
    1. Harbors—New York (State)—New York—History—20th century.
I. Title.
HE554.N7C83   1997
387.1′09747′1—dc21   96-50263
                                                                                          CIP

Printed in the United States of America

Contents

Introduction

This book contains six different stories about six different maritime subjects, each involving the port of New York in a central and important way. A second theme common to all six stories—perhaps the only other one—is sheer personal interest on my part. I do not profess that these six tales deal with the six most central or important developments in the overall history of the port of New York. I simply assert they are six stories that I believe are interesting and deserve telling. The sequence in which they are told here is quite arbitrary.

Chapter 1 is a history of around-Manhattan Island sightseeing service and was written to help commemorate the fiftieth anniversary of the Circle Line in 1995. An earlier and somewhat shorter version of this chapter was published in the Fall 1995 issue of *Steamboat Bill.* I must acknowledge the encouragement that William Rau, that journal's editor, gave me in preparing the original version. I must also thank Joseph A. Moran, president of Circle Line–Statue of Liberty Ferry, Inc., for taking time to share his recollections of Circle Line's early days. Circle Line's current leadership—Chairman Karl Andren and President August Cerridini—were generous in discussing current policy and future plans. And for insights into actual Circle Line operations—both in the wheelhouse and below decks in the engine room—Captain Ken Cochran must be thanked for his assistance.

Two inanimate objects are also worthy of mention with respect to chapter 1: a red and white bicycle and a battered old rowboat. The bicycle was mine, and on it I would ride from my home in Flatbush to a place called Mill Basin, there to keep tabs on the Circle Line sightseeing fleet while the boats were laid up over the winter. Once, as winter was ending, my brother Roger and I decided we needed a closer look at the fleet, so we hired a rowboat at a marina along Flatbush Avenue. The owner of the marina was understandably perplexed when his two customers left the dock and, instead of heading out toward the open water of Jamaica Bay where the fish were biting, proceeded further inland into the brackish waters of Mill Basin.

Our trip proved to be quite rewarding. Because when we maneuvered the rowboat up close to where the sightseeing yachts were tied up, we saw something that couldn't be seen from our usual shoreside vantage point: an old surplus Coast Guard cutter. "I wonder what Circle Line is going to use that for?" we asked each other as we returned the rowboat to the marina. We would soon find out.

Chapter 2 is simply a vignette, a snapshot of a brief moment in the history of the port of New York. In July 1952, the brand new superliner *SS United States* sailed out of New York Harbor on her maiden voyage and totally obliterated all previous speed records on the North Atlantic Ocean. In more recent years, glorified speedboats have eclipsed the *United States*'s record-shattering transatlantic crossing. But this is of little consequence. The voyage we hear about in chapter 2 was the culmination—and the finale, as it turned out—of a glorious maritime tradition that involves the likes of the original *Mauritania*, the *Rex*, the *Normandie*, and the *Queen Mary*.

I am sorry to say that I was never fortunate enough to have sailed on the *United States*; I did, however, visit aboard her on several occasions during the 1950s while she was laying over in New York at Pier 86, and I watched her head out to sea on many occasions. If protracted plans to convert the *United States* into a cruise ship ever reach fruition, perhaps one day I will get to sail aboard this magnificent vessel, although as I write this, in the summer of 1996, such a possibility is so remote that it must be called a virtual impossibility.

Her most glorious moment, though, will always and ever be back in the summer of 1952, whe she steamed out of New York for the channel ports of Europe for the very first time.

Chapter 3 concerns the fireboats that have long protected the New York waterfront from a variety of perils. Today's fireboat fleet is a mere shadow of its former self, and that is because changing patterns of commerce around the port of New York have removed many of the fire-prone structures that once ensured work for the fireboats. Fewer wooden piers along the Manhattan waterfront, and less commercial traffic in the Hudson and East Rivers, mean fewer incidents that require the specialized assistance only a fireboat can provide.

I must acknowledge the awesome research into the history of the New York fireboats that my friend Al Trojanowicz has long been undertaking. My most important file of information about New York fireboats are personal letters from Al, a Supervising Dispatcher with the New York City Fire Department (FDNY). One day he will write a definitive history of this subject and we will be the richer for it.

I must also harken back to a marvelous Saturday morning in August 1954 when my father—a career member of the FDNY who served in the Marine Division for a short time—made arrangements for my brother and me to be in the pilothouse of *Fire Fighter* when she went out from Pier 1 to put on a water display and help welcome the Italian Line's new *Christoforo Columbo* on her maiden voyage into New York. "Engine 57 to citywide . . . leaving berth for a water display."

About our experience I will say this: We saw the *Christoforo Columbo* coming up the bay, and we saw her later heading up the Hudson. But while she was abreast of *Fire Fighter* off the Statue of Liberty, when we should have gotten our very best view of the new sister-ship to the year-old *Andrea Doria*, we didn't see a blessed thing. Because once the pilot told the engineer down below to "start the water," the display that *Fire Fighter* was throwing skyward from her deck monitors fell back and enveloped the wheelhouse in such a way that, despite the fact that it was a cloudless summer day, we were engulfed in a torrential downpour of monsoon proportions and couldn't see five feet beyond the wheelhouse window.

Chapter 4 deals with a long-departed New York maritime institution, the Iron Steamboat Company (1881–1932), whose graceful sidewheelers were once the principal link between Manhattan and a magical place called Coney Island. Harken back to the summers of 1955 and 1956 for the key acknowledgment with respect to this chapter. During those days I worked in the office of Steeplechase Park in Coney Island. One day, while talking to the man who ran Steeplechase—his name was James J. Onorato, but absolutely everybody called him "Jimmy the manager"—I learned about a file drawer in the upstairs office that contained material from the days when the "steamboats from New York" docked at the end of Steeplechase Pier.

"Go up and take a look at it, if you want to," Jimmy the manager said. Later, when I asked if I could borrow several photographs I found in the file drawer to have copy negatives made, he was most cooperative.

Chapter 5 tells a story that is a follow-on to something in chapter 1. In fact, it's something I learned about only while doing research for chapter 1. A vessel that makes a mere cameo appearance in the story of around-Manhattan Island sightseeing service is a little two-deck steamboat whose final name was *Observation*. After her brief sighseeing career was over, *Observation* kicked around the harbor for a variety of owners until she was purchased by the Forsyth family of Staten Island, around 1930. Several months later, in the depths of the Great Depression, the Forsyths were lucky enough to land a contract with the P. J. Carlin Construction Company to haul workers to a new city penitentiary Carlin was building on Rikers Island. On September 9, 1932, while making ther third trip of the morning out to Rikers Island, *Observation*'s boiler exploded and 72 of the workmen aboard the little steamer were killed.

This is a terrible story. Yet it is one that is filled with strange ironies. *Observation* exploded within yards of the spot where on June 15, 1904, the excursion boat *General Slocum* was beached after suffering an all-consuming fire. The disaster aboard *General Slocum* claimed 1,025 lives, the worst New York accident of all time, and one that has been written about often over the years. The tragedy aboard *Observation* deserves to be written about as well.

As to chapter 6: maritime historian John Maxtone-Graham has popularized the coinage "crossing and cruising" (see John Maxtone-Graham, *Crossing and Cruising* [New York: Scribners, 1992]). Maxtone-Graham has in mind the evolution in ocean travel from being primarily a means of basic transportation—crossing the North

Atlantic in order to get to Europe—to a more leisure-oriented activity where such things as one's destination aren't really all that important—cruising the Caribbean for seven days, for instance.

One oceangoing service very much associated with the port of New York has nicely survived the evolution from crossing to cruising and to this day retains an element of both. This is the 697-mile voyage to Bermuda. It can look back on a classic era when ships of the Furness Bermuda Line sailed for Hamilton twice each week from Pier 95 on the Hudson River. But while the typical Caribbean cruise ship on a leisurely sail out of Miami or Port Everglades today bears little relationship to the days when North Atlantic mailboats were the principal link between New York and Europe, when a vessel such as Norwegian Cruise Line's 1992-built *Dreamward* heads down the Hudson and out to sea today bound for Bermuda, the days of the Furness Bermuda Line can be effectively recaptured—maybe even surpassed.

Several acknowledgments are in order for chapter 6. Nan Godet and Karen Ashbury at the Bermuda Maritime Museum provided considerable material to help tell the Furness, Withy part of the story. Within the fortresslike walls of the museum is to be found a treasure trove of information about steamship service between New York and Bermuda. Fran Szick of Norwegian Cruise Line most generously arranged an introduction to Staff Captain Jostein Kalvoy aboard *MS Dreamward*, and Captain Kalvoy was patient beyond belief in answering my questions about contemporary cruise ship operations. His invitation to join him on the bridge early on the morning of August 26, 1995, as *Dreamward* sailed into the port of New York on our return trip from Bermuda, resulted in an experience I will remember for the rest of my life.

A final acknowledgment with respect to New York–Bermuda steamship service must go to my late parents. On the morning of Saturday, March 2, 1935, they were joined in matrimony in Brooklyn. Later that afternoon they sailed out of New York aboard *Monarch of Bermuda* and over the years would frequently talk about their honeymoon voyage to and from Hamilton. "Down on the *Monarch*, back on the *Queen*" was the way my mother always put it. The fact that New York–Bermuda steamship service remains an important maritime constant explains why, more than sixty years later, I was able to retrace their 1935 voyage.

All of the six stories that follow contain notes with suggestions for further reading. The stories also include one or more appendices comprising various kinds of technical information; these are to be found at the end of the book (before the Index).

Finally, one acknowledgement that pertains to several of the stories involves assistance I continually receive from Angie Vande-reedt of the National Archives, who has searched out official enrollment certificates for many of the vessels discussed in the various chapters.

So join me, please, in these six tales of six different aspects of the maritime heritage of New York Harbor.

Burke, Virginia
July 1996

AROUND MANHATTAN ISLAND

Circle Line XV heads down the Hudson River on the around-Manhattan tour. The 1913-built Woolworth Building is flanked by the twin towers of the World Trade Center.

1

Around Manhattan Island: Circle Line's First Fifty Years

On June 15, 1995, several weeks after the world at large had commemorated the fiftieth anniversary of the end of World War II in Europe, a celebration was held on Pier 83 and the Hudson River in the City of New York to mark a different kind of golden jubilee. Circle Line—a company whose stock in trade is the operation of narrated three-hour cruises around Manhattan Island—took a few moments out from the ordinary routine of business to call attention to the fact that its sightseeing boats carried their first paying passengers in the same year World War II came to an end.

Appropriate speeches and a spirited rendition of "Old Man River" took place under a tent on shore. Mayor Rudolph Giuliani was on hand to intone a proclamation saying that June 15, 1995, is hereby and forever declared to be Circle Line Appreciation Day. And *Fire Fighter*—the city's veteran fireboat that has protected lives and property along the New York waterfront for more years than Circle Line has been in business—came by to deliver a dramatic water display with her powerful deck monitors.[1]

To top it all off, several hundred invited guests boarded two of the company's sightseeing boats—one of which was unofficially rechristened *Circle Line 50* for the day—and were treated to a leisurely luncheon cruise down to the Statue of Liberty and back under a delightfully blue spring sky that was filled from horizon to horizon with big fluffy white clouds.

But while Circle Line itself has been in business for half of a century, and around-Manhattan Island sightseeing cruises of one sort or another have been continuously operating for almost ninety years, the little slice of New York maritime history and heritage such service represents is not terribly well known.

Perhaps this is understandable. During the early years, Circle Line sightseeing yachts were overshadowed in New York by larger excursion boats operating for the likes of the Hudson River Day Line, the Meseck Line, the Wilson Line, and others. Furthermore, in a harbor that was then the principal North American port of call for transatlantic ocean liners flying a dozen or more flags, how could a small fleet of little sightseeing boats expect to receive any attention in the face of such glamorous competition?

Circle Line has *demanded* attention, though, and the way it has done so is by surviving—and thriving—where more illustrious maritime institutions have long since failed. The sidewheel steamboats of the Hudson River Day Line, and its *Hendrick Hudson* and *Robert Fulton*, are no more. Gone, too, are *Queen Mary, Ile de France, United States.* The dozen or so crossings to England that *Queen Elizabeth 2* now makes in a full season are a pale shadow of a transatlantic passenger service that could often see that many ocean liners departing New York for Europe during a single summer weekend.

The Chelsea piers, the Liberty Street ferry, and so much more that once characterized the port of New York have given way to new institutions and new activities geared to the needs of a new age: South Street Seaport, Battery Park City, Gateway National Park. But Circle Line sightseeing boats offering seasonal three-hour cruises around Manhattan Island remain a permanent and stable New York tradition. Here's how it all happened.

THE EARLY YEARS

Unfortunately, it is not possible to say with any kind of confidence or precision exactly when sightseeing service by boat around Manhattan Island was first offered. Nor can we tell by whom it was first offered or what was the name of the first vessel used. What is known for certain, however, is that it couldn't possibly have happened before June 1895. That was when something called the Harlem Ship Canal was completed, linking the navigable portion of the Harlem River with Spuyten Duyvil Creek and the Hudson River and making circumnavigation of Manhattan Island possible—possible in anything larger than a boat one was prepared to portage for a portion of the distance.

The Harlem Ship Canal had been talked about in New York for almost one hundred years before it finally became a reality. The project was seen as providing an important link for trade and commerce between towns along the Hudson River Valley and towns along the Connecticut shore of Long Island Sound; elected officials from these municipalities greeted the new waterway with enthusiasm. After a fashion—and with any necessary apologies—the Harlem Ship Canal could be called the Cross Bronx Expressway of its day.

The new canal was inaugurated with appropriate civic celebration on June 17, 1895. The cruiser *USS Cincinnati* fired a salute at the Hudson River end of the new waterway off Spuyten Duyvil, and though the warship was too large herself to negotiate the canal, the City of New York had a brand new police boat by the name of *Patrol* that herded a flotilla of smaller craft—tugs and steamboats of all kinds, including the fireboat *New Yorker*—into a massive and festive tour through the new canal and down the Harlem River. (Remember the police boat *Patrol*, for fifty years later she will make another cameo appearance in our story.)

Sometime during the year 1905—or close to it—one John P. Roberts is thought to have offered the very first around-Manhattan Island sightseeing service. He *probably* used a vessel by the name of *Herman S. Caswell*, a wooden-hull steamboat that measured 82 feet from stem to stern. Built in Noank, Connecticut, in 1878, the boat was powered by a single-cylinder steam engine with a diameter of 16 inches and a stroke of 17. Roberts promoted his service as the "Seeing New York Yacht." Lacking a better claimant for the title—and acknowledging the possibility that one might exist—we can declare (albeit provisionally) *Herman S. Caswell* the very first vessel to offer around-Manhattan Island sightseeing service.

This unassuming little steamboat, the *Herman S. Caswell*, may well have been the first vessel to offer around-Manhattan sightseeing service, circa 1905. (Courtesy of the Mariners' Museum, Newport News, Virginia.)

Captain Roberts's sightseeing fleet eventually expanded to include four different vessels, though all did not necessarily operate in the around-Manhattan Island service. Beginning about 1909, for instance, Roberts ran a two-deck launch named *Observation* on a sightseeing tour from Manhattan out to *Ambrose* lightship and back, although *Observation* was also used in around-Manhattan Island service from time to time. (See chapter 5 for a discussion of *Observation*'s tragic demise in 1932.) In 1913 Roberts added a trim little wooden steamboat by the name of *Sapphire* to his fleet, renamed her *Tourist*, and put her to work around Manhattan Island. *Tourist* was built in Bath, Maine, in 1888, had statutory dimensions of 118.8 feet by 26.1 feet by 10.2 feet, measured 260 gross tons, and was powered by a three-cylinder triple-expansion steam engine.[2]

After Roberts died suddenly sometime around 1918 (while riding on the New York subway), a man by the name of Thomas J. Goodwin purchased the entire Roberts fleet and continued to operate sightseeing service under the house flag of his Goodwin Steamboat Company. Under Goodwin, "Str. Tourist," as she was often identified in newspaper advertisements, sailed twice each day, in season, from a point near the Battery at the southern tip of

Manhattan. She stayed on the route until the early 1940s and, in doing so, established an interesting tradition: longevity of service would become a hallmark of many vessels that followed her in the around-Manhattan Island trade.

The first serious competition *Tourist* faced was probably in 1939; it came from two different quarters. Two men who had previously been partners in a Sheepshead Bay fishing boat venture, Jeremiah T. Driscoll and John W. Nugent, put their vessel *Sylph* into service hauling passengers between the exclusive Coney Island residential community of Sea Gate and downtown Manhattan. As this was a commuter service operating around ordinary working hours, Driscoll and Nugent had an opportunity to look for other revenue-generating work for *Sylph* while her Sea Gate passengers were busy in their offices. Nominally, they advertised a sightseeing tour from lower Manhattan to see—but not land at—the site of the 1939 World's Fair in Flushing Meadow. Instead of returning directly via the East River, though, Driscoll and Nugent headed *Sylph* up the Harlem River, through the Harlem Ship Canal, and back to lower Manhattan via the Hudson. And with that, *Tourist* was no longer the only vessel offering around-Manhattan Island sightseeing service.

The year 1939 also saw the advent of around-Manhattan Island sightseeing service by a firm called Manhattan Yacht Cruises. Of three vessels the company owned and operated, one bore the name *Marilda II*. This boat was actually the old *Herman S. Caswell*, once owned by both Roberts and Goodwin and a likely candidate for being the very first vessel ever to offer around-Manhattan Island sightseeing service. Another was called *Manhattan*, the first of four sightseeing boats to bear the name of the island around which they sailed.

Goodwin responded to the competitive challenge by obtaining another vessel, a former Maine-coast ferry named *Islander*, since the fifty-year-old *Tourist* was past her prime and in poor repair; Driscoll and Nugent supplemented their original *Sylph* with a running mate they brought east from the Great Lakes and christened *Sylph II*. Around the same time, a man named Joseph Moran started yet another around-Manhattan Island service, a venture he called the Battery Sightseeing Boat Company and whose initial vessel was a wooden-hull coal-burner that had been built in Albany in the year "naught-one" and that Moran rechristened *Manhattan*.

It was Moran's company, incidentally, that in 1944 offered what appeared to be the winning bid of $3,150.00 on an old police steamer named *Macom*, auctioned off by the City of New York. Moran never put *Macom* into sightseeing service; she was reported to be tied up north of the Grand Street Bridge in Brooklyn later in 1944, for instance, and soon thereafter was removed from the rolls of documented U.S. merchant vessels. But *Macom* deserves passing mention; built at Sparrows Point, Maryland, in 1894, she was formerly the New York police boat *Patrol*, which played a ceremonial role on the day the Harlem Ship Canal opened in 1895 and around-Manhattan Island sightseeing service became an operational possibility.

(*Macom* remained technically a police launch during all of her years of municipal service. But her name was a foreshortening of Mayor's Committee, a semipolitical organization in charge of planning and executing all manner of civic celebrations in New York, including many that required the mayor to travel by water; for this he used *Macom*, which was specially maintained for the purpose. His Honor James J. Walker, whose term as mayor ran from 1925 to 1932, is the city hall incumbent most identified with *Macom*.[3])

The Second World War, and the fuel shortages it caused, put a serious crimp in any further expansion of around-Manhattan Island service in the early 1940s; in fact, operations had to be curtailed. Goodwin's *Islander*, for example, came out for the 1943 excursion-boat season but made her final trip of the year on June 19 before being laid up once again. Driscoll and Nugent suspended their operation entirely, as both *Sylph* and *Sylph II* were conscripted for wartime service with the U.S. Navy. Manhattan Yacht Cruises disappeared during the war, never to be seen again. Moran, however, was able to keep *Manhattan* in service for the entire duration. Goodwin, too, kept his boats running, but hardly on a full or robust schedule.

As the war was drawing to a close, something important happened that would influence the course of around-Manhattan Island sightseeing service forever. A group of men, relatively young in years and with a variety of experience running boats of one sort or another in and around New York, formed a partnership—a corporation, actually—to operate sightseeing yachts around Manhattan Island. Out of this venture the Circle Line would soon emerge.

Circle Line Gets Started

The company was formed in April 1945 and began to run sight-seeing boats around Manhattan Island that very season, when the worst of wartime fuel rationing had begun to ease off. The original principals were five in number: the brothers Gerald and Jeremiah Driscoll (though the former identified himself as O'Driscoll, while the latter merely used Driscoll); Frank Clair, an earlier partner of Driscoll and Nugent when *Sylph* was a Sheepshead Bay fishing boat; Joseph Moran, of Battery Sightseeing; and a man by the name of Frank Barry, then in the early years of a career as a New York customs broker.

Each of the partners contributed to the enterprise his own interest in one or another vessel, or cash, or some combination of the two. The boats then became the core of the company's operating fleet and each man received, in exchange, a 20-percent stake in the new cooperative venture. By 1945, Barry, for example, owned all or part of Goodwin's old *Tourist*, and she was included in his contribution. It is doubtful, though, if this vessel ever sailed in revenue passenger service for Circle Line. (Another boat sometimes mentioned as being part of the early Circle Line fleet is a former yacht named *Placida*. Sold to the Navy in 1942 and mustered out of service after the war, she was never documented as a U.S. merchant vessel and never ran in Circle Line sightseeing service, even though one or another of the partners may have held full or partial interest in her.)

During that first season of 1945, the new company lacked any smart or catchy corporate identity; newspaper advertisements used the bland term "Sightseeing Boats," for example, with little concern as to whether this was a proper name or a mere description.[4] Whatever it was, though, it was able to offer daily sightseeing service around Manhattan Island from two different locations—

basically, four daily trips from Pier 1, adjacent to Battery Park at the southern tip of Manhattan Island, and two daily trips from the Hudson River near the foot of West 42nd Street, a site that was just a short bus or streetcar ride from midtown hotels and railroad stations and, consequently, the visitors and tourists the new company immediately, and correctly, recognized as its principal market. (Today, for example, Circle Line estimates that 75 percent or more of its around-Manhattan Island passengers are from outside the metropolitan area.)

The next year, 1946, three important things happened. First, the new company began to call itself the Circle Line. Second, while it still operated from the same two locations, now the midtown location saw the larger number of daily departures, with only minimal service from Pier 1. Eventually, sightseeing service from lower Manhattan was eliminated entirely by the Circle Line. And finally, 1946 was the year the partners were able to obtain from the U.S. Navy a one-time fishing boat whose distinctive profile would become the company's signature on brochures and advertisements for the next quarter century.

For an enterprise whose founders were so thoroughly Irish, it seems totally appropriate that the vessel in question was once called *Celt*. *Celt* was built in 1902 at the famous Pusey and Jones yard at Wilmington, Delaware, as a private yacht for industrialist J. Rogers Maxwell. *Celt* was conscripted for military service during the First World War, but by the Great Depression of the 1930s the former luxury yacht had devolved into *Sachem*, a fishing boat operating out of Brooklyn's Sheepshead Bay. Cocktail parties and formal dinners had given way to rods, reels, and buckets of bait.

In 1935–1936, *Sachem*'s original steam engine was replaced by a seven-cylinder Fairbanks-Morse diesel, and along with many other civilian craft she was recruited for coastal patrol work by the Navy during the Second World War, her second tour of duty for Uncle Sam; she was assigned to south Florida waters for the duration.

Following hostilities, Circle Line purchased the ex-yacht, and, once refitted for around-Manhattan Island service, she emerged as *Sightseer*. An earlier *Sightseer* that ran for the new company during its inaugural season was renamed *Visitor* (see fleet roster in Appendix A).

SIGHTSEEING BOATS
3 Hour Lectured Cruise
Around Manhattan Island

LEAVE BATTERY
PIER 1
10:30 & 11:30 A.M.
2:30 & 3:30 P.M.

LEAVE FT. W.
42ND ST.
10:30 A.M. &
2:30 P.M.

6:00 P.M. ◄─◄SPECIAL·CRUISE►─► 5:30 P.M.

PHONES: BO. 9-3474 · 3475 · 5054   LO. 5-3306

CIRCLE *Line* **AROUND MANHATTAN ISLAND**

SIGHTSEEING YACHTS

3 Hour LECTURED CRUISE
Daily and Sunday from:

FOOT of W. 42nd ST { 10:30 & 11:00 a.m.
2:30 & 3:00 p.m.

PIER 1 NORTH RIVER ..... { 10:30 a.m.
2:30 p.m.

EVENING CRUISE (Except Monday)
Foot of W. 42nd St._____6:00 p. m.

Tel. BOwling Green 9-3474, 3475, 5054

Circle Line's identity saw a change from 1945, the company's inaugural season, to 1946—from the bland "Sightseeing Boats" to "Circle Line Sightseeing Yachts."

The new *Sightseer* first sailed for Circle Line in 1946. Her fleet-mates in those immediate postwar years included the ex-Maine coaster *Islander* which Goodwin had sold to Jeremiah Driscoll in 1944 and which Driscoll, in turn, had contributed to the partnership; Moran's *Manhattan*; and three other secondhand craft the company was able to secure and which were given the names *Traveler*, *Visitor*, and *Tourist*. All were painted traditional steamboat white; all but *Traveler* were built as steam-powered and later converted to diesel; *Traveler* retained her original steam engine for all of her days. (In 1954, sailing under the name *Harbor Queen* for a short-lived independent operator, Circle Line's ex-*Traveler* would become the last steam-powered vessel to offer around-Manhattan Island service.) Circle Line's *Tourist*, incidentally, was not the old *Tourist* from the days of Roberts and Goodwin; though bearing the same name, she was a different and slightly newer vessel that was launched in Boston in 1906.

The name Circle Line seemed quite appropriate for the service the company was offering. Its stock in trade was to sail around Manhattan Island, and while the route was hardly a true circle when traced out on a map, the name was sensible and quickly caught on. In fact, though, it was also derivative, having been suggested by a rapid-transit rail line in London, the Circle Line, that circumnavigates (so to speak) the British capital.[5]

Traveler, a steam-powered luxury yacht that joined the Circle Line sightseeing fleet shortly after the company's founding in 1945.

Around-Manhattan Island sightseeing tours—circular or otherwise—were not the only services the new company offered. Then as now, boats were available for special charter work, and in 1949 *Islander* and *Visitor* were put to work on a ferry-style route between Brooklyn's Canarsie Beach Park and Rockaway Beach, on the opposite side of Jamaica Bay.

In 1947 the Circle Line partnership saw the departure of one of its original members: Jeremiah T. Driscoll, an irascible and independent-minded mariner whose constitution seems to have been totally incompatible with any kind of bureaucratic process or constraint, left the organization. Following Driscoll's departure, a man by the name of George Sanders bought into the Circle Line venture, so the number of principals remained at five.[6]

Driscoll journeyed north to Rockland, Maine, and there took title to a marvelous little wooden-hull steamboat called *North Haven*. Towed back to New York and her steam engine replaced by a diesel, she was put into around-Manhattan Island service for Driscoll's new Panorama Line, formed to compete with his former partners.

Rechristened *Manhattan*—the third sightseeing yacht to bear the name—Driscoll's vessel was an especially good-looking boat, with enclosed all-weather cabins on the first and second decks, and a second deck that extended all the way to the bow. Her profile had to be altered a bit from her Maine-coast days, though: to pass under the various Harlem River bridges without their having to open, a vessel's height could not exceed 24 feet, so funnels and masts had to be drastically foreshortened (or removed) before a vessel could enter the specialized around-Manhattan Island trade. Thus adapted, Driscoll's *Manhattan* became a fixture for many years, operating primarily out of Battery Park in lower Manhattan.

(Excursion boats had long docked in lower Manhattan along a sea wall at the edge of Battery Park. Between 1939 and 1952, while the Brooklyn-Battery Tunnel was under construction, Battery Park was closed and such vessels were forced to use either Pier A or Pier 1 at the northern end of Battery Park.)

Jeremiah Driscoll's independent streak—not to mention his temper—boiled over from time to time. Once, a local political organization arranged a seemingly routine charter trip aboard *Manhattan*. But when told that the city's mayor, William O'Dwyer, was part of the group that was ready to come aboard, Captain

Captain Jeremiah Driscoll's *Manhattan* approaches Battery Park after a leisurely cruise around Manhattan in 1957.

Driscoll took a fire axe from a bulkhead rack and threatened to swing away if His Honor so much as set foot on *his* boat. (It would seem that Driscoll was not among the more enthusiastic supporters of Mayor O'Dwyer and his municipal administration.)

In later years, Driscoll wrote a book about his sightseeing career, a book that treats some of his former associates rather uncharitably. The privately published *Crime Circles Manhattan* is long on vicious charges, short on documentation, quick to jump to unwarranted conclusions, and, like many accounts based largely on personal recollection, often incorrect on factual matters.[7]

Circle Line would send a boat south to Battery Park to compete directly with Driscoll's *Manhattan* from time to time over the years, although the company's principal landing remained uptown in the West 42nd Street area. Steadier competition with Driscoll in lower Manhattan was provided by a company headed by Driscoll's old partner, John W. Nugent, and generally known as Normandy Sightseeing.

In 1946 Nugent put an old steamboat, *Col. Frank H. Adams*, into around-Manhattan Island service from Pier A, adjacent to Battery Park. Nugent's operation would continue for more than a decade, although *Adams* would not become a permanent fixture on the route. Instead, Nugent became the first around-Manhattan Island operator to see the potential of something the U.S. Navy put up for sale in quantity at the end of World War II. It was a mass-produced vessel designated Landing Craft Infantry (Large), otherwise known as the LCI(L). Four different companies would operate LCI(L)s around Manhattan Island following Nugent's lead.

The Landing Craft Infantry (Large)

The LCI(L) was a product of wartime necessity for transporting battle-ready troops across open water and landing them on hostile, enemy-held beaches. A flotilla of LCI(L)s was designed to substitute for a large transport steamer and its associated landing craft during such assaults; the first action the LCI(L)s saw was Operation Husky, the cross-Mediterranean invasion of Sicily. The little ships were built to haul about two hundred troops each, and although accommodations were anything but luxurious, they were tolerable for the four or five days the soldiers might be aboard. One military historian has advanced the contention, with tongue only partly in cheek, that the LCI(L) was so uncomfortable—and made its passengers so miserable—so as to ensure properly aggressive behavior once forces left the boat to face the enemy in battle.

From the outset, the LCI(L) was a craft that was intended to be produced in large numbers. Under the overall supervision of Rear Admiral Daniel E. Barbey, one of the key figures in the development of U.S. amphibious strategy, the design developed around several critical concepts.[8] First, it had to be capable of being built by workers with minimum skills, not trained shipwrights whose talents were more critical to other assignments. Second, the LCI(L)s had to be built someplace other than on existing shipbuilding ways, which were needed for heavier maritime construction. Third, propulsion had to make use of a dependable off-the-shelf engine that was already in production.

All the criteria met, the LCI(L)s—or "lice," as they were sometimes affectionately called—were turned out by the hundreds all over the United States. They featured all-welded construction, and launching usually involved nothing more ceremonial than shoving a finished hull into the water with a bulldozer, or even a couple of old trucks. An LCI(L) displaced 380 tons; it was 157 feet long and just over 23 feet at the beam. Everything about the vessel was severely straight and angular, from the flat-bottomed hull to the squared-off stern. One eventual admirer described LCI(L)s this way: "There wasn't a curved line in them that could be left straight."

The power plant, rated at 1,600 horsepower, was rather unusual. Each LCI(L) featured eight separate diesel engines arranged in two sets of four—"twin quads," as they are sometimes called—with each set linked to its own variable-pitch propeller. Variable-pitch propellers may sound like needless complexity in a boat whose design philosophy supposedly stressed simplicity. They were selected not for operational reasons but because the kind of straight-cut gears they employed could be produced by a wider spectrum of industrial suppliers than could the specialized gears needed for a typical maritime reduction/reversing unit. In a similar vein of utilizing readily available components whose production did not put added strain on marine suppliers, the engines were adaptations of stock six-cylinder General Motors diesel bus engines with cylinder diameter of 4.25 inches and stroke 5 inches. And while the thought of eight prime movers in one 157-foot-long hull may at first seem overwhelming, LCI(L) engine rooms were, in fact, small and compact. At first glance, the eight diesels actually look more like four— and four small ones, at that—since each engine is mounted immediately side by side with another. But with 48 pistons cycling up and down inside 48 cylinders—and doing so at relatively high RPM— LCI(L) engine rooms were never known as especially quiet places.

The rudder was electrically operated, and, in another clever use of equipment from the civilian sector, it was controlled not by a conventional ship's wheel but by a streetcar-like control handle that must have made some LCI(L) quartermasters think they had become seafaring motormen.

Each LCI(L) had a ship's company of two officers and about twenty seamen. Armament consisted of five 20-mm guns mounted in small deck turrets, and a few depth charges were usually carried for good measure. On early LCI(L)s, troops went ashore from a pair of awkward-looking gangways mounted outboard on either side and immediately abaft of the bow. Later models did away with this arrangement, because when LCI(L)s were navigating in close quarters—often with inexperienced crews—the outrigger-like gangways and their assorted hardware kept punching holes in the hulls of adjacent vessels. The solution was to substitute a bow door in the hull itself, much like those used in larger U.S. landing craft such as the LST. This also served to provide added protection for soldiers during assaults on enemy-held beaches.

A raised pilothouse amidships—square on early models, round on later ones—gave the LCI(L) the unfortunate look of a submarine running on surface. There are stories—but no documented cases— of LCI(L)s coming under "friendly fire" as a result. From some angles the LCI(L) also bore some resemblance to the Navy's somewhat larger LSM, a 558-vessel class of 203-foot landing craft that displaced just under 900 tons.

However much the LCI(L) seems to have been designed and built in calculated disregard of naval and maritime traditions, the overriding fact is that, from 1943 on, the class of just over eight hundred vessels made a significant contribution to the war effort on three separate fronts. They proved to be seaworthy craft—in fact, extremely so—and participated first in the various amphibious assaults that were involved in the invasions of Sicily and Italy and, later, southern France. Meanwhile, in Great Britain, 245 LCI(L)s were part of the allied fleet that was assembled for the D-Day assault on Normandy, and no serious account of that "longest day" fails to credit the little landing craft for its role in that success. After the beachhead was secure, LCI(L)s were deployed in cross-channel ferry and supply work in support of the Allied advance into Germany.

LCI(L)s were also active in the Far East, where they were involved in the invasion of Okinawa and various assaults required to recapture the Philippines. A total of seventeen LCI(L)s were reported by the Navy as lost during the war, including seven at Normandy on D-Day. All in all, though, this would have to be regarded as a very low casualty rate for a class of vessel that participated in some of the fiercest assaults of the war.

The first person to be put in charge of any LCI(L)s was Commander Alan Villiers of the Royal Navy, a man who would number among his later accomplishments sailing *Mayflower II* across the North Atlantic to Plymouth, Massachusetts, in the mid-1950s. While the United States built and owned all the LCI(L)s, in operation some were manned by U.S. Navy crews, others by U.S. Coast Guardsmen, and still others by His Majesty's forces under the lend-lease program—hence Villiers's role in the piece. He left Norfolk, Virginia, in early 1943 with a squadron of twenty-one LCI(L)s and shepherded them across a hostile Atlantic, under their own power, to Gibraltar, with a stopover in Bermuda. Crews were virtually untrained, and for many an LCI(L) officer, the very first time in his life he ever sailed out of sight of land he did so while in command of his very own vessel. Villiers remained with a Royal Navy squadron of LCI(L)s until the vessels were formally returned to the U.S. Navy at Subic Bay, in the Philippines, following VJ Day.[9]

One further point about the LCI(L): the same hull and power plant was utilized for at least two variations, the LCI(G) gun ship and the LCI(R) rocket-firing ship. The great bulk of LCIs, however, were LCI(L) landing craft.

The design parameters that made the LCI so successful during the war—simple construction and stock components—enabled it to adapt easily to peacetime functions. Converted to civilian use, LCI(L)s have performed any number of different maritime tasks:

they have hauled freight on the Delaware River and in Alaskan waters; they have carried passengers between Hyannis and Nantucket Island and on cruises around New York's Lake George; they have worked as tow boats in the Gulf of Mexico and as fishing boats out of Charleston, South Carolina. A full decade after the end of World War II, no fewer than forty-one ex-LCIs of all classes were still carried on the rolls as documented U.S. merchant vessels, and others remained active in various undocumented categories, working out of both U.S. and foreign ports.

In many cases, the military-to-civilian conversion of an LCI(L) involved little more than a fresh coat of paint. For service around Manhattan Island, though, definite conversion specifications were developed. The original pilothouse amidships would not clear the Harlem River bridges. It had to be replaced with a lower structure, and the obvious place to put it was further forward. This fortunate happenstance gave those LCI(L)s converted for around-Manhattan Island service a distinctive and very balanced low and long look of their own, one that was quite unlike the ships' appearance in their wartime configuration. Postwar LCI(L) conversions that retained the original pilothouse amidships—and many did—produced some rather awkward-looking civilian vessels.

The first LCI(L) to be converted for around-Manhattan Island sightseeing service was the 646, and when Nugent executed his conversion he included a new second deck from immediately abaft of the new forward pilothouse all the way to the stern. On Nugent's boat, this second deck was fully open and exposed; later it was partially covered with a canvas awning, and when Circle Line subsequently got into the business of turning LCI(L)s into around-Manhattan Island sightseeing yachts, semipermanent enclosures were included on newly built upper decks.

LCI(L) 646 entered sightseeing service in the spring of 1947 bearing the name *Normandy*, a reference to presumed wartime exploits. In fact, though, LCI(L) 646 never participated in the Normandy invasion—never even crossed the North Atlantic. Converted into an LCI(R) vessel shortly after being built, she made her principal contribution to the Allied cause by performing fire-support work during the invasion of Okinawa. Nugent was likely taking some harmless poetic license when he selected the name.

Four years later, in 1951, Nugent added another ex-LCI(L), the

758, to his fleet; he called this boat *Normandy Two*, and again the vessel's new civilian name was not a valid reflection of her military career. This LCI(L) was built on the West Coast and, like the 646, served exclusively in the Pacific—served with considerable distinction, in fact. By war's end she had been awarded three battle stars and was credited with shooting down two enemy planes; in early 1945 she became the very first Allied vessel to return to Corregidor when that island fortress at the entrance to Manila Bay was recaptured.

CIRCLE LINE'S LCI(L)s

Circle Line quickly saw the potential the LCI(L) design held for conversion into a sightseeing yacht. Over the winter of 1951–1952 they went to work and turned LCI(L) 191 into such a vessel and put her into sightseeing service as *New Yorker*. As LCI(L) 191 she had participated in five different Allied invasions in the Mediterranean,

U.S. Navy LCI(L)-class landing craft No. 191. After the Second World War, the vessel was converted into a Circle Line sightseeing yacht.

The classic shape of a Circle Line LCI(L) is exhibited by *Circle Line-Sightseer VII* (formerly *New Yorker*, now *Circle Line VII*) in this 1955 view in the lower Harlem River.

including Sicily, Salerno, and Anzio. (See Appendix B for additional information about the military careers of Circle Line boats.) *New Yorker* was not only Circle Line's first LCI(L); she also pioneered a distinctive Circle Line look that would become a steady fixture in the port of New York for many decades (and still counting).

When Nugent converted LCI(L) 646 into his first *Normandy*, he was working with a later-model vessel, one that had a main-deck cabin extending the full width of the boat. He retained much of this cabin work as he executed his design, and it was not difficult to see the LCI(L) in *Normandy*. Circle Line, on the other hand, used earlier-model LCI(L)s that featured a narrower main-deck cabin; as a result, there is much less about a Circle Line conversion that recalls a boat's earlier career. Everything from the main deck up is the product of a new and balanced Circle Line design.

The most distinctive feature of that design is clearly the pilothouse. Sharp and angular and anything but big, it is a perfect compliment to the LCI(L) hull on which it rides, as well as to the equally sharp lines Circle Line used for cabin work on its converted landing craft. So perfect, in fact, was the pilothouse design that Circle Line developed for its first LCI(L) conversion that it would be repeated eleven more times in following years—on converted LCI(L)s as well as on other kinds of vessels. It became a genuine trademark for both the company and for New York Harbor itself—not in the same league, obviously, as the Statue of Liberty and the Brooklyn Bridge, but distinctive and jaunty nonetheless. Of course, while the pilothouse Circle Line designed for its converted landing craft was new and different on the outside, on the inside it contained much of the standard equipment from LCI(L) days, including those streetcar-like control handles for steering the boat.

Sadly, it has not been possible to identify the naval architect from whose imagination this wonderful design flowed. It is more than probable that Circle Line partner Gerald O'Driscoll played a key role in the whole business—O'Driscoll's title in later years at Circle Line was First Vice President and Marine Superintendent. Once the company realized how good and distinctive its design was, Frank Barry was undoubtedly instrumental in making sure it was not discarded in favor of something more contemporary.

Circle Line's first LCI(L) conversion went into service in 1952 and was followed by another a year later, a vessel that bore the somewhat confusing name *Circle Line*. In 1955 the company purchased Nugent's *Normandy Two*—of Corregidor fame—and rebuilt her to Circle Line standards at the company's maintenance facility in Brooklyn's Mill Basin, where the fleet was laid up in the off season.

Meanwhile, the company's older sightseeing Yachts—*Traveler*, *Visitor*, *Tourist*, and *Islander*—were sold off as the converted LCI(L)s came on line. *Sightseer*, though, remained active with the company into the 1970s and served as the unofficial flagship of the fleet for most of that time, even though her profile was quite different from the new company design featured on the converted landing craft.

Sightseer's master during the early years was Norwegian-born Captain Harold Log, the company's senior officer, who is remembered today every time a Circle Line vessel refuels. A little forty-six-ton company minitanker that regularly pulls alongside the sightseeing yachts to top off fuel bears the name *Capt. Log*. (Given the fleet's military origins, Circle Line craft have comparatively large fuel tanks; on the average, a sightseeing boat has to be serviced by *Capt. Log* only about once a month.)

Sightseer would inevitably be moored at the end of Pier 83 closest to land. Her sharply raked hull recalled her days as the luxury yacht *Celt*, and metal footings welded to the forward part of her main deck were the remnants of a gun mount from her years of service with the U.S. Navy during the Second World War. Interestingly, in her final years with Circle Line, *Sightseer*'s original wheelhouse was replaced, and when she made her final trip around Manhattan Island, she, too, featured the same angular wheelhouse that had by then become the company's standard.

While Circle Line was largely ridding itself of ex-yachts during the 1950s, there was one exception to the rule (besides *Sightseer*). The company acquired such a vessel, converted it into a sightseeing boat, and added it to the fleet as *Circle Line II*. Smaller than the LCI(L)s, she still featured the same general design that had by then become the company standard. *Circle Line II* was sold in 1958 and enjoyed a long post-Circle Line career. In fact, on the day Circle Line celebrated its fiftieth anniversary—June 15, 1995—tied up at nearby Pier 84 amid a cluster of independently owned charter and party

Circle Line-Sightseer moored in the head position at Pier 83.

Resplendant in old-fashioned "steamboat white," *Circle Line Sightseer* heads up the Harlem River in this 1955 photo taken from the bridge that once carried the Third Avenue E1 from Manhattan into the Bronx.

Circle Line II was a former yacht that was added to the fleet in the mid-1950s. She is shown here making a special call at Battery Park in 1955.

boats was a vessel with the name *Diplomat* on her bow. *Diplomat* is the current identity of an ex-yacht that was once called *Circle Line II.*

Circle Line thus entered a new and more mature phase. With

Circle Line VII at North River Pier 83, the company's base of operations.

Sightseer in the lead and the rest of the fleet composed largely of recently converted LCI(L)s, the company settled in for what would become many years of steady and dependable service. Vessel nomenclature was simplified: all units in the fleet were given numerical names—*Sightseer*, for example, eventually became *Circle Line V*, while the company's original LCI(L) conversion, *New Yorker*, was renamed *Circle Line VII*.

The year 1953 saw important expansion. The company successfully bid to take over the ferry service between Battery Park and the Statue of Liberty and created a separate company, Circle Line-Statue of Liberty Ferry, Inc., to handle this work. Circle Line replaced an excursion boat operator by the name of B. B. Wills on the Statue ferry run on October 1, 1953, and, in the following spring,

"There wasn't a curved line in them that could be left straight" is the way someone once described the LCI(L) landing craft. Even after conversion to a sightseeing yacht, the dictum largely holds true, as can be seen in this 1958 view of *Circle Line VII* heading north in the Harlem River.

took delivery of a brand new three-deck boat for the service. *Miss Liberty* was built by Blount Marine, of Warren, Rhode Island, and her distinctive profile would also become a New York classic, a classic that would be repeated four more times over the next forty years.[10]

DAY LINE ENTERS THE FRAY

The Hudson River Day Line—or at least a post-1948 corporate reincarnation of the original Day Line—entered the around-Manhattan Island sightseeing business in 1953.[11] The company acquired the very first ex-LCI(L) ever to run in around—Manhattan Island service, Nugent's first *Normandy*, and, after renaming her *Gotham*, set up shop at Day Line's Manhattan landing, North River Pier 81. Day Line's first revenue trip around Manhattan Island was made on May 23, 1953. What this meant was that the Circle Line, whose vessels departed from nearby Pier 83 on the north side of the Weehawkeen ferry slips, now had direct competition at its very doorstep. Later in the same year, Day Line added a second converted LCI(L) to its fleet and christened her *Knickerbocker*.

Despite the distinctive design Circle Line developed for its converted LCI(L)s, a good case can be made that Day Line's *Knickerbocker* was the smartest-looking LCI(L) conversion of them all, the only problem being that it turned out to be a one-of-a-kind effort. *Gotham*, for instance, more or less retained the look Nugent gave her in 1947, and a third sightseeing boat Day Line added in 1957, as we shall see, did not imitate *Knickerbocker*'s external design.

In any event, Day Line and Circle Line then settled in for several years of spirited competition. In a tableau straight out of the legendary "steamboat wars" of bygone years, potential sightseeing passengers stepping off a crosstown bus in front of the West 42nd Street ferry terminal and midway between the docks of the two sightseeing companies would face rival hawkers extolling the virtues of each service. Other hawkers selling sightseeing trips on street corners throughout midtown Manhattan would also represent one, but never both, of the rival companies.

Perhaps the strangest aspect of the competition was this: Circle Line always ran more service than Day Line, but it usually scheduled a departure at exactly the same time as the Day Line trips. Two rival boats thus completed a thirty-five-mile trip around Manhattan Island running virtually in tandem. Indeed, if the wind was right, passengers on one boat could sometimes even hear the lecturer on the other one. But competition was competition, and while the lecturers on each vessel would call attention to countless items of maritime and shoreside detail throughout the trip, one thing no lecturer would ever identify, describe, or even acknowledge the presence of was that *other* sightseeing boat of that *other* company that was continually just a few hundred yards away. (I don't recall exactly how I made my point, but I remember using this as an example in a high school history class one day as to why the United States should recognize Red China.)

Like Circle Line, Day Line inaugurated sightseeing service with its yachts painted traditional steamboat white. This lasted only a

A 1953 advertisement for Hudson RIver Day Line's around-Manhattan sightseeing service.

season or two, though, presumably because the rigors of competition demanded vessels whose ownership was obvious at first glance, and what was more obvious than a distinctive color scheme? Day Line first tried a grey, white, and yellow design and later went for a black hull with buff-orange and white trim. Captain Driscoll dealt with this identity problem by painting *Manhattan* several shades of blue, while Circle Line adopted a green and yellow color scheme on one of its early LCI(L) conversions and soon made it standard for the fleet. Circle Line's owners were never happy with the green and yellow—"too drab," one of them said in later years— so a design consultant was called in and, after he presented several alternatives, a decision was made to go with a green and white scheme with touches of red trim, and this is the way Circle Line vessels are painted to this day. Out of this same era of Day Line-Circle Line competition emerged the practice of each company rendering its corporate name in the largest possible letters along the sides of every boat's hull, a decorative scheme the Circle Line fleet still features.

Some time during the day on August 27, 1956, the tugboat *H. A. Wood*, hailing port of Miami, Florida, delivered two additional LCI(L)s to the Day Line's Pier 81 in New York. One of these, the 766, emerged for the 1957 sightseeing season as *Knickerbocker VII*, the Day Line's third around-Manhattan Island sightseeing boat. At the same time, *Gotham* was renamed *Knickerbocker II* and the original *Knickerbocker* remained *Knickerbocker*. Precisely why these three vessels were identified by three unconsecutive numerals (I, II, VII) remains unclear four decades after the fact.[12]

Knickerbocker VII bore a slight external resemblance to the original *Knickerbocker*, but it had a harshness to its lines that rendered it not nearly as attractive as the older vessel. The second LCI(L) delivered to Pier 81 on August 27, 1956, was never converted into an around-Manhattan Island sightseeing vessel, and its disposition is unknown.

In 1961 the "Knickerbocker" names were dropped and the three boats became *Day Line I*, *Day Line II*, and *Day Line VII*, but not for long. Day Line's around-Manhattan Island sightseeing business lasted only through the excursion season of 1962. Then, beginning in 1963, the whole Day Line operation—sightseeing as well as what steamboat service up the Hudson as was still in operation—was

Day line sightseeing yacht *Knickbocker II* backs out from Pier 81 for a cruise around Manhattan.

bought out by the Circle Line. All three Day Line sightseeing boats worked for Circle Line for a number of years. Although painted Circle Line colors and given proper Circle Line names, not a single one was ever rebuilt to Circle Line specifications. Soon enough, all three were retired.

The sightseeing subsidiary of the Hudson River Day Line gave Circle Line some of its best competition over the years. Like Circle Line, Day Line ran from midtown Manhattan; also like Circle Line, Day Line offered a cruise that proceeded a mile or so out into Upper New York Bay for a close encounter with the Statue of Liberty. By contrast, sightseeing services that departed downtown from the Battery Park seawall were shorter in both time and distance, because they eschewed sailing into the bay toward Liberty Island. Battery Park services normally charged a slightly lower fare than the two uptown competitors.

Day Line's *Knickerbocker VII*. Note the welded outline of bow doors from the vessel's earlier career as an LCI(L) landing craft.

ARGO-CLASS COAST GUARD CUTTERS

As its business continued to expand in the 1960s, Circle Line needed not only more tonnage but also a boat that was a tad bigger than a converted LCI(L). It found just the thing in yet another class of vessels that once toiled for the military: the *Argo*-class cutters of the U.S. Coast Guard.[13]

This eighteen-boat class of twin-diesel, 165-foot vessels was built in the early 1930s with an eye toward combating the Prohibition-era problem of "mother ships" at sea off-loading cases of whiskey into speed boats for delivery to thirsty customers ashore. Armament included two three-inch deck guns, supplemented by smaller-calibre weapons. During World War II the *Argo*s were active in convoy protection and in anti-submarine work; they were especially helpful in rescuing survivors of merchant ships torpedoed off the East Coast of the United States during the worst of the U-boat assaults of 1942. When the tanker *China Arrow* was sunk by a German submarine southeast of Ocean City, Maryland, on February 5, 1942, for example, the *Argo*-class cutter *Nike*—later to become a Circle Line sightseeing boat—rescued her entire thirty-eight-man crew and landed them safely in Lewes, Delaware. (*China Arrow*'s captain told a harrowing story of his ship's being torpedoed, remaining afloat, and finally being dispatched by the U-boat's deck gun.) *Nike* initiated attacks on three German submarines during the war; but there was no immediate confirmation of any damage she may have inflicted, nor did a postwar review of German naval records suggest that *Nike*'s attacks were successful.

Another *Argo*-class boat—WPC-110, *Icarus*—is credited with sinking a German U-boat, the U-352. (Actually, the captain and crew abandoned and scuttled their submarine—but that "counts" as a sinking.) The action on May 9, 1942, off Cape Lookout, North Carolina, was only the second recorded kill of a German U-boat by any U.S. forces during World War II. The vessel WPC-115, *Thetis*, is also credited with sinking the German submarine U-157 off Key West on June 13, 1942; this was the third U-boat sunk by American forces. Neither *Icarus* nor *Thetis* was among the cutters that Circle Line later obtained, though. The entire *Argo* class was retired from Coast Guard service after the war, and the final active vessel, WPC-101, *Ariadne*, was decommissioned in December 1968.[14] (See Appendix B for further information about the military careers of Circle Line's ex-*Argo*-class Coast Guard cutters.)

Converted to Circle Line configuration, the *Argo*s—five of them, including *Argo* herself, WPC- 100—provide for larger passenger loads than an LCI(L): six hundred versus five hundred, approximately. And while they include the distinctive "Circle Line look" that was developed at the time of the LCI(L) conversions, they have more traditional nautical lines to them, including a pronounced sheer and rounded sterns. The five vessels were introduced into Circle Line service, one by one, between 1960 and 1974 after each had undergone conversion at the company's maintenance facility in Mill Basin.

Coast Guard cutter *Triton* (WPC 116) in wartime grey. This vessel would later become *Circle Line XVII.* (United States Naval Institute).

Mechanically, Circle Line's ex-*Argos* feature some interesting variations one from another. Two boats, *Circle Line XI* and *Circle Line XV*, are still powered by their original twin six-cylinder Winton diesels from Coast Guard days. Another, *Circle Line XVI*, had its original Winton engines replaced by a pair of Cummins V-12 diesels, and the other two former cutters, *Circle Line XII* and *Circle Line XVII*, were outfitted with surplus LCI(L)-style "twin quad" power plants.

An important improvement in Circle Line service was effected by the City of New York in 1965 when a $1.5 million program was begun to rehabilitate Pier 83. For almost twenty years Circle Line vessels had tied up to one side of an inadequate and fire-gutted wooden pier that afforded passengers no weather protection at all. The new pier is a two-deck concrete structure with parking for 270 automobiles, facilities for company offices, and sheltered loading berths for sightseeing boats on both the north and the south side of the pier. The old terminal for the New York Central Railroad's Weehawkeen ferry—out of business since 1959—was demolished as part of the same project.

When Circle Line bought out Day Line Sightseeing after the 1962

Coast Guard cutter *Nike* (WPC 112), shown here in peacetime white, with buff funnels topped by black bands. Later, this vessel would be converted into *Circle Line XVI*. (United States Naval Institute).

Circle Line XVI, an ex-*Argo*-class Coast Guard cutter, heads down the Hudson River.

Sidewheel steamboat *Alexander Hamilton* heads up the Hudson. The *Hamilton* was the only former Day Liner to operate under Circle Line auspices.

season, it also became the owner and operator of the ex-Hudson River Day Line steamer *Alexander Hamilton*, the last vestige of regularly scheduled seasonal passenger service on the Hudson between New York and such upriver points as Bear Mountain and West Point. (Circle Line organized Day Line as a *subsidiary* company. Earlier, in 1953, when Circle Line branched out to serve the Statue of Liberty, it established Circle Line–Statue of Liberty Ferry, Inc., as a *separate* company.)

Circle Line operated the 1924-built *Hamilton* through the excursion-boat season of 1971, when the old sidewheeler was retired. She was replaced the next year by a brand new four-deck, diesel-powered excursion boat that Circle Line designed and called *Dayliner*. Sadly, the kind of upriver excursions for which *Dayliner* was built lacked the customer base needed to render them economically viable. *Dayliner* was removed from service after the 1989 season and, following extensive conversion, was returned to service in New York by new owners, World Yacht, as the luxury dinner

cruiser *New Yorker*. (More on World Yacht later—there's an important Circle Line connection here.) However, *New Yorker, née Dayliner*, has moved on yet again; sold by World Yacht, she underwent
still more conversion and now works as a gambling ship under a
new name in a port far from New York.

Circle Line retains all rights to the Hudson River Day Line
corporate name, and there is occasional talk of restoring some kind
of upriver passenger service, perhaps more in the style of luxury
week-long river cruises that have become quite popular in Europe.

THE WORLD'S FAIR OF 1964–1965

Just as the 1939–1940 World's Fair in New York saw the emergence
of the first around-Manhattan Island sightseeing service to offer competition to the established operator, so did the 1964–1965 World's
Fair see a new entrant into the market. Fairwater Cruises was established to link downtown Manhattan with the fair grounds in Flushing Meadow, for which purpose the company obtained a pair of
smallish—but new—vessels from Blount Marine. In addition to ferry
trips to the fair, Fairwater took a flyer on around-Manhattan Island
sightseeing service from Battery Park as well. Alas, the service lasted
no longer than the two summers the World's Fair lasted.

Interestingly, Fairwater sold off one of their boats, *Fairmaid*, to a
sightseeing company in Savannah, where she continues to operate
in sightseeing service as *Waving Girl*. Circle Line's *Visitor* was also
sold off to Savannah interests when her New York sightseeing days
were over, a decade or so earlier. In fact, *Waving Girl* can be
regarded as *Visitor*'s replacement in Savannah.

A further assertion can also be advanced with respect to *Fairmaid*: of the more than two dozen vessels that have worked in
around-Manhattan Island service over the years, she is the only one
to have done so as a brand new boat sailing for her original owner.
All the others came to the trade after earlier work elsewhere under
somebody else's house flag.

At Battery Park, Fairwater had to compete directly with Jeremiah
Driscoll's Panorama Sightseeing, which continued to offer around-
Manhattan Island sightseeing service through the excursion-boat

Waving Girl today runs sightseeing tours in Savannah. In 1964–65 she operated around-Manhattan service.

season of 1969. The original wooden-hull *Manhattan* was at first supplemented, and eventually replaced, by an ex-LCI(L) that was christened *Manhattan II*. Of *Manhattan II* this may be suggested: Seven ex-LCI(L)s were converted into around-Manhattan Island sightseeing yachts over the years, and without question she turned out to be the ugliest of them all.

Actually, government records of enrolled U.S. merchant vessels fail to identify *Manhattan II* as a former LCI(L). Her date and place of construction, however, are consistent with the LCI(L) program, and she certainly looked like an ex-LCI(L) prior to her conversion into an around-Manhattan Island sightseeing boat. It is known that 270 LCI(L)s were canceled by the Navy prior to their completion toward war's end; perhaps Jeremiah Driscoll's *Manhattan II* is one of them, an ex-LCI(L) that was never commissioned by the Navy. (See chapter 4 for a discussion of *Manhattan II's* pre-sightseeing career as the excursion boat *San Jacinto*.)

The irrepressible Driscoll continued his independent ways. In 1960, for example, the cruise liner *Victoria* was unable to berth at a conventional Manhattan pier because of some kind of labor dispute.

Driscoll jumped in and turned *Manhattan II* into a tender for cruise ship passengers between Battery Park and *Victoria*'s Staten Island anchorage, pocketing $1,000.00 for his effort.

New York Parks Commissioner Newbold Morris then stepped in and suspended Driscoll's rights to land at Battery Park for *any* purpose, claiming that the run out to the cruise ship was in violation of his contract with the city to operate only sightseeing service from Battery Park. Much contretemps followed, including the inevitable filing of multiple law suits, the exchange of heated charges, countercharges, and denials, and complaints to the newspapers from Driscoll that thousands of hot dogs he had purchased for the upcoming Memorial Day weekend would go bad. Eventually—and thankfully—the matter was allowed to drop.

Manhattan II—and Captain Driscoll—last sailed around Manhattan Island in 1969, leaving Circle Line the sole company offering the popular service. It was thirty-one years earlier that the same Jeremiah Driscoll put the ex-fishing boat *Sylph* into around-Manhattan Island service, the first known competitor to challenge Budd Goodwin's *Tourist* on the route.

CIRCLE LINE TODAY

Circle Line evolved, with founding partner Frank Barry emerging as chairman of the privately held corporation. Then, in July 1981, came more change—not so much in the day-to-day operations of the sightseeing yachts as in the organizational structure of the business.

Essentially, the sightseeing service was taken over by new investors while the people associated with the old company continued to run an expanded Statue Ferry operation. It was a very amicable sale—the remaining partners were getting on in years and felt it was time to realize some appreciation from their work and investment—and the two companies remain on the best of terms. Frank Barry and Gerald O'Driscoll actually stayed on and worked for the new owners for a few years to ensure a smooth transition. Statue Ferry chartered one of Circle Line Sightseeing's ex-LCI(L)s for a spell when business expanded but its own new boats had yet to be delivered. The most poignant moment during the fiftieth anniversary celebration on June 15, 1995, came when Circle Line president

August Ceradini Jr. presented gold medals to descendants of the founding Circle Line partners.

The Statue Ferry is formally called Circle Line–Statue of Liberty Ferry, Inc., although, in the interest of avoiding passenger confusion, the name "Circle Line" no longer appears in big letters on the ferry company's vessels. But because Statue Ferry continues to be run by a second generation of Barrys and Morans and Clairs and O'Driscolls—either as day-to-day corporate officers or as members of the board of directors—the proud name Circle Line and the familiar logo are featured prominently on business cards, corporate letterhead, and other official documents. For that matter, the flagship of the company's seven-boat fleet continues to bear the name *Miss Circle Line*.

The new owners of the sightseeing company—that is to say, the *real* Circle Line, Circle Line Sightseeing Yachts—are headed by a man named Karl Andren. The same people also own World Yacht, a company that operates upscale luncheon and dinner cruises around the port of New York. A firm called New York Cruise Lines, Inc., is the parent company of both Circle Line and World Yacht.

In 1985, sightseeing competition once again emerged in New York, although not on the full three-hour, around-Manhattan Island route. Rather, shorter, one- and two-hour cruises were scheduled out of the newly redeveloped South Street Seaport, along the East River below the Brooklyn Bridge. A company called Seaport Line designed a marvelous-looking diesel-powered sidewheeler, *Andrew Fletcher*, and supplemented her with an equally attractive propeller boat, *DeWitt Clinton*.[15]

Seaport Line operated through the 1992 season and then lowered its flag. Circle Line picked up the slack and began to offer such shorter sightseeing trips from South Street Seaport beginning in the summer of 1993, in addition to its regular schedule of trips from West 43rd Street and the Hudson River. *Circle Line XII*—USCGC *Argo*, herself—is regularly assigned to this service. While still owned by Circle Line Sightseeing, and while operated by Circle Line personnel, the vessel has been renamed *Sightseer XII*, her color scheme has been changed to a very traditional steamboat white with a dash of blue trim, and she has the words "Seaport Liberty Cruises" painted on her sides, not "Circle Line—America's Favorite Boat Ride."

Circle Line has also begun to offer a limited schedule of shorter sightseeing cruises from Pier 83, including a popular two-hour evening sailing that follows the conventional around-Manhattan Island route as far as the United Nations Building, where the vessel turns around and heads back to Pier 83.

As for Circle Line's bread-and-butter operation, around-Manhattan Island cruises usually get underway each year in mid-to- late March. Service increases as the days grow longer, until as many as ten regularly scheduled departures cast off from Pier 83 each day in high summer, with extra service operated as traffic warrants. A variation Circle Line recently worked into its around-Manhattan Island schedule is to have a few trips each day stop to pick up passengers at the old Lackawanna Railroad terminal in Hoboken, New Jersey, across the river and downstream from Pier 83. After Labor Day the frequency of service decreases, until the season finale in late November or early December. The fleet is then laid up for the winter at Pier 83 (the old Mill Basin facility was given up some years ago). A boat or two is usually kept available for any late-season charter work, but by the time mid-December rolls around, the entire fleet has been deactivated and winterized. Many Circle Line captains (and crew) head south for Florida and environs to practice their trade in warm water as they await the start of another sightseeing season in New York.

Something noteworthy happened before Circle Line and Statue Ferry went their separate ways in 1981. For decades, the Statue Ferry was simply an over-and-back service between Battery Park and Liberty Island. But as the federal government began to renovate historical buildings on Ellis Island, and as the former Jersey Central Railroad depot in Jersey City was converted into an attractive waterfront park, more-complicated waterborne service patterns developed and additional vessels were needed to work them.

In 1977, Circle Line–Statue Ferry took delivery of a new boat from Blount Marine that was christened *Miss Freedom* and was intended to inaugurate service to Ellis Island. Instead of building a three-deck vessel along the lines of *Miss Liberty* of 1954 or *Miss Circle Line* of 1964, *Miss Freedom* is a lesser-capacity two-decker that looks, for all the world, like an around-Manhattan Island sightseeing vessel.

Miss Freedom—and a 1982-built sister ship, *Miss Gateway*—even

Miss New Jersey is one of the triple-deckers that Circle Line-Statue of Liberty Ferry, Inc., runs between Battery Park, Liberty Island, Ellis Island, and Jersey City. Corporate ties between the Statue ferry and the sightseeing operation were broken in 1981.

include the distinctive Circle Line pilothouse design and were delivered in the same green, white, and red livery as the sightseeing fleet. But they work Upper New York Bay ferry routes for Statue Ferry, not around Manhattan Island for Circle Line.

And what of the five *Argo*-class cutters and three ex-LCI(L)s that still form the Circle Line passenger fleet? All are kept in excellent repair, the seasonal service they are called upon to provide is not overly demanding, and the eight vessels are little changed since they were first reconfigured to Circle Line specifications many decades ago. There have been some modifications, though. Direct pilothouse engine controls have been installed on all the ex-LCI(L)s and on three of the five ex-*Argo* class boats. (With such controls, the captain up on the bridge doesn't merely *request* the engineer down in the engine room to execute certain maneuvers with the engine ["slow ahead" and so forth]; he actually controls the engines himself, much as would a Sunday skipper out for a spin in a sixteen-foot outboard.)

The two ex-*Argo*s still powered by their original Coast Guard Engines—*Circle Line XI* and *Circle Line XV*—cannot be readily converted to direct pilothouse engine controls, for some technical reason. In any event, old-fashioned polished brass engine room telegraphs remain in place as backup communication between bridge and engine room on all vessels equipped with direct pilot-house controls—all except one. *Circle Line XVII*'s original system for sending commands to the engine room featured large dials mounted on a console, not a free-standing telegraph, and this was left in place as the backup system when direct pilothouse engine controls were installed. The two boats that lack direct pilothouse controls, of course, use the engine room telegraph as their primary system of bridge-to-engine room communication.

There have been other changes. Variable-pitch propellers have been replaced with conventional ones on *Circle Line VIII* and *Circle Line X*, leaving *Circle Line VII*, the company's very first converted landing craft, as the sole ex-LCI(L) that still utilizes a complete and authentic World War II-style power and propulsion system. Most of the fleet has been equipped with fold-down masts atop the second deck that are extended to full height when a vessel is working an assignment—e.g., a charter trip, the South Street Seaport service—that does not require navigating the Harlem River, with its minimal clearances. Two boats—*Circle Line X* and *Sightseer XII*—have been outfitted with navigational radar. Minor changes have been made to cabin work, exhaust ducting, plumbing, wiring, and the like.

The question, though, is how long the current fleet can be expected to last. On the day Circle Line celebrated its fiftieth anniversary, not a single one of its passenger-carrying boats was less than fifty years old, and, indeed, two of the ex-*Argo*-class cutters were a robust sixty-two.

There are no firm plans for replacement vessels, although some years back there was talk of new boats, and concepts are starting to develop about what they should be like. Management wants a slightly larger craft that is a little faster than the current fleet and that will be able to cut today's three-hour running time down to two-and-a-half or less—and do so without kicking up a lot of troublesome wake. Environmental damage to mud flats along the Harlem River was not high on the list of naval architects' considerations when they worked up hull designs for *Argo*-class Coast Guard cutters and LCI(L)s many decades ago.

So while there is nothing definite on the horizon for now, one of these years—or maybe one of these decades—we'll read about an order for some new vessels, and the LCI(L)s and the *Argos* will sail into the sunset. It will be a retirement they will have earned many times over, from the beaches of Sicily and Anzio and convoy protection up and down the East Coast to the assault on Okinawa and the liberation of the Philippines and culminating in generations of faithful service on a peaceful thirty-five-mile cruise around the island of Manhattan.

From this quarter there is but a single suggestion advanced for any new sightseeing yachts Circle Line might decide to build. Make them as modern as tomorrow, if you want to. Hire the best naval architects in the world to work up specifications. Include every high-tech device known to humankind. Just don't waste any time— or money—designing a new wheelhouse. The old one's just fine!

Odds and Ends

An interesting story from pre-Circle Line days involves the sightseeing vessel *Islander*. Wartime security required on-board tour guides to instruct passengers, in those days, not to take any photographs of the Brooklyn Navy Yard as the sightseeing boats passed by in the East River. (The prohibition actually continued well into the postwar era.) To enforce the edict, a Navy observer on shore gave each passing vessel a careful once-over with binoculars. One day, passengers aboard *Islander* were seen to be taking such photos, so a swift launch was sent out to intercept the sightseeing yacht and bring her back to the Navy Yard, where all film was seized from the offending passengers. The story has a courteous ending, though, as the Navy developed the film and returned prints and negatives to their rightful owners at no charge—minus, of course, any photographs of destroyers or battleships.

Circle Line crews are very much aware of the military heritage their fleet of sightseeing boats represents, and they enjoy collecting stories about wartime exploits. Oddly enough, this phenomenon seems to be more pronounced among younger employees—people who weren't even born when World War II was being fought. Hanging in the crew's quarters below decks, for instance, is a marvelous photograph of *Sightseer XII* as USCGC *Argo* escorting what is said to be a captured German submarine in the Atlantic.

Then there is the story of the couple from Norway in 1971 who spoke little or no English but wanted to take a trip around Manhattan Island aboard the Circle Line. They made their way to Pier 83 and purchased tickets for the next departure, but instead of a regular sightseeing cruise, they accidentally wandered aboard a Circle Line vessel that had been chartered by a fraternal order to conduct an initiation ceremony. The couple became genuinely frightened when people whom they thought were, like themselves, ordinary sightseeing passengers began donning strange robes, uttering unintelligible incantations, and lighting purple candles.

Let's not forget how New York Mayor Abraham Beame and a party of political dignitaries celebrated the nation's Bicentennial on July 4, 1976. The Port of New York put on a big bash that day that was called Operation Sail '76, a massive assembly of tall ships that the mayor and his party planned to view from aboard a chartered Circle Line vessel. The boat wandered into some kind of restricted area, however, and was ordered by the Coast Guard to put in at Governor's Island because of the transgression. A skillful and fast-talking Circle Line captain soon negotiated the release both of his hostage passengers and of his vessel.

Circle Line passengers are linked to the myriad sights and wonders along the route by what may well be the company's greatest single contribution to New York folklore: talking heads called tour guides.

In pre-Circle Line days, lectures aboard sightseeing boats were handled on a concession basis. The vessel owner concentrated his attention on navigational matters while the concessionaire delivered the lecture and even sold coffee, soda, sandwiches, and souvenirs as part of the deal. Soon enough, the various sightseeing companies assumed responsibility themselves for this work and the lecturers became direct employees.

With Circle Line, Frank Barry himself was reported to have been the personal custodian of a big looseleaf binder that contained all the facts the tour guides needed to ensure an accurate presentation. But the charm of a Circle Line lecture has little to do with facts—it's all in the delivery.

When Day Line was in the around-Manhattan Island sightseeing business, it hired only women tour guides, outfitted them like airline stewardesses of the era, and took it all quite seriously. Circle Line, on the other hand, has always recognized the need for more color in the delivery and has consistently recruited a group of show-business types—men and women—who can be counted on to add a personal touch to the delivery of otherwise factual material. Be accurate— that's a given; be utterly respectful when talking about Ellis Island and the Statue of Liberty; but otherwise try not to confuse a Circle Line tour narration with a graduate school seminar on monetary policy or a presidential address on the state of the federal union.

In the year of its fiftieth anniversary, Circle Line gave its tour guides a piece of new equipment: wireless microphones so they can deliver their spiel as they roam around the boat and not have to sit stationary in one spot, as had long been the case. Move over, Phil and Oprah![16]

As Circle Line begins its second half-century of service, there are plans to compliment the live on-board lectures with prerecorded video treatments of New York sights that are beyond a passenger's line of sight from the deck of a sightseeing boat. "We have to remember we're in the entertainment business, not just the boat business," Circle Line chairman Karl Andren says.

Like any recreational enterprise that is conducted seasonally and out of doors, Circle Line depends on good weather for economic success. One year, toward the end of his career, Frank Barry was asked how business was going. "This year I might just as well be selling umbrellas" was the sum and substance of his reply.

Still, the customers keep heading down to the Hudson River at West 43rd Street—and they arrive by the millions. Sometime over the 1961 Fourth of July weekend, Circle Line calculated that the sightseeing yachts carried passenger number 10 million since the service was inaugurated back in 1945. By the end of the century, the grand total will be in the range of 60 million people—60 million 35-mile rides around Manhattan Island. That means over two *billion* passenger miles. And except for a few seasons of clockwise operation in the early years, all 2 billion will have been in the same direction!

Today, all Circle Line sightseeing trips operate around Manhattan Island in counterclockwise fashion; that is to say, they start at the foot of West 43rd Street and go down the Hudson to the Statue of Liberty, then up the East and Harlem Rivers, and back down the Hudson. This tends to frontload many of the more interesting sights early in the trip, with the final portion being more of a relaxed cruise. In its early days, though, Circle Line operated clockwise; north up the Hudson first, then back south via the Harlem Ship Canal and the Harlem and East Rivers, and finally north again up the Hudson River to Pier 83.

As to the original five young men who formed the Circle Line partnership in 1945, all are now deceased. Frank Barry became chairman of the board of directors of the Circle Line; it was Barry who saw the once fledgling company grow into the dominant force it eventually became. Barry, who was also active in Democratic Party work in New York, died on June 7, 1986. His daughter, Beverly, served as an active corporate officer for many years before "retiring" to a position on the board of directors of the Statue Ferry operation.

Frank Clair also spent many years with Circle Line, eventually holding the positions of treasurer of Circle Line Sightseeing Yachts and president of Circle Line-Statue of Liberty Ferry. It was one of Clair's sons who, returning from World War II, told his father about a subway service in London that had a catchy name—it was called the Circle Line. Frank Clair died on March 31, 1992.

Gerald O'Driscoll also stayed with the company for many years; his contribution was largely in technical areas associated with vessel design. It is difficult to have a conversation with an engineer aboard any Circle Line vessel today without O'Driscoll's name coming up, and always in a respectful manner. Gerald O'Driscoll died on November 18, 1992.

Joseph Moran, the very first president of Circle Line, remained with the company until his death on January 3, 1968. His son—also named Joseph—later became president of Circle Line-Statue of Liberty Ferry, Inc., and was among those honored during the Circle Line anniversary celebration in 1995. (The Circle Line Morans are no kin to the Moran family of tugboat fame.)

Of the five men who formed a sightseeing partnership in April 1945, Jeremiah Driscoll—the brother of Gerald O'Driscoll—lived the longest. Of course, he left the fold in 1947 and formed Panorama Sightseeing, an enterprise that continued to operate in competition with Circle Line until 1969. One of these days, perhaps Driscoll will be remembered more for the contributions he made to around-Manhattan Island sightseeing, with vessels like *Sylph* and *Islander* and *Manhattan*, and less for the unfortunate battles he waged against his former colleagues. Jeremiah Driscoll died in January 1994.

These five men—together with countless other people, from captains and engineers to ticket sellers and line handlers—have given New York a marvelous maritime heritage, one that has genuinely earned the right to be called "America's Favorite Boat Ride."[17]

NOTES

1. *Fire Fighter* was joined during the Circle Line celebration by her newer (and much smaller) fleetmate, the *Kevin C. Kane*. (See chapter 3 for further treatment of New York fireboats.)
2. A triple-expansion engine was the epitome of maritime conventionality in the steam era. Cylinders were of different diameter because exhausted steam from one cylinder was fed into a second and then a third; the variation in cylinder size compensated for the fact that the steam lost some of its energy at each stage of the process.
3. See John I. Griffin, "The Passing of the Hostess of New York Harbor," *Steamboat Bill* 29 (March 1949), 405, for general information about *Macom*; for commentary about the political aspects of the vessel's history, see *The New Yorker*, January 29, 1944, p. 21.
4. The formal name of the new firm was Sightseeing Yachts, Incorporated, although the general public had no need to be aware of it.
5. That portion of London's rapid transit Circle Line that runs between Bishop's Rock and Paddington can lay claim to being the oldest subway line in the world, having opened for revenue service on January 10, 1863. The first U.S. subway opened (in Boston) on September 1, 1897.
6. Before assuming Driscoll's interest in Circle Line, Sanders—a New York excursion boat operator who also held a "dollar-a-year" political position in Mayor William O'Dwyer's municipal administration—formed a partnership with B. B. Wills to establish a separate around-Manhattan Island sightseeing company. Called Sightseeing Around New York Waterways, Inc., it is unlikely the firm operated for even a full season, if at all. At the time, Wills was the operator of the Statue of Liberty ferry service as well as excursion-boat companies in Boston, Baltimore, and Washington.
7. Jeremiah T. Driscoll, *Crime Circles Manhattan* (New York: the author, 1980).
8. Barbey's importance in the development of the LCI(L) was suggested in a recent study. See Walter J. Boyne, *Clash of the Titans; World War II at Sea* (New York: Simon and Schuster, 1995), p. 283.
9. Villiers has written of his LCI(L) experiences. See Alan Villiers, "The Story of the Lice," *Ships and the Sea* (August 1952), 46–53.
10. For information on service to the Statue of Liberty, see Peter T. Eisele, "Fifty Years of Service to Miss Liberty," *Steamboat Bill* 130 (Summer 1974), 77–85. The Circle Line partners were interested in the Statue of Liberty route for many years before taking it over in 1953. While recently studying the private

papers of B. B. Wills, the man who ran the service before Circle Line, I discovered a letter to Wills dated August 3, 1946, asking if he might be "interested in selling the Statue of Liberty run." The communication is on the letterhead of Cambell & Gardiner, Custom House Brokers; it was signed by Francis J. Barry.

11. For a full history of this company, see Donald C. Ringwald, *Hudson River Day Line* (New York: Fordham University Press, 1990).

12. Some have speculated that the "missing numbers" in the I, II, VII sequence are accounted for by the other excursion boats owned by the Hudson River Day Line, Inc., between 1948 and 1962; see Franklin B. Roberts and John Gillespie, *The Boats We Rode* (New York: Quadrant, 1974), p. 44. This book deserves broader mention for its treatment of all post-Second World War around-Manhattan Island sightseeing boats.

13. The 165-foot cutters have also been called the *Thetis*-class, since this vessel, although numbered WPC-115, was the first to be launched. See Robert Erwin Johnson, *Guardians of the Sea; History of the United States Coast Guard* (Annapolis, MD: U.S. Naval Institute, 1987), p. 92.

14. For more information about the *Argo*-class cutters, see Malcolm F. Willoughby, *The U.S. Coast Guard in World War II* (Annapolis: U.S. Naval Institute, 1957); also, Robert Scheina, *U.S. Coast Guard Cutters and Craft of World War II* (Annapolis: U.S. Naval Institute, 1982). See also "United States Coast Guard Patrol Boats," *Marine Engineering and Shipping Age* 37(9) (September 1932), 382–86.

15. *Andrew Fletcher* was lengthened and her paddlewheels were deactivated and removed; she now works as a river casino boat in the Midwest under the name *Diamond Jo. Dewitt Clinton* likewise became a "river gambler" some place out in the heartland.

16. Circle Line tour guides have often been the subject of feature stories in local newspapers. See, for example, *New York Newsday*, June 15, 1995, B1, B4–B5, B23; *The New York Times*, October 6, 1974, sect. X, pp. 1, 18; *The New York Times*, June 29, 1964, p. 27.

17. The slogan "America's Favorite Boat Ride" has long been used by Circle Line. Marketing efforts associated with the fiftieth anniversary in 1995 seem to be moving away from its use, however. The phrase was coined as the title of a magazine article many years ago. See Don Wharton, "America's Favorite Boat Ride," *Saturday Evening Post* 225 (August 9, 1952), 34–35.

5 gala days to Europe
—on the fastest ship afloat!

There's just time for the time of your life on the s.s. United States

s.s. United States World's fastest liner, sails from New York 12 noon: Jan. 16*; Feb. 3*, 19*; Mar. 6*, 24*; Apr. 9*, 24; May 8, 22, and regularly thereafter. Arrives Havre early morning the 5th day, Southampton, same afternoon. *First Class $367 up; Cabin $232 up; Tourist $181 up.*

Also arrives Bremerhaven 6th day

s.s. America Offers extra hours of leisure at sea. Air-conditioned public rooms. Sails from New York: Jan. 9, 29; Feb. 21; Mar. 14; Apr. 3, 25; May 15, and regularly thereafter. 5½ days to Cobh, 6½ to Havre, 7 to Southampton, 8 to Bremerhaven. *First Class $312 up; Cabin $212 up; Tourist $174 up.*

No finer food and service afloat or ashore

"Such a wonderful welcome," declare Mr. and Mrs. Grover A. Whalen. "The staff seemed to anticipate our every need." The ship is air-conditioned, and your stateroom is apartment-size. Mr. Whalen is a Director of Coty, Inc. and Coty International.

"The fastest five days I ever spent," says glamorous motion picture actress Merle Oberon. There are three Meyer Davis orchestras, deck sports of every description, pre-release films, and an internationally renowned cuisine.

Consult our authorized travel agents or **United States Lines**

One Broadway, New York 4, N. Y. Tel.: DIgby 4-5800

Offices also in: Baltimore, Boston, Chicago, Cleveland, Detroit, Los Angeles, Montreal, Norfolk, Philadelphia, St. Louis, San Francisco, Seattle, Toronto, Vancouver, Washington, D. C.

UNITED STATES

2

When the *SS United States* Won the North Atlantic Blue Riband

The year 1977 marked the twenty-fifth anniversary of the capture of the North Atlantic Blue Riband by the superliner *SS United States*; the prize is traditionally awarded to the commercial vessel that has crossed the Atlantic faster than any other.[1] In one of those strange quirks of happenstance that cause one to pause now and again to ponder the passing of the years, 1977 was also the fiftieth anniversary of Charles Lindbergh's solo flight across the very same North Atlantic in an airplane he called the *Spirit of St. Louis*.

Both events, one by air and the other by sea, have much in common beyond the fact that each involved a daring and unprecedented crossing of the most hostile ocean on earth. In 1927, and a quarter-century later, in 1952, genuine excellence was on display, excellence that bore the indelible stamp "Made in the U.S.A." In 1927 that excellence marked the emergence of something new that would grow and prosper in the decades following, something that would radically change not merely intercontinental travel habits but, indeed, the very relationship of peoples and nations. In 1952, the excellence on display was a culmination and a finale of something that had been no less an agent of social transformation in its day but that would never be repeated again.

United States was unable to bask in the glory of the twenty-fifth anniversary of her record-setting performance, for she had long since been removed from active steamship service by her owners, the United States Lines, and was passing her days in quiet retirement in the peaceful tidewater country of Virginia where she had been built.

Eight years earlier, on November 14, 1969, as *Apollo 12* was streaking toward the moon, a somber announcement was released at Number One Broadway in New York, headquarters of the United States Lines. Because of steadily rising costs, lower-than-ever transatlantic airfares, and uncertainty over the Nixon Administration's policies on continuing maritime subsidies, the new owners of the company were canceling three future sailings of the *SS United States* and placing the seventeen-year-old superliner in indefinite lay-up.

A twenty-one-day Christmas cruise to the West Indies and Africa, an early-January transatlantic crossing, and a fifty-five-day cruise to the Far East, leaving from New York on January 22, 1970, were all being canceled outright. (This last cruise would have involved the vessel's first transit of the Panama Canal.) *United States* would instead remain in Newport News, where she had gone for a regular annual inspection and dry docking after completing an otherwise routine transatlantic crossing in New York on Friday, November 7, 1969.[2] That crossing proved not at all routine: it turned out to be her final crossing and her last voyage. Shortly afterward, all subsequent sailings were canceled and she would remain in Newport News, or nearby Norfolk, for the next twenty-two and a half years. She actually spent more time in inactive lay-up than she did on the North Atlantic, and while *United States* may yet return to service as a leisure-oriented cruise ship, her days of glory will always and ever be back in the summer of 1952, when she first steamed majestically into New York Harbor, full of promise, larger than life, and raring to go.

LAUNCHING

Let's begin our little tale a year earlier, though, in the summer of 1951. The temperature in Newport News rose above one hundred degrees that June 23, the day *United States* was launched. The wife of U.S. Senator Tom Connolly of Texas smashed a bottle of cham-

Newport News, Virginia, June 23, 1951. The christening having been completed, the new superliner *SS United States* is being eased out into the James River from the graving dock where she was built. The vessel to the right is CV 39, the Essex-class carrier *USS Lake Champlain*. (Courtesy of the Mariners' Museum, Newport News, Virginia.)

pagne across the vessel's prow at 12:43 P.M. This symbolically turned what had previously been hull number 488 of the Newport News Shipbuilding and Dry Dock Company into the *SS United States*. Senator Connolly chaired a committee with jurisdiction over merchant marine issues, and his spouse was selected for the honor after Bess Truman, the President's wife, earlier sent her regrets.

In a traditional launching, the vessel slides stern-first down inclined ways into the water. But the *United States* was built in a graving dock, where "launching" simply involved flooding the enclosure until the new liner achieved buoyancy. Water had begun flowing into the graving dock the previous afternoon; at approximately 5:00 A.M. on the day of her christening—almost eight hours before Mrs. Connolly let fly the champagne—the *United States* floated free of her keel blocks. As she was christened, a huge red, white, and blue bunting was billowing away from the top of her bow in much the fashion of a spinnaker on a fast sailboat sprinting for the finish line.

Because her hull never had to be subjected to the one-time stress associated with a conventional down-the-ways launching, *United States* was considerably more complete on the day she was christened than were most vessels; by common estimate she was more than 70 percent finished. Her twin red, white, and blue "sampan" funnels, perhaps her most distinctive visual characteristic, were in place on June 23, 1951, and other than a few tell-tale signs here and there—she was riding higher in the water than she would later, the windows of her wheelhouse were covered over, and the lifeboat davits were empty—on the day she was christened, *United States* looked as if she were ready for sea.

The new superliner was moved out of the graving docks into the James River by a fleet of tugboats that very afternoon. Fitting out took another year; in May 1952, the about-to-be-crowned queen of the American merchant marine was ready for her sea trials.

With many earlier ocean greyhounds, the question of speed, though important, was of less concern than were styling, interior appointments, and even the quality of food service. With *United States*, though, speed had always been the dominant consideration. During trials off the Virginia Capes in May and June of 1952, it was announced that *United States* held 34 knots for eight hours, and even managed 20 knots while going astern. There was considerable speculation that the vessel's true performance had been even more impressive than announced. Twenty-five years later the speculation would be confirmed.[3]

HOME PORT

Arriving in New York, her home port, preparatory to departure on her maiden voyage to the channel ports of Europe, *United States* was accorded a lusty harbor welcome, longer and louder and more enthusiastic than her reception two weeks later when she returned from Europe after actually capturing the North Atlantic Blue Riband. It seems everyone just assumed *United States* would win the coveted prize—news stories and Sunday supplement accounts were very matter-of-fact in their predictions—so why delay the celebration?

The weather was anything but auspicious on Tuesday, June 24, 1952, when *United States* steamed into New York Harbor for the very first time. It was cloudy and overcast, and intermittent showers fell throughout the day. The new superliner had departed Newport News early on the morning of June 23, carrying 1,400 specially invited guests. Though indeed guests of the company, these passengers also afforded the vessel's serving staff an opportunity to have a bit of a "dress rehearsal" before facing their first paying customers on the maiden voyage to Europe several days hence.[4]

United States emerged from the overcast fifty miles south of the lightship *Ambrose* shortly after dawn. She was met there by four Navy warships, the *Gearing*-class destroyers *USS Warrington* (DD-843), *USS Perry* (DD-844), *USS Goodrich* (DD-831), and *USS William W. Wood* (DD-715). The five vessels then formed a convoy and

Tuesday, June 24, 1952. The *United States* is off Governor's Island as she heads into New York Harbor for the very first time. A fleet of tugboats escorts the new superliner while *Fire Fighter* throws streams of water skyward. Both the *United States* and *Fire Fighter* were designed by the same man: William Francis Gibbs. (Courtesy of the Mariners' Museum, Newport News, Virginia.)

proceeded north, two destroyers leading the new superliner, two off her stern. As the ships neared *Ambrose* and the entrance to Ambrose Channel, a pair of Navy blimps from Lakehurst, New Jersey, appeared overhead. Outbound from New York came the Coast Guard cutter *Tuckahoe* with Mayor Vincent Impelliteri and United States Lines president John M. Franklin leading a welcoming party that boarded the new liner around 11:00 A.M. near Gravesend Bay.

The procession then continued through the narrows and the convoy grew in size. Tugboats of virtually every company working in the harbor were the principal participants, while various units of the city's fireboat fleet threw streams of water skyward in the city's traditional welcome for a vessel entering New York for the first time. Ferryboats whose over-and-back routes intersected the path being taken by the inbound *United States* altered course to give the superliner clear sailing, and any vessel at all that came anywhere near the new ship let out three long blasts on its whistle in greeting. Up on the bridge of *United States*, Commodore Harry Manning, the vessel's captain, had specially assigned Third Officer John Tucker to answer each and every greeting with three thunderous return salutes from the new liner's deep and powerful whistles.

Excursion boats traditionally joined such arrival processions. (Photographs of the arrival in New York of, say, the *Queen Mary* or the *Normandie* include many day-excursion boats steaming up the bay along with the new liner.) By 1952, though, the harbor's excursion-boat fleet had dwindled to a precious few, and because it was the last week in June leading up to the Fourth of July weekend, most New York excursion boats were at work on their assigned routes on the day *United States* first came to town, and were thus unavailable for escort duty. *Liberty*—one of the boats that ran to the Statue of Liberty—fell in behind *United States* for a portion of the inbound procession, and Meseck Line's *Americana* passed near the new superliner on a regular trip to Rye Beach. But of the dozens of vessels that escorted *United States* into port on the morning of June 24, 1952, the great majority were tugboats.

At 12:10 P.M., *United States* steamed past the Battery and entered the Hudson River; the rain fell all the harder. As the procession approached the deep-water passenger piers north of West 42nd Street, the various escorting vessels dispersed; now there was serious work to be done, and five Moran tugs had drawn the assignment to help dock the new superliner. *Eugene Moran* and *Doris Moran* took the port bow of *United States*, *Carol Moran*, and *Barbara Moran* were assigned aft on the starboard side, and *Grace Moran* was at the port quarter.

Moran docking pilot Captain Chester Evans had come aboard *United States* and was in charge of the operation, assisted by Fred Snyder. "Back the port engines," Evans ordered. "Port engines backing, sir," came the reply. Fresh new hawsers were let out and made fast to Pier 86. More orders back and forth; the five tugs pushed and pulled in unison under Captain Evans's direction. Finally, at 1:41 P.M., the process was completed. "Docked her in less than twenty-five minutes," Snyder said. "She sure handles easy."[5]

It was widely assumed that *United States* would win the North Atlantic Blue Riband as soon as she entered regular transatlantic service. An aura of mystery surrounded the myriad "secret features" incorporated into her design at the direction of the U.S. Navy to make her, during any future war, the most effective troopship of all time. With the lessons of World War II mobilization and supply still fresh, she was built for rapid conversion into a troopship that could carry 14,000 soldiers—virtually a full division—nonstop from North America to any port on earth. Kitchens aboard *United States*, for example, were designed so they could as easily turn out basic meals for 14,000 hungry servicemen as they could haute cuisine for 2,000 finicky passengers. The total cost of *United States* was reported to be $79.4 million, of which total the federal government contributed 65 percent and United States Lines the remaining 35 percent.

The cost-sharing ratio was arrived at in this way: (1) United States Lines was required to pay what a similar ocean liner might cost if built by one of its foreign-flag competitors in an overseas shipyard; (2) the U.S. government put up the difference between this figure and the actual price bid by an American shipbuilding company; (3) in addition, the government fully funded all the high-performance features included in the vessel to make her an effective troop transport in time of war.[6]

In any event, shrouded in deep secrecy were her true top speed, the shape of her hull below the waterline, and the performance specifications of the four powerful Westinghouse steam turbines with which she was equipped. It wasn't revealed until a decade later that the engines of *United States* were rated at a whopping 240,000 horsepower, almost 100,000 greater than any previous ocean liner. For all of her years, *United States*'s listing in the annual government publication *Merchant Vessels of the United States* left a telling blank in the horsepower column.

As to speed, in 1977—eight years after *United States* had been withdrawn from service—an official from Newport News Shipbuilding and Dry Dock delivered a paper that finally told the world the superliner had sustained 38.32 knots during her 1952 sea trials, a level of performance that can only be called breathtaking.[7]

Concerning all the secrecy associated with the shape of her hull, this anecdote should suffice: Plastic models of many famous ships have been produced over the years for sale in hobby shops and toy stores. Whether it was the *Queen Mary*, the battleship *Missouri*, or, in later years, *Los Angeles*-class nuclear submarines, these models always include a rendition, to scale, of the entire vessel—that is to say, the full hull configuration, both above and below the waterline, was accurately portrayed. When a plastic model of *United States* came onto the market, though, it was a waterline model only—in other words, the full shape of the hull was not rendered. (In the first decade of the superliner's active life, more than 500,000 such models of *United States* were sold.)

In any event, it was widely assumed that all these mystery features would enable *United States* to wrest the North Atlantic Blue Riband from Cunard-White Star's *Queen Mary* and better that vessel's 1938 mark of 3 days, 20 hours, and 42 minutes—and 31.69 knots—for an Atlantic crossing.

MAIDEN VOYAGE

After spending eight days in port—with the general public invited to come aboard for tours on one of those eight days—the new superliner was scheduled to leave for Europe at high noon on Thursday, July 3, 1952. Her larder was stocked with appropriate comestibles for the transatlantic voyage: 123,811 pounds of meat, 5,820 dozen eggs, 12,468 quarts of milk, 58,585 pounds of vegetables. (From time immemorial, there has been a strange fascination with quantifying the foodstuffs put aboard a ship, any ship.)

The *SS United States* is eased away from North River Pier 86 in New York for yet another trip to the Channel ports of Europe.

As noon hour approached on July 3, uniformed staff made their rounds, sounding the usual calls for visitors to go ashore. A Sandy Hook Harbor pilot came aboard and headed up to the bridge. Gangways were drawn back onto Pier 86. The last lines were let go at exactly 12:07 P.M., and, with a bevy of Moran tugs assisting the new superliner, she backed away from Pier 86 out into the Hudson River and turned her bow south toward the sea. There were 1,660 passengers aboard for the maiden voyage; they would be ministered to by a staff of 1,000. The new vessel had a passenger capacity of 1,928 (usually spoken of as 2,000), but because many ordinary double cabins were occupied by passengers traveling alone, only 1,660 people sailed that historic day. (The 1,000-person crew is also a rounded figure. While it changed marginally over the years, at one point the vessel's crew included 97 officers and 946 other personnel, for a total of 1,043. Three-quarters of this complement attended to passenger needs; the rest ran the ship.)

July 1952 would go down as one of the hottest summer months in New York history, but at noon on the day *United States* sailed on her maiden voyage, the temperature was a comfortable seventy-eight degrees in midtown Manhattan. As she headed down the Hudson, *United States* was greeted by countless harbor craft. On the bridge, Commodore Manning ensured that all were answered with a return salute on the new liner's booming whistle.

Interestingly, the departure of the new American superliner for Europe was not the only important and unusual trip to get underway in the United States that day. In Denver, Colorado, a special train pulled out of Union Station there, bound for Chicago. Aboard was retired General Dwight D. Eisenhower; his destination was the Republican National Convention, soon to be called to order in the Windy City. The whistle-stop tour from Denver to Chicago was part of Ike's strategy for wresting the party's presidential nomination away from Senator Robert Taft, of Ohio. As *United States* was making its first transatlantic voyage, Eisenhower won the G.O.P. nomination.

Near the Narrows, *United States* passed Cunard–White Star Line's *Mauritania*, inbound from Europe. Captain Donald Sorrell was in command of the British vessel and he saluted the Blue Riband contender with this message: "God speed to all on board."

It was fitting that the first Cunarder the new vessel met while under way was one that carried the name of a famous and long-time holder of the Atlantic Blue Riband. The original *Mauritania*—sister ship of the *Lusitania*—held the title for 22 years after winning it in 1907, longer than any other vessel. *United States* would break that longevity mark in 1974. Unfortunately, she would be five years into retirement at the time. (See Appendix C for a chronology of twentieth-century Blue Riband winners.)

United States slowed to let off her Sandy Hook Harbor pilot a little after 2:00 P.M. Then, at exactly 2:36 P.M., as she was resuming speed, *United States* steamed past *Ambrose* lightship, the traditional starting point for ocean voyages out of New York. The time was noted, clocks were started, and the try for the Blue Riband was underway—even though United States Lines officials had been refusing all day long to confirm that the maiden crossing would be the one that would try for any speed records. "I've been instructed to keep to schedule," Captain Manning earlier told reporters before leaving Pier 86. "After all, the main thing is a safe passage."[8] He had a big grin on his face when he said it, though, and it is a pose that steamship companies traditionally adopted whenever a new vessel hoped to contend for the Blue Riband.

There were ample giveaway signs, though. Earlier in the day, for example, a number of cabin-class passengers whose accommodations were on lower decks immediately adjacent to the four propellers were moved into different quarters. "The noise of the propellers at high speed would be great," a company official said.[9]

United States would use what is called "Track C" for her crossing, a northern sea lane popular during the summer. By 5:00 P.M., even before passengers had begun to enjoy early-seating dinner on the first night of the crossing, *United States* was comfortably making 30 knots. Manning's plan was to increase his vessel's speed very gradually over a period of several hours.

The 55-year-old Manning, incidentally, was himself a notable mariner. He first went to sea on a sailing ship in the years before World War I, and he skippered the United States Lines's *America* on her first commercial voyage to Europe, in late 1946. Perhaps his most notable achievement at sea happened during the early days of World War II, while the United States was still a neutral nation. He was the master of the United States Lines's *Washington* when she was stopped by a German U-boat intent on sinking the vessel. While passengers were actually taking to the lifeboats, Manning managed to talk the U-boat commander out of his proposed course of action by signal lamp, and his ship was allowed to continue.

An airplane pilot as well as a mariner, Manning took leave from the sea for a time in 1937 and served as a navigator for Amelia Earhart. Had United States Lines given Manning additional leave, he likely would have been Earhart's navigator on her tragic around-the-world flight in July 1937. (Who knows? Perhaps Earhart's last flight would have ended differently.)

Each day of the maiden voyage, reporters aboard ship radioed accounts back to New York telling of the assault on *Queen Mary*'s record; such stories inevitably made the front page, in big cities and small, along with stories about the Republican Convention in Chicago. British journalists, on the other hand, sent dispatches ahead to Fleet Street whose common theme was that, yes, the new ship was quite fast, but *Queen Mary* and *Queen Elizabeth* are still the best in the world for service, food, and general style. Throughout the voyage, other liners on the North Atlantic run greeted the newcomer with appropriate radio messages.

The Fourth of July—the first full day at sea—was celebrated with the new liner averaging 35.6 knots, a new record for a single day. It was a record that would prove to be extremely short-lived, though, because the very next day, July 5, *United States* averaged 36.2 knots to set another new mark. By mid-voyage a theme that began to be repeated in news accounts of the crossing was this: Only the onset of heavy fog will prevent *United States* from setting a new transatlantic speed record, and doing so in rather dramatic fashion.

The following day, July 6, a poignant thing happened. At 5:00 P.M. that Sunday afternoon, *United States* was still a half day's sail west of the Scilly Islands and Land's End when she passed Cunard-White Star's *RMS Queen Mary* seven miles to starboard, outbound for New York from Cherbourg and Southampton. Passengers on the Cunarder flocked to the ship's railing—even the movie theater emptied out—to get a look at the newest superliner on the western ocean. *Queen Mary*'s officers did some calculations and estimated that *United States* was making 36 knots, and after dipping his colors in salute, Captain Grattidge signaled *United States*: "God speed. Welcome to the Atlantic. Am sacking my chief engineer."

Another Blue Riband winner: Cunard-White Star's *RMS Queen Mary*, shown in New York after completing her maiden voyage in 1936.

A New Record

Many passengers stayed up until dawn that last night at sea. And at 5:16 A.M. Greenwich Mean Time on Monday, July 7, 1952—it was 2:16 in the morning back in New York—the *SS United States* came abreast of Bishop's Rock off Land's End on the southern coast of England, 2,942 nautical miles from *Ambrose* lightship. It was overcast and raining and a full gale was raging, with wind gusts reported as high as 60 knots. (An aluminum ping-pong table on one of the upper decks had earlier been picked up and blown overboard.) But neither the weather nor the hour made any difference, because on board *United States* champagne toasts were being raised, the ship's whistle roared back at the wind, the band played "The Star Spangled Banner," and passengers danced a conga line.[10]

Up on the bridge, Captain Manning was entertaining a VIP passenger: Margaret Truman, daughter of the President of the country after which the new ocean liner was named. Margaret Truman had taken the helm of the superliner for a few minutes the previous day; she was on her way to a six-week holiday in Scandinavia. In later years, Margaret Truman Daniel would write of that day when she was on the bridge of the *SS United States*: "I've never been so thrilled in all my life."[11]

Manning's celebrity passenger, though, in no way overshadowed his celebrity ship this July morning. "I feel like a pitcher who just pitched a no-hit game," said the master of what had just become the fastest ocean liner of all time.[12] The *SS United States* established a new eastbound Atlantic record of 3 days, 10 hours, and 40 minutes at an average speed of 35.59 knots. This beat *Queen Mary*'s old mark by a very comfortable 10 hours and 2 minutes—and 4.90 knots. In fact, in the competition for the North Atlantic Blue Riband, no challenger had ever bettered an earlier mark by such a wide margin since the early days of steam navigation in the 1830s. And *United States* did so with ample reserves to set a new and even faster mark at some future time, should her own record ever be challenged. Not to put too fine a point on it, but *United States* even used a course from *Ambrose* to Land's End that was four miles longer than *Queen Mary*'s 1938 route, 2,942 nautical miles versus 2,938.

United States was welcomed in both Le Havre and Southampton later in the day, even though she arrived in each port hours ahead of published schedules. The greeting she received in Southampton was said to be the warmest and loudest ever given to any vessel, any time, anywhere, for any reason. She was led into port by a U.S. Navy destroyer, a fireboat threw streams of water into the late afternoon sky, the Lord Mayor of Southampton came aboard to extend an official welcome, and a telegram was delivered to Captain Manning from a British subject whose knowledge of maritime matters was fully the equal of his rare skill in the use of the English language: "Congratulations on your magnificent achievement," wired Prime Minister Winston Churchill.[13]

Perhaps the most interesting passenger who went ashore and boarded the boat train for London at Southampton Ocean Terminal that day was a gentleman by the name of Juan Trippe. Trippe was the long-time president of a corporation called Pan American World Airways, and the purpose of his visit to England was to inspect the new deHavilland Comet, the world's very first jet-powered passenger plane. Considering that it would be similar jet airplanes— flying for Trippe's company, as well as others—that ultimately forced *United States* into premature retirement, perhaps Captain Manning should have put his passenger in irons and never let him go ashore!

(Something interesting about the London that Trippe and the other passengers reached on the evening of July 7, 1952, was that two days earlier the last of the city's double-deck electric trams had been withdrawn and replaced by motor buses. Between *Queen Mary*'s record being broken by *United States* and the last trams making their final run, for many British traditionalists, July 1952 must have seemed doubly unkind.)

On her first westbound voyage, *United States* again smashed the previous speed record, coming abreast of *Ambrose* lightship 3 days, 12 hours, and 12 minutes after clearing Bishop's Rock End at an average speed of 34.51 knots, 1.08 knots slower than her own eastbound crossing but a convincing 9 hours and 36 minutes faster than the previous record set by *Queen Mary*. The man in charge of the engine room aboard *United States*, Chief Engineer William Kaiser, said that were it not for the fog the ship encountered on Saturday and Sunday, the westbound crossing would have been even faster than the eastbound.

After reaching *Ambrose* lightship at 4:29 P.M. on Monday, July 14,

United States anchored at Quarantine overnight before proceeding ceremonially up the Hudson and docking at Pier 86 the next morning. Then, at 7:10 A.M. on Tuesday, July 15, 1952, *United States* raised her anchor, lowered her quarantine flag, and let out three loud salutes on her mighty whistle. The final phase of the fastest transatlantic round trip of all time had begun, although from here on into its berth it would travel at little more than five knots.

At 7:35 A.M., *United States* steamed past the Statue of Liberty; at 7:45 she was off the Battery. The municipal tugboat *Brooklyn* assumed a position close to the inbound ocean liner, and on the tug's fantail the marching band of the Department of Sanitation vainly attempted to add a musical note to the celebration. (The band's melodies were hopelessly drowned out by whistle salutes from welcoming vessels.) Fireboats threw streams of water skyward, led by the flagship of the municipal fleet, *Fire Fighter*, then assigned to the "Engine 57" post adjacent to the Battery; tugs and other harbor craft escorted the Blue Riband winner. Once again the docking pilot was Captain Chester Evans of Moran Towing and Transport, and just before the new ocean liner was eased into Pier 86, whistle salutes were sounded by two ocean liners that were tied up at nearby piers. Italian Line's *Vulcania* was moored at Pier 84, and Cunard–White Star's *Queen Elizabeth* at Pier 90; each delivered three long salutes to the new American superliner.

Then, with the Fire Department of New York band providing music from the end of Pier 86, *United States* was slowly turned with the aid of a fleet of Moran tugs and eased into her berth on the north side of Pier 86. At 9:12 A.M. lines had been set and the ship was safely tied up to the pier.

In all her seventeen years on the North Atlantic, *United States* would never again sail as fast as she did on her maiden voyage in July 1952. There is one story from her second crossing, though, that bears retelling.

Was It a Race?

Cunard-White Star's *Queen Elizabeth* had quietly entered commercial passenger service after the war, and while the scuttlebutt from her days as a British troopship during the war suggested she had the

Looking forward (top) and aft (bottom) from the starboard bridge wing of the *United States* while moored at North River Pier 86.

Fuel was pumped aboard the *United States* at New York shortly after completion of each transatlantic crossing.

ability to beat *Queen Mary*'s prewar records, the late 1940s were just not a proper time to worry about such seeming frivolity as transatlantic speed records, never mind the extraordinary fuel costs that efforts to set speed records necessarily entailed.

Queen Elizabeth was actually completed in 1940, and her first voyage brought her to New York in March of that year. But this was a crossing under wartime security measures, not a traditional maiden voyage. She was then outfitted for troopship service in North America, away from the threat of German aerial attack. It was not until *United States* came on the scene in 1952 that the British maritime world realized their "second Queen" might never get a chance to compete for the Blue Riband.

Cunard publicly discounted all talk of unlimbering *Queen Elizabeth* and making a try for the record. Even the British press played down the idea of having *Queen Elizabeth* try to reclaim the Blue Riband.[14] Perhaps the most revealing glimpse into Cunard's inten-

A Blue Riband non-winner: the original *RMS Queen Elizabeth* of the Cunard-White Star Line, shown in 1955.

tions comes from an Associated Press interview with Commodore George E. Cove, the master of the *Queen Elizabeth*, conducted in early July. Cove, whose own retirement was imminent, allowed as how it would be a very fine idea indeed if he could cap off his career with a "memorable fast crossing" on the bridge of the 83,673-ton British liner.[15]

Late on Thursday morning, July 31, 1952, *Queen Elizabeth* sailed out of Cherbourg bound for New York. A half hour later, *United States* left Le Havre on her second westbound crossing. Both vessels had departed Southampton earlier in the day.

The next morning off Land's End, an observer on the Cornwall coast said that *Queen Elizabeth* seemed to slow down, almost as if she were waiting for something. The "something" was the new American superliner, and once she appeared, *Queen Elizabeth* resumed speed. As the two vessels came abreast of each other off Bishop's Rock, Cove and Manning exchanged greetings.[16]

The Cunard-White Star Line has since issued all manner of denial that anything like a race was intended or ever took place on that midsummer crossing—and perhaps the denials are accurate and truthful. But there are others who insist that on August 1, 1952, the Royal Mail Steamer *Queen Elizabeth* made her first, last, and only try for the North Atlantic Blue Riband.[17]

The contest, if ever there was one, proved to be a first-round knock-out. For the *Queen Elizabeth* it was too late, and for *United States* it was too easy. Within four hours *United States* was out of sight of *Queen Elizabeth* and so, with the outcome of the "race" quite clear, Commodore Cove eased off on his engines and continued the crossing at service speed. *United States* reached *Ambrose* lightship 10 hours and 40 minutes ahead of *Queen Elizabeth*. "There was no race. We just raced away from her," Manning said when he reached New York.[18]

Captain Manning stepped down as master of *United States* after that second crossing. His assignment had been simply to put the new superliner into service, and for her third crossing, Captain John W. Anderson was moved over onto *United States* from *America*. He stayed with the ship for many years.[19]

The advent of *United States* into transatlantic service gave United States Lines a chance to realign its schedules and service. At the end of the summer season in 1951, as *United States* was being fitted out in Newport News, the company terminated its charter of the 1933-built *Washington* from the Maritime Commission. The *Washington*—which United States Lines had owned outright before the war but afterward only leased from the federal government—had been deployed since 1948 on a single-class and very much economy-style service between New York and Cobh, Le Havre, Southampton, and Cuxhaven. Since the new superliner would serve only Le Havre and Southampton, the company's previous flagship, the *America* of 1940, was redeployed on *Washington*'s old route, albeit with traditional three-class service and the substitution of Bremerhaven for Cuxhaven. In July 1952, *United States* and *America* became United States Lines's sole transatlantic passenger liners. Because *America* lacked the speed of her newer fleetmate, plus the fact that she

United States Lines' *SS Washington*, of which Commodore Harry Manning, the first skipper of the *United States*, had earlier been master.

serviced twice as many European ports on a typical crossing, *America* was generally able to make only three round trips in the time it took *United States* to make four.

RETROSPECTIVE

The *SS United States* remains one of the most memorable ships ever to sail the North Atlantic mailboat route, a service that is distinguished by the calibre of vessels that have crossed between Europe and North America over the years; in many categories she was simply the best. Designed by William Francis Gibbs—a fascinating man who was also responsible for *America* and for the city of New York's classic fireboat, *Fire Fighter*—*United States* may have lacked some of the lavish interior touches that gave European-built ocean liners much of their distinction and charm, but she was second to none in the basic engineering that made her not only the fastest liner of all times but also a ship able to manage such performance while being virtually vibration free. Gibbs also took great pains to ensure that *United States* was the most fire-proof passenger ship of all time, carrying to legendary proportions his concerns that there be no material aboard the vessel that would support combustion, such as wood.[20]

United States quickly became a very popular ship. In 1955, for example, at the height of her career, she made twenty-two round trips between Europe and New York, averaged 95 percent utilization, and carried more passengers—70,194—than any other vessel on the North Atlantic. Cunard-White Star's *Queen Elizabeth*, marginally larger than *United States*, came in second that year, with 66,600 transatlantic passengers.

United States can also be called the last high-performance ocean liner to be built especially, and exclusively, for fast North Atlantic service. Latter-day ocean liners such as Cunard's *Queen Elizabeth 2* and French Line's *France*, while designed to cross the North Atlantic at close to 30-knot speed, lacked the ability to push their performance into the 35-knot-plus range that would have been necessary to challenge the mark set by *United States* in 1952.

On her maiden voyage in May of 1969, for instance, the *QE2* averaged 28.02 knots from Le Havre to Ambrose light tower, considerably less than *Queen Mary*'s best prewar performance of 31.69 knots, not to mention the speed of 35.59 knots that stands as *United States*'s best performance. *France* reportedly made 35-knot speed during her sea trials in 1961, but required maximum output from her boilers to do so. *United States* set her records without ever being pushed to maximum performance.

Furthermore, both *France* and *Queen Elizabeth 2*, while noble vessels that occupy their own special niches in the long history of transatlantic express service, were designed to be equally at home in more-leisurely cruise service to warm-water ports. *United States*, on the other hand, though she was deployed on various cruises later in her career in an effort to help the bottom line, was from the outset designed to maintain express mailboat service across the North Atlantic on a year-round basis, and to that extent she can correctly be called the last of her kind.[21] A lighted map aboard *United States* that kept passengers informed of the ship's position during a voyage had the ability to indicate but a single route: New York to the channel ports of Europe. (This map is today on display in the Mariners' Museum in Newport News, Virginia.)

Contemporary cruise ships that spend their time in warm water have no need for an enclosed promenade. On a ship designed for all-weather crossings of the North Atlantic, however, such a facility was an absolute necessity.

Later in the summer of 1952, *United States* carried an unusual piece of cargo from Southampton to New York. It was the actual Blue Riband trophy, an artifact that took even some steamship fanciers by total surprise since many were unaware there was such a trophy and assumed the Blue Riband was merely an honorary prize and title. Among those who did know about the trophy there was some doubt it had survived the war intact. But the trophy was quite real—and undamaged. It had been commissioned by a member of the British Parliament from Hanley by the name of Harold Hales in 1933, when that honorable member felt it was singularly unfortunate that so significant an accomplishment as a record-fast crossing of the North Atlantic Ocean carried no formal award.

Cunard-White Star never took possession of the trophy following

Another Blue Riband winner: French Line's *Normandie* heads down the Hudson.

Queen Mary's record- setting performance, and it had spent the war years in a jewelry shop in Hanley, England.[22] A committee headed by the Duke of Sutherland is responsible for validating claims for what has come to be called the Hales Trophy, and it was formally presented to United States Lines by the duke during a dinner aboard the new superliner while she was docked in New York on November 10, 1952.

The Hales Trophy remained with United States Lines as long as *United States* herself was active, and for much of that time it was displayed under glass in the company's New York offices. After *United States* was retired from service in 1969, the company felt the U.S. Merchant Marine Academy at Kings Point, New York, was a more appropriate place for the trophy, and that's where it was sent. Many thought it would stay there forever.

It didn't. In 1990, a 213-foot catamaran bearing the name *Hoverspeed Great Britain* set out across the North Atlantic from New York, reached Bishop's Rock 2 hours and 45 minutes faster than *United States* did in 1952, and thereby laid claim to the Hales Trophy. But this new mark would not last long. In August 1992, a 222-foot vessel powered by three high-performance water jet engines, *Destriero*, made the run from Ambrose light to Bishop's Rock 21 hours faster than *Hoverspeed Great Britain*, and the Hales Trophy changed hands once again. The new record is 2 days, 20 hours, 34 minutes, and 50 seconds, for an average speed of 53 knots.

While not at all discounting the fact that both *Hoverspeed Great Britain* and *Destriero* represent notable achievements of both technology and seamanship in their fast crossings of the North Atlantic, a voice of protest does have to be raised if these specialized voyages are purported to be bona fide betterings of the achievement recorded by *United States* in the summer of 1952. *Hoverspeed Great Britain* and *Destriero* are glorified speed boats, not ocean liners, and it remains an article of unquestioned faith that no commercial displacement hull of any serious size will ever equal or exceed the accomplishment turned in by *United States* on the July day in 1952 when she steamed proudly out of New York Harbor, picked up speed as she passed *Ambrose* lightship, and headed east.

Well, there might be one qualification to this article of otherwise unquestioned faith. Once upon a time there was a marvelous ocean liner that was fully capable of bettering the records that were set in July 1952—perhaps by a rather wide margin, too. This potential record-setter was towed away to Turkey for conversion into a cruise ship in June of 1992 by the oceangoing tugboat *Smit Rotterdam*.[23] As she disappeared into the ocean mists off Cape Charles, Virginia, sans serif aluminum letters across her stern were still very visible, very vivid:

UNITED STATES
New York

A 1996 postscript: Converting *United States* into a contemporary cruise ship in Turkey proved to be a formidable task. Removal of layer upon layer of asbestos fire-proofing was itself a major challenge, and as the overall project moved along, its eventual completion grew less and less likely. It was finally abandoned, and in the summer of 1996, *United States* was towed back across the western ocean and up the Delaware River to the port of Philadelphia. If this fine ship will never again sail the seas, neither will she be reduced to scrap. Her future will likely involve conversion into some kind of stationary facility.

It's the spring of 1969 and in six months the active career of the *SS United States* would be over. Here she calls at Boston to board additional transatlantic passengers while enroute to Europe. It was her first—and possibly only—visit to the Hub.

NOTES

1. "Riband" is an older English spelling of "ribbon" and particularly connotes prize or honor. One sometimes finds a reference to the North Atlantic Blue *Ribband*; this would seem to be incorrect usage, since a "ribband" is a structural part of a ship.
2. See "*SS United States* Heads for Layup," *Marine Digest* 48(13) (November 22, 1969), 3, 38. The final transatlantic crossing of *United States*, "Voyage No. 400," was as follows:

lv. New York	October 25, 1969; noon
ar. Le Havre	October 30, 1969; morning
ar. Southampton	October 30, 1969; afternoon
ar. Bremerhaven	October 31, 1969; morning
lv. Bremerhaven	November 1, 1969; afternoon
lv. Southampton	November 2, 1969; morning
lv. Le Havre	November 2, 1969; afternoon
ar. New York	November 7, 1969; 8:00 A.M.

She left New York on the evening of November 7 and tied up in Newport News on November 8.

3. There were two sets of sea trials. Between May 14 and May 16, a series of builder's trials were conducted, and May 14, 1952, marked the first time that *United States* ran under her own power. On June 10 additional sea trials were conducted under the auspices of the U.S. Maritime Commission.

4. This trip generated some controversy. Was the luxury cruise for specially invited guests paid for with taxpayer funds? Not at all, said United States Lines; only company funds were used. See *The New York Times*, June 21, 1952, p. 33; see also Frank O. Braynard, *The Big Ship* (Newport News, VA: Mariners Museum, 1981), 107–111. Braynard's work, let it be noted, is a *tour de force* that does full justice to its magnificent subject, the *SS United States*.

5. *The New York Times*, June 24, 1952, p. 15.

6. Some federal officials felt that because the cost of the new vessel had escalated, some renegotiation of the 1949 contract between the government and United States Lines was called for, and threatened not to turn the vessel over to the company unless a new agreement was forthcoming. United States Lines refused. The impasse was broken when all parties agreed to discuss financial matters at a later time and let the new superliner enter service as scheduled. President Truman had this to say about United States Lines's refusal to renegotiate the contract: "I deplore this attitude on the part of the company" (*The New York Times*, June 21, 1952, p. 33). See also Braynard, *The Big Ship*, pp. 80–106.

7. See John R. Kane, "The Speed of the SS *United States*,"*Marine Technology* 15(2) (April 1978), 119–39. Although delivered to a professional audience in 1977, this paper contains much information that a general reader can understand and appreciate.

8. *The New York Times*, July 4, 1952, p. 6.

9. Ibid.

10. One newspaper ran a front-age story telling of *United States*'s capture of the Blue Riband that included a rather serious misstatement about the weather. "The eastern Atlantic was enjoying fine summer weather, with a southwesterly wind of 5 miles an hour," claimed the *Washington Post* on July 7, 1952.

11. Margaret Truman Daniel wrote the foreword to William G. Miller's fine book about *United States*; see Miller, *SS "United States"* (Sparkford, U.K.: Patrick Stephens, 1991), p. 9.

12. *The New York Times*, July 7, 1952, p. 1.

13. *London Times*, July 9, 1952, p. 4.

14. *Manchester Guardian*, July 7, 1952, p. 7 and July 8, 1952, p. 6.

15. *The New York Times*, July , 1952, p. 6.

16. *New York Sunday News*, August 3, 1952, p. 2; *New York Daily News*, August 5, 1952, p. 5.

17. Braynard presents further perspectives on this whole matter of whether there was or wasn't a race; see *The Big Ship*, 166–67.

18. *The New York Times*, August 5, 1952, p. 43.

19. Captain John W. Anderson, the vessel's second master, should not be confused with Captain Leroy Alexanderson, the vessel's third and last master.

20. Gibbs made only a single crossing aboard *United States*: the maiden voyage, in July 1952. For a detailed study of his contribution to the U.S. maritime industry, see Frank O. Braynard, *By Their Works Ye Shall Know Them* (New York: Gibbs and Cox, 1968). For a shorter treatment of Gibbs, see Bill Ross,

"Mr. Merchant Marine," *Ships & Sailing* 2(1) (June 1952), 52–55.

21. The very first cruise ever operated by *United States* was in January 1962, a two-week trip to Nassau, St. Thomas, Trinidad, Curaçao, and Cristobal. The following statistics give some sense of how much of her time was spent on and off the North Atlantic: When she ended her active career in 1969, she had carried 1,025,691 passengers—98 percent in transatlantic service and 2 percent on cruises. For more details, see Miller, *SS "United States,"* 180.

22. One published report even raised the possibility that the Hales Trophy had been aboard the ill-fated *Normandie* when, as *USS Lafayette*, that superliner burned and capsized in New York in February 1942. (See *The New York Times*, July 16, 1951, p. 37.) French Line had quietly returned the Hales Trophy to the jewelry store in Surrey where it had been crafted, and that's where it spent the war years. See Braynard, *The Big Ship*, p. 83.

23. During her inactive years, the home port of *United States* was changed on two different occasions, first to Washington, D.C., after she was purchased by the federal government, then to Seattle, reflecting her sale to a West Coast company intending to use her in a cruise service that never materialized. "Seattle" had actually been painted onto her stern, but prior to departure from Norfolk for Turkey, "Seattle" was removed and when she returned to sea on June 4, 1992, her home port as shown was "NEW YORK." It was an insignificant gesture, but a totally marvelous one!

John J. Harvey puts on a water display.

3

FDNY Fireboats

Over the years, many fleets of specialized vessels have called the port of New York home. Few, however, can lay claim to the traditions of valor and heroism that are routinely associated with the fireboats of the Fire Department of New York.

Most of us, if we even notice a fireboat at all, see a quiet vessel sitting peacefully at its berth, lightly bobbing up and down with the tide. Or maybe we see it out in the bay, throwing streams of water skyward as part of some kind of harbor celebration—the first visit to New York of a magnificent new cruise liner, or an important civic anniversary of one sort or another. What few people ever see are the times when New York fireboats truly earn their keep: These are times of disaster—*terror* is not too strong a word—when the scourge of uncontrolled fire is devouring property and posing a threat to life and limb for the people of New York. This is when the fireboats of the FDNY sail unhesitatingly in harm's way to control a raging inferno and, just as often, to rescue innocent people from danger.

Many brave men have given their lives while fighting fires from the decks of the city's fireboats; others have suffered serious injury. Their story not only deserves to be told. It is a story that has earned a very special place in the history—and in the legends—of the port of New York.

Early Fireboats

The very first "fireboat" in New York was nothing more than a barge that was outfitted with hand-powered pumping apparatus, not unlike the kind seen today during firemen's musters at county fairs. Since the volunteers who manned the pumps also had to row the barge from its berth to the scene of a fire—and were, consequently, exhausted when they got there—it is not difficult to understand why this "floating engine," as it was called, proved to be no great success. It was introduced in 1800 and withdrawn in 1818.

Almost fifty years later, in 1866—the year after the first paid fire department was established in New York—the Metropolitan Board of Fire Commissioners contracted with the Baxter Wrecking Company for the services of their tugboat, the *John Fuller*, which was equipped with fire-fighting gear. The *Fuller* would be called out whenever the specialized skills of a waterborne "fire engine" were needed, and she remained under contract to the Fire Department until 1875, when the wooden-hulled *William F. Havemeyer* became the first city-owned fireboat. According to some reports, the *John Fuller* remained active with the department even after the *Havemeyer* came on the scene.[1]

Delivered at a cost of $23,800.00, the *Havemeyer* was built in Camden, New Jersey, by Wood, Dialogue, and Company. Its statutory measurements were 102.5 feet by 20.6 feet by 9.8 feet, and it was equipped with two Amoskeag steam pumps. Entering service on May 12, 1875, it was the first of ten FDNY fireboats to be named after a former mayor of the City of New York. (See Appendix E for identification of the namesake of each FDNY vessel; Appendix D is a more conventional vessel roster.) In 1882 the iron-hulled *Zophar Mills* became the second FDNY fireboat, and in 1898, when the City of New York expanded to its current size and shape by amalgamation with previously independent jurisdictions, two fireboats that had been built by and for the Fire Department of the City of Brooklyn were absorbed into an expanded FDNY fleet. These were the 1885-built *Seth Low* and the 1892-built *David A. Boody*. *Seth Low* bears an interesting distinction with respect to her name. When christened, she bore the name of a former mayor of the City of Brooklyn. (The Honorable David A. Boody also once served as Mayor of Brooklyn.) But in 1899 Seth Low would also be elected the second mayor of the newly amalgamated City of New York. Thus it can be said that when *Seth Low* joined the FDNY fleet in 1898, she became the only fireboat to bear the name of a mayor of New York more than a year before he was elected.

THE NEW YORKER

Prior to the 1898 amalgamation a very notable fireboat was added to the fleet, a vessel that was christened *New Yorker* but shortly afterward had her name officially and formally changed to *The New Yorker*. Described by *Harper's* magazine at the time of her launching as "the final development of the most efficient New York Fire Department," *The New Yorker* would serve for more than three decades as the flagship of the FDNY fleet holding down the prestigious assignment as "Engine 57"[2] adjacent to Castle Garden at the Battery, followed by nine years in other assignments. Her career would begin during the presidential administration of Benjamin Harrison and end midway through that of Herbert Hoover.

The New Yorker was designed by William Cowells and built at the Jonson Foundry and Machine Company, East 118th Street and the Harlem River. Powered by a three-cylinder triple-expansion steam engine, the 243-gross-ton fireboat was the FDNY fleet's first vessel

The New Yorker tied up at the old Engine 57 fire house at the Battery. For many years this fireboat exceeded all other FDNY vessels in pumping capacity, the traditional measure of fireboat performance.

with a steel hull, an obvious advantage in fire-fighting work. She was launched amid much pomp and ceremony on April 5, 1890. During a luncheon reception held afterward at the foundry, former Judge Gildersleeve delighted those in attendance by reciting from Henry Wadsworth Longfellow's "The Building of the Ship":

Choose the timbers with greatest care;
Of all that is unsound beware;
For only what is sound and strong
To this vessel shall belong.

The New Yorker was big. A standard measure of fireboat performance is a vessel's pumping capacity, routinely expressed as the number of gallons of water per minute (GPM) a vessel can deliver.[3] *The New Yorker* could pour 13,000 GPM on a burning ship or pier; by contrast, *William F. Havemeyer*'s pumping capacity was 3,000 GPM, and *Zophar Mills*'s was 6,000. It would not be until 1931, forty-one years later, that FDNY designed and built a fireboat that could outperform *The New Yorker* in sheer pumping capacity.

The New Yorker also *looked* big. She had an oversized wheelhouse and a funnel that seemed disproportionately large on a hull that was only 112 feet long. (The funnel seen in most photographs of the vessel is not the original; it is a larger one that was retrofitted, probably during her first decade of service.)

In addition, *The New Yorker* ushered in a new era in fireboat operations: while the vessel's marine officers would always remain on board, her firefighting crew would await the call to duty in a shoreside firehouse adjacent to the boat's berth. With previous fireboats, everybody—ship's crew and firefighters—stayed on board all of the time.

This raises another point: just as an aircraft carrier requires two separate crews to make it fully operational—a ship's company to run the vessel and an air wing to fly the planes—so does a fireboat need the services of people with maritime ratings, such as pilot and engineer, to operate the boat, and traditional firefighters to man the deck monitors, stretch hose, and overhaul after a fire has been put out. Neither aircraft carriers nor fireboats can hope to perform their respective missions unless the two groups work in a coordinated manner.

New Yorker, the new flagship of the FDNY fleet, with Captain Archie Watt in command, entered service at the Battery as Engine 57 on February 1, 1891; her acceptance trials had been completed on the Hudson River on January 22.[4]

EARLY EXPLOITS

One cold night during the winter of 1905, when the telegraph operator at Sandy Hook looked out to sea, his heart jumped at the sight of a ship on fire. He quickly activated his telegraph circuits and tapped out the following message: "Ocean steamer loaded with passengers going to destruction at the gateway to the new world; frenzied passengers rushing about the deck."

The alarm was picked by *The New Yorker* and the powerful fireboat quickly cast off from the Battery and steamed down the bay, her crew fully expecting to face an awful shipboard holocaust. But the alarm proved to be a false one. The vessel was merely a tramp steamer, and the "fire" the Sandy Hook telegraph operator observed from shore was the crew using kerosene torches to remove caked ice from the vessel's railings in preparation for the unloading of cargo the next morning.

On another occasion, a steamer from Brazil was anchored off Swinburne Island just below the Narrows. Fire had erupted in her hold and *The New Yorker* arrived to render assistance. While some of the fireboat's crew held the blaze at bay, others led passengers to safety. As *The New Yorker* was preparing to return to shore with rescued passengers, a woman cried out, "You have forgotten my baby, Eva!" Firemen reboarded and made their way through smoke-filled passageways to the woman's cabin. And there, hiding under a sofa, was Eva—a large white cat.[5]

Over and above such humorous stories, two serious turn-of-the-century tragedies stand out: one was the awful fire that destroyed the excursion steamboat *General Slocum* in 1904, and the other was a fire in Hoboken in the summer of 1900.

Saturday, June 30, 1900: Four ships of North German Lloyd were docked at their usual piers in Hoboken, New Jersey; visitors and guests were being welcomed to tour the various ships on the first weekend of summer. Sometime around 4:00 P.M., fire broke out among bales of cotton stored on Pier 3; the flames quickly spread to nearby barrels of turpentine and oil, and within 15 minutes the pier was completely involved. Then, before anyone could do anything about it, fire spread to the four ships: *Bremen, Saale, Main,* and *Kaiser Wilhelm der Grosse.* The latter was then the fastest passenger liner operating between New York and Europe; she was also the first of the memorable "four stackers" that would come to dominate transatlantic travel for the next quarter century. (See Appendix C for a chronology of transatlantic speed champions.)

Hoboken firemen concentrated on the piers. Three of the four ships were cut loose from their moorings and set adrift on the Hudson. *Kaiser Wilhelm* was able to move on her own, as she had steam up; she would be the least damaged of the four. The other three were totally destroyed.

The New Yorker and *Robert A. Van Wyk* were dispatched to assist, later followed by *Zophar Mills.* While they would perform yeoman work in rescuing passengers and crew from the four vessels, in large measure they confronted a situation that rendered even a powerful fireboat helpless. People aboard several ships were trapped below decks by the fire and were unable to squeeze themselves through the ship's small portholes. A fireman aboard the *Van Wyk* told this story about the situation they found when they tried to come to the aid of *Saale*: "Finding it impossible to get the poor people out, we handed cups of water to some of them who cried for a drink."[6]

The fireboats helped keep the flaming ships from inflicting damage to other vessels in the port, and *The New Yorker* took twenty-eight people off *Bremen*; but the fireboats also had to stand by helplessly while people died. The death toll in the Hoboken dock (and ship) fire of 1900 was 326 people.[7]

If FDNY fireboats performed bravely and heroically during the Hoboken pier fire in 1900, they played a very minor role when *General Slocum* caught fire in Hell Gate on June 15, 1904. This is not to fault the performance of the fireboats; the wooden excursion steamer simply went up in flames so quickly that by the time the first fireboat was on the scene—*Zophar Mills*, then assigned to a berth on the Manhattan side of the East River near Hell Gate—the disaster was over. *Zophar Mills* pursued *General Slocum* from a distance but was never able to close in on the swiftly moving excursion steamer.

Instead, the fireboat directed her efforts to rescuing people who had fallen or jumped overboard into the East River as fire consumed the ill-fated vessel. Of the first thirty-one people brought aboard *Zophar Mills*, twenty-seven were already dead. But the fireboat was able to put her unique abilities to good use on that awful day. The master of the tugboat *John Wade* had steamed in close to the *Slocum* in an effort to rescue some of her passengers, and his boat was herself in danger of catching fire. Fast work by the men of *Zophar Mills* ensured that the gallant tug did not become another casualty. In all, 1,030 people lost their lives in the *General Slocum* fire, by far the worst tragedy ever to befall New York—on land, on sea, or in the air.[8]

What Is a Fireboat?

A fireboat isn't simply a fire engine that happens to float and can therefore fight fires in places where land-based apparatus can't. A fireboat is also—and perhaps primarily—a massive and overpowering fire engine that can bring huge quantities of water to bear on any fire to which it can gain access. *The New Yorker* came on the scene in 1891 with a 13,000 GPM pumping capacity. The typical land-based FDNY pumper *today* has a capacity of only 1,000 GPM, meaning that a nineteenth-century fireboat could outperform more than a dozen contemporary engines. Imagine what a fire-fighting weapon *The New Yorker* was in the 1890s, when the comparison on land was a horse-drawn pumper whose capacity was only a few hundred gallons per minute. In 1904, the city's seven fireboats had a pumping capacity that was virtually double that of all the land-based fire engines stationed on Manhattan Island.

A simple comparison of pumping capacity does not tell the full story, though, for land-based fire equipment is also restricted in its ability to pump water by whatever volume a city's hydrant system can supply. By contrast, fireboats have access to unlimited quantities of water, which makes their overpowering pumping capacity all that more valuable an asset.

So powerful is a fireboat that its deck monitors are seen not merely as sources of water to extinguish an inferno but also as brute physical force that is capable of knocking down brick walls to gain access to the interior of an otherwise inaccessible building. (Deck monitors are cannonlike devices aboard fireboats—ordinary fire engines today feature similar equipment, but of a somewhat smaller calibre—that discharge powerful streams of water.)

Given such overpowering force, it should not be surprising to learn that when modern fireboats came on the scene in the latter years of the nineteenth century, it was suggested in some quarters that they could also prove useful in quelling civil disturbances, such as those the newly organized labor unions were frequently seen as fomenting. There are no known instances of civil authorities ordering a fireboat into action as a form of crowd control. Had a boat like *The New Yorker* ever trained its deck monitors on a gathering of people at fairly close range—and run the pumps at anything remotely approaching full power—it would have resulted in as bloody a slaughter as if the crew opened fire with Gatling guns.

Because fireboats had such powerful pumping capacity, fighters of waterfront fires quickly developed the strategy of linking the hoses of land-based fire companies directly into high-pressure manifolds aboard the boats and letting the boats do the pumping, even if the boats' deck monitors could not themselves be brought to bear. A major fire on a pier or in a waterfront warehouse might see ten or fifteen land-based companies respond, along with two fireboats, and yet the fireboats would supply 90 percent of the water used to bring the blaze under control.

1890 THROUGH 1931

After *The New Yorker* entered service in 1891, more new boats were added to the fleet. Interestingly, though, no effort was made to equal, much less exceed, *The New Yorker*'s pumping capacity. Instead, the new fireboats added to the fleet in the years while *The New Yorker* served as Engine 57 were all smaller than the flagship.

An important theory was at work here. The preeminent fireboat architect of the period was a man by the name of Harry deBerkely Parsons, and it was Parsons's belief that the ideal fireboat was a vessel with a pumping capacity somewhat less than 10,000 GPM. There was no technical impediment against building a fireboat with double—or even triple—*The New Yorker*'s 13,000 GPM capacity.

Such firepower would have meant building a much bigger boat, of course. "There is little or no benefit to be derived from [fire] boats exceeding a certain size," Parsons said. "Large boats become un-handy and slow in maneuvering, both of which are requisites of the greatest importance in fighting a fire."[9]

Among the Parsons-designed fireboats that joined the FDNY fleet after *The New Yorker* were *William L. Strong* of 1898 (6,500 GPM), *Abram S. Hewitt* of 1903 (7,000 GPM), and *George B. McClellan* of 1904 (7,000 GPM).[10]

In addition to being smaller than *The New Yorker*, the new boats Parsons designed used a different kind of steam engine than did the older and larger vessel. *The New Yorker* was powered by a three-cylinder, triple-expansion engine, a popular style of power plant during the steam era. Parsons felt, though, that for the unique demands of fireboat work, a two-cylinder compound engine was a better choice. Why? A triple-expansion engine took longer to reach optimal operating temperature—and, therefore, maximum effi-ciency—than a two-cylinder compound, and when a fireboat was getting away from its berth and heading to the scene of a waterfront blaze, minutes, even seconds, were important. All subsequent FDNY steam-powered fireboats would be powered by two-cylinder compound engines.

Parsons, an independent naval architect and professor of engi-neering at Rensselaer Polytechnic Institute whose interests ex-

William L. Strong, shown in the all-grey paint scheme that was used during the Second World War.

tended to the world of racing yachts as well as fireboats, found a ready ally for his theories within the FDNY at the turn of the century, in the person of Chief of Department Charles Croker. Croker, more than any other FDNY official, saw the potential that fireboats represented and was a staunch advocate of expanding the fleet. He also had ideas of his own about fireboat design: "The decks should be flush fore and aft, and as clear as possible of all obstructions. The common practice of providing a large pilot house should be avoided," Croker insisted.[11] Fireboats of the FDNY came to reflect Parsons's thinking in technical areas of naval architecture and Croker's in practical matters relating to firefighting.

In 1905, under Croker, the fireboats were removed from the jurisdiction of FDNY's conventional battalion structure and turned into an independent Marine Battalion, headed by its own battalion chief. In 1909 this battalion was elevated into a Marine Division, headed by its own deputy chief, and the man whom Croker selected to serve as chief of marine operations—first battalion, then deputy— was John Kenlon. Kenlon would later go on to be Chief of Department; he also proved to be an erudite firefighter and sailor: he wrote an important book on the history of firefighting and a delightful volume about such seafaring adventures as sailing around Cape Horn.[12]

The year before Chief Croker established the FDNY's Marine Division, 1908, saw the construction and delivery of *three* brand new fireboats. Two were full-size vessels that incorporated important advances in fireboat design; the third was a somewhat smaller vessel that could move swiftly up and down the Harlem River without having to wait for the many swing bridges along that waterway to open.

Cornelius W. Lawrence was the name selected for the boat to be stationed along the Harlem. It honored a former mayor who served between 1834 and 1837 and who can lay claim to this interesting distinction: Mayor Lawrence was the first City Hall chief executive to ascend to the post as the result of direct popular election. The earliest mayors were simply appointed; later they were elected by vote not of the people but of the Common Council. The *Lawrence* was 104 feet long and had a pumping capacity of 7,000 GPM.

The other two boats that joined the fleet in 1908, *Thomas Willett* and *James Duane*, were the first New York fireboats to feature water pumps driven by steam turbines rather than reciprocating steam engines; they were rated at 9,000 GPM. The 1908 sister-ships were also equipped with mastlike towers toward the stern, featuring monitor guns mounted atop; this gave the boats more angles of attack for bringing streams of water to play against fires, particularly down into the holds of blazing ships, a feature that would have been especially helpful during the Hoboken fire in 1900. (After a fashion, the towers on *Willett* and *Duane* resembled the "birdcage" masts then popular on naval ships of the line.)

Both *Willett* and *Duane* honored the memories of former mayors, Mayor Willett being the very first individual who ever held the office. He was appointed to two nonconsecutive one-year terms in 1665 and 1667, more than one hundred years before the American Revolution and 243 years before a municipal fireboat would be launched bearing his name.

James Duane served from 1908 through 1969. Throughout that period she was assigned to Engine 85, West 35th Street and the Hudson River.

The two sister-ships were built in Newburgh, New York, at the famous T. J. Marvel yard, and were welcomed to the fleet with a most unusual ceremony. On May 21, 1908, a maritime parade was staged with all of the city's fireboats participating: *The New Yorker, William L. Strong, George B. McClellan, Abram S. Hewitt, Seth Low,* and *David L. Boody.* The fireboats proceeded up the Hudson River from the Battery in single file for a mile or so and returned. Then, with all the fireboats except the two newcomers lashed to each other in side-by-side fashion, their pumps were engaged and plumes of water were thrown skyward as the six boats slowly made their way in unison toward the Battery sea wall.

With the arrival of so many new fireboats, it was time for the oldest unit in the FDNY fleet to be retired. The wooden-hulled *William F. Havemeyer* was stricken from the roster in 1901.

The FDNY would add two more steam-powered fireboats to its fleet: *William J. Gaynor* of 1915, which allowed *Seth Low* to be retired, and *John Purroy Mitchel* of 1922. *Mitchel* was the only FDNY steam-powered fireboat that was designed and built to burn oil fuel, all earlier vessels being coal-burners, at least originally.[13] Following *Mitchel*'s lead, *Duane, Willett,* and *Gaynor* were converted from coal to oil fuel. *John Purroy Mitchel,* with a pumping capacity of 9,000 GPM, joined the active fleet on December 1, 1922 and took over the Engine 57 "flagship" assignment from *The New Yorker.* The latter was reassigned to Engine 77 on the Brooklyn waterfront close by the Brooklyn Bridge.

When delivered, both the *Abram S. Hewitt* and the *George B. McClellan* featured two smokestacks. Both vessels were rebuilt as single-stackers.

William J. Gaynor protecting the Brooklyn waterfront at the foot of Fulton Street under the Brooklyn Bridge.

Fighting Fire with Gasoline?

As the FDNY fleet expanded during the early years of the twentieth century, there was no workable alternative to steam power as a source of propulsion for the fireboats. Once internal-combustion engines began to be perfected, though, an ordinary feature of steam power began to be seen more and more as a liability that might be eliminated. The fact of the matter was that whether a fireboat was fighting fires or merely awaiting a call to action at its berth, if it were steam-powered, pressure in the boilers had to be maintained constantly at workable levels. This meant fuel was being consumed whether the boat was fighting fires or not; it also meant that wear and tear—and, consequently, maintenance, repairs, and their associated costs—were unrelated to how much work a steam-powered fireboat performed. Wouldn't it be better, FDNY officials began to ask themselves, if a fireboat could be powered by an engine that was shut down during those long hours when the boat was at its berth?

William J. Gaynor turns her monitor guns on an after-dark fire along the Brooklyn waterfront, c. 1954.

Eventually, of course, diesel engines would become conventional for fireboats—not just citywide, but worldwide. But before FDNY took delivery of its first diesel-powered fireboat in 1938, it added to the fleet in 1931 a unit powered by gasoline engines.

The keel of the new boat was laid in Brooklyn at the Tebo Yacht Basin of the Todd Shipbuilding Corporation on June 23, 1931. Fire Commissioner John J. Dorman operated the machine that capped the first bolt, and less than four months later, on October 6, the brand new *John J. Harvey* was ready for launching. William H. Todd, president of the corporation that built the boat, had been a rivet heater at the Pusey and Jones shipyard in Wilmington fifty years earlier when the fireboat *Zophar Mills* was constructed there, and he recalled working on that craft. To add a proper note to the festivities, *Zophar Mills* was on hand when *Harvey* slid down the ways. *Mills* had a pumping capacity of 6,000 GPM; *John J. Harvey*, with a capacity of 16,000 GPM, was the first FDNY boat to exceed *The New Yorker*'s 13,000 GPM capacity.

There was another dimension to the *John J. Harvey–Zophar Mills*

John Purroy Mitchel, the last steam-powered fireboat in the FDNY fleet— last to be built, last to be retired.

contrast: neither fireboat was named after a mayor; each was named after a firefighter. Zophar Mills was a nineteenth-century New York volunteer who supposedly never missed a call in more than forty-five years; John Harvey was the pilot aboard the fireboat *Thomas Willett* on February 11, 1930, when he lost his life following an explosion aboard the 13,3275-ton North German Lloyd passenger liner *Muenchen* which had caught fire while tied up at Morton Street and the Hudson River. *Zophar Mills*, the fireboat, was retired in 1934 shortly after *John J. Harvey* entered service.

   John J. Harvey was powered by five eight-cylinder 548-

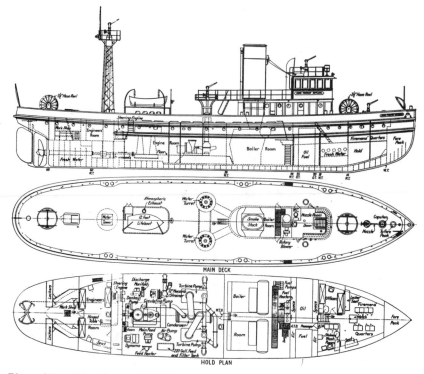

Plan of the *John Purroy Mitchel.*

horsepower Sterling-Viking II gasoline engines. Each engine drove its own electric generator, and the vessel's twin screws were run by electric motors. Her fire pumps, however, were directly driven by her four outboard engines, through clutch drives.

It was claimed that there was no wood whatsoever aboard *Har-*

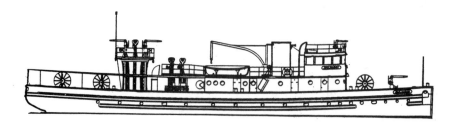

John J. Harvey in her as-built configuration.

vey. What the new fireboat did have, though, were elaborate detection systems for ensuring that no troublesome gasoline vapors would ever emerge from below decks to cause problems. Many maritime observers in New York remained quite skeptical of the idea of building a gasoline-powered fireboat in the first place.[14]

Harvey passed her acceptance trials with flying colors, including heading up the Hudson River on December 17, 1931, to the site of the George Washington Memorial Bridge and throwing a stream of water skyward from its forward deck monitor that sprayed the roadway of the new span. Both the world's most powerful fireboat and the world's longest suspension bridge—both built in 1931— were destined to lose their respective crowns before the decade was over: *Harvey* to another New York fireboat and the George Washington Bridge to one spanning the Golden Gate in San Francisco.

The *John J. Harvey* was both accepted and placed in service that very day; she took over the flagship position as Engine 57 at 6:00 P.M., as *John Purroy Mitchel* was reassigned as Engine 232 in Greenpoint, *Abram S. Hewitt* moved from Engine 232 to Engine 77 at the foot of Brooklyn's Fulton Street, and *The New Yorker*, which had reactivated the Fulton Street berth earlier in the year, was withdrawn from service and retired.

The first major fire that *Harvey* worked almost turned out to be her last. North River Pier 53—one of New York's famed "Chelsea Piers" and the one from which *RMS Lusitania* sailed on her tragic voyage in 1915—caught fire in early May 1932. It proved to be a long and troublesome five-alarm blaze, one which the FDNY unhesitatingly cited for many years as a standard of comparison when discussing any New York pier fires. (Among the problems were burning timbers that were *underneath* the pier's concrete and asphalt deck; firemen had to use jackhammers to open up access ports in the deck before heading below with hand-held hoses to battle the flames.)

Thomas Willett, stationed at the foot of Bloomfield Street and but a single pier away, was the first fireboat on the scene; she was quickly followed by *Duane*, *Hewitt*, and five-month-old *Harvey*. The initial alarm was placed early on the morning of Friday, May 6, 1932. More than eight hundred firemen would battle the blaze for almost thirty-six hours; on the afternoon of that first day, sections of roof began to collapse and fall in. A section of flaming roof fell from a structure adjacent to the pier where *Harvey* was tied; the temperature in her engine room rose quickly, and the crew feared the boat's tanks of gasoline would explode. With burning timbers falling all around them, firemen moved onto the deck and hacked through the lines that fastened *Harvey* to the pier; she backed away from the threat, let her hull cool down a bit, and then continued to work the fire.[15]

THE FINEST FIREBOAT OF ALL TIME

John J. Harvey held down the flagship position as Engine 57 for only six years; that's when she was replaced by an even newer and more powerful vessel with a 20,000-GPM pumping capacity, one that would go on to become the best known and most respected fireboat of all time. Designed by the firm of Gibbs and Cox (see chapter 2 for discussion of another Gibbs and Cox-designed vessel, *SS United States*), she was named in honor of all the brave New York firemen who died in the line of duty. She was christened *Fire Fighter*; to her crews over the years, she has been known simply as *Fighter*.

She cost the city $924,000 in 1938; she has paid back that amount countless times over in the way of waterfront property she has spared from destruction, and there is no possible way to estimate the number of people whose lives she has saved during her career with the FDNY. Maybe it's dozens; more likely it's hundreds.

Unlike *Harvey*, with her gasoline engines, *Fire Fighter* is powered by a pair of Winton sixteen-cylinder diesel engines. These do not directly drive the boat, though; like the system used on *Harvey*, each powers an electric generator and each of *Fire Fighter*'s twin screws is turned by a 1,000-horsepower electric motor. Each of her four water pumps is driven by a 600-horsepower electric motor. But like previous FDNY fireboats, steam and internal combustion alike, *Fire Fighter* had to apportion power between propulsion and water pumping; neither could operate at maximum capacity if the other was also engaged.

Fire Fighter also featured a fifty-five-foot water tower that could be hydraulically lowered into a horizontal position when not in use. In 1962 it was removed, as it had by then become in need of too much maintenance.[16]

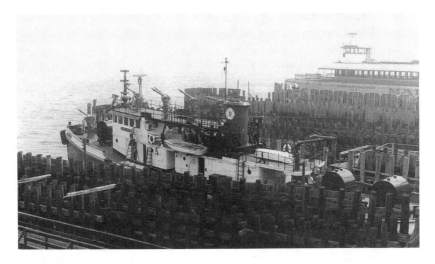

Fire Fighter holding down the assignment as Marine Company No. 9. The slip at St. George, Staten Island, was once used by a ferryboat line that linked Brooklyn and Staten Island.

Fire Fighter's launching at the United Shipyard in Staten Island was not without a touch of style and flair. To find an appropriate sponsor for a vessel that was not to be named after any specific individual, a contest was held among daughters of FDNY members in the Marine Division. The young woman with the highest grades throughout her high school career would earn the right to christen the new fireboat, and thus was eighteen-year-old Eleanor Flanagan—whose father, Lieutenant John Flanagan was an officer aboard *George B. McClellan*—selected to smash the champagne against *Fire Fighter*'s prow. And when Miss Flanagan ascended the platform at the United Shipyard on August 26, 1938, she was wearing a white gown and red cape especially designed for the occasion—the handiwork of a part-time couturier who earned his principal paycheck serving as the mayor of the City of New York. Said *The New York Times* of the multitalented Mayor Fiorello La Guardia at the time of *Fire Fighter*'s launching: "Art critic, lawyer, soldier, flyer, steam-shovel operator, assistant to surgeons, statesman—and none of it done with mirrors, either, but easily and gracefully and in five languages if necessary. He may be Chief

Rising Cloud to the Cheyennes and the Arapahoes, but to us his versatility remains a pillar of flame."[17]

Fire Fighter was completed at the United yard in the weeks following her launching. She finished her acceptance testing in early November—including tossing a stream of water higher than the George Washington Bridge, as did *John J. Harvey* in 1931—and she entered service as Engine 57 on November 16, 1938. The old wooden firehouse at the Battery that was once *The New Yorker*'s base was reaching the end of its days, and Battery Park itself was about to be closed for a number of years while the Brooklyn-Battery Tunnel was constructed. The quarters of Engine 57 were therefore moved to nearby Pier 1 in 1941, a wharf that for many years had been the lower-Manhattan landing for excursion-boat service to Coney Island, operated by the Iron Steamboat Company, but was available for FDNY use after that company went out of business in 1933. (See chapter 4 for further discussion of Iron Steamboat.)

Before *Fire Fighter* joined the fleet in 1938, the FDNY equipped its fireboats with a piece of technology that would greatly facilitate their work: two-way radios. On August 29, 1936, Commissioner John J. McElligott announced that specifications were complete, money had been set aside, and the new radio system would soon be operational. "This policy is in keeping with that of the present administration to take advantage of the latest developments in communicating intelligence by radio," McElligott said. The commissioner concluded his remarks with a statement that countless public officials have put forth over the years in announcing new spending programs: "I believe the equipment will pay for itself within the first year of operation."[18]

WORLD WAR II

During World War II, FDNY fireboats played a critical role in the overall war effort by protecting the nation's most strategic harbor from the peril of fire. It has been estimated, for example, that during the war, one-half of all American troops en route to Europe, and one-third of their supplies, sailed from the port of New York.

Many things changed for the FDNY fleet between Pearl Harbor

and VJ Day. For example, the new and highly touted two-way radio system that had been installed aboard the fireboats in 1936 was used on a very limited basis during the war, and was not to be used at all during fire-fighting operations. The Navy was afraid that with enemy U-boats lurking just outside the harbor, transmissions from one fireboat to another might be overheard and potentially valuable pieces of intelligence wind up in the enemy's hands.

Since most piers in the harbor were turned into *de facto* military installations, FDNY personnel reporting for work aboard fireboats moored at the end of such piers had to present military-issued identification to armed sentries before they could begin a tour of duty. The fireboat fleet itself, per edict of the U.S. Navy, was repainted from its prewar livery of black and white with buff funnels into a uniform navy grey; even brasswork aboard the fireboats was painted over for the duration, since there was fear that brightly polished metal might give off reflections during an after-dark air raid and help enemy pilots plot locations inside the harbor.

Some otherwise routine fireboat operations were subject to unusual changes during the war. For example, New York Harbor was protected by a submarine net strung across the Narrows. Fire, though, would still erupt in places like the Rockaways and Jamaica Bay from time to time, requiring a fireboat to be dispatched to assist in putting it out. Before the war, the only problem in sending a boat to such a location was the time it would take to get there, but during the war the fireboat also had to wait while coded messages were exchanged and the submarine nets swung open to let it pass.

Early in the war, before the Navy and the Coast Guard had adequate numbers of harbor craft on station in New York, FDNY fireboats stayed on active patrol twenty-four hours a day, pausing only to change crews and refuel. Once the Navy and Coast Guard were able to conduct this patrol work themselves, fireboats returned to their more traditional role. FDNY fireboats were also supplied with sets of plans for every ship that made port in New York to which they might respond in case of fire. Obviously, it was useful for fireboats to know the general layout of a ship for general firefighting purposes, especially with so many new and strange vessels visiting the port. But the most critical piece of information fireboat crews had to be familiar with was the location of the magazine aboard every visiting vessel; here was where seconds were critical, not for saving any particular ship, but for saving the port itself from devastation.[19]

Among several incidents that took place in wartime New York to which FDNY fireboats responded, the fire that destroyed the former French superliner *Normandie* is perhaps the best known. What the men of the Marine Division did on April 24, 1943, though, when a completely unknown cargo ship by the name of *El Estro* suddenly caught fire, ranks with the most heroic exploits of World War II.

The 11,500-ton *El Estro* was loading ammunition, incendiary bombs, depth charges, and drums of aviation fuel at the Caven Point Pier in Bayonne, New Jersey. Nearby were two other ships, each as lethally loaded as *El Estro*. Despite elaborate safety precautions, at 5:40 on that spring afternoon a flashback from one of the ship's boilers ignited oil in the bilge water beneath the engine room. The danger this fire represented for the entire metropolitan area was perhaps the most serious and imminent threat of devastation that New York experienced in all of World War II. If the fire touched off *El Estro*'s cargo, it would trigger secondary explosions in the tons of ammunition and gasoline stored nearby—and loaded on other ships—and inflict more destruction on New York than the Nazi High Command could ever have hoped to achieve. Shortly before 9:00 that evening, radio stations throughout New York interrupted regular programs and instructed residents to open their windows and then stay away from them.

While continuing to pour water into the burning *El Estro*, *Fire Fighter*, *Harvey*, and a flotilla of tugs and Coast Guard boats pulled the blazing ship away from its berth and out to the safety of open water, where she was scuttled. Every minute that the two fireboats were lashed to the side of the burning ship, there was the threat of instant devastation. Yet the FDNY crews never hesitated.[20]

The wartime fire aboard the *Normandie* on February 9, 1942, is a textbook case of just about everything going wrong that possibly could. It wasn't enemy sabotage; it was just plain carelessness, carelessness that was compounded by the absence of proper shipboard discipline, a chain of command that had too many missing links, and critical shortcuts taken to meet an impossible deadline for getting the big ship ready for sea. (She was scheduled to leave New York on February 14.)

The story of the loss of *Normandie* has been told many times and need not be repeated.[21] Three FDNY fireboats labored long and hard to put out the fire aboard *Normandie*—*James Duane, John J. Harvey*, and *Fire Fighter*. A large number of harbor tugboats equipped with small monitor guns atop their pilothouses also pitched in, but the three FDNY vessels supplied the bulk of the firepower. And they actually completed the job; the fire that began around 2:30 P.M. was under control and pretty much out by 6:30. But over those four hours, the three fireboats had pumped almost 850,000 gallons of water onto *Normandie*'s superstructure; her stability had been fatally compromised. What began as a slight list grew progressively worse through the night, and at 2:45 the next morning, *Normandie* rolled over on her port side. The FDNY put out the fire, but it would have taken a miracle on February 9 and 10 to have saved the beautiful French superliner, and a miracle was a little more than *Duane, Harvey*, and *Fire Fighter* were able to deliver that day.

Engine 57 Becomes Marine Company No. 1

After the war, the FDNY designed a new vessel that may well represent the epitome of conventional fireboat design in New York, in the United States, and maybe in the world. *John D. McKean* has a pumping capacity that is a tad less than *Fire Fighter*'s—19,000 GPM vs. 20,000 GPM—but because she is equipped with two separate sets of diesel engines, one for propulsion and the other for running the fire pumps, she never has to apportion power between the two functions. Her pumps can run at full power even while she is making way.

The *McKean* was launched from the John H. Mathis shipyard in Camden, New Jersey, on March 19, 1954; her sponsor was the wife of New York Mayor Robert F. Wagner Jr., and two Philadelphia fireboats welcomed FDNY's newest vessel by throwing streams of Delaware River water skyward during the launching ceremony. *John D. McKean* arrived in New York six months later and was given an enthusiastic greeting by *Fire Fighter* and *William J. Gaynor*. After some minor vibration problems encountered during acceptance trials were corrected, she joined the fleet and replaced *Fire Fighter* as Engine 57 on May 1, 1955.

Dressed in ceremonial flags, *Fire Fighter* (left) throws water skyward to welcome the new *John D. McKean* (right) to the FDNY fleet.

Fire Fighter shifted to Engine 223 at the foot of 37th Street in Brooklyn after spending more than sixteen years as Engine 57. The *McKean* would go on to set a new mark for longevity of service as flagship of the FDNY fleet, eclipsing *The New Yorker*'s old record.[22]

John D. McKean was designed by John H. Wells. For propulsion she relies on two 1,000-horsepower eight-cylinder Enterprise diesels that are directly linked to twin screws. (No "electric drive," as on *Harvey* and *Fire Fighter*.) Her fire pumps are driven by a pair of six-cylinder Enterprise diesels, although each is also rated at 1,000 horsepower, like the propulsion engines. Each pumping diesel is attached to two Worthington centrifugal pumps.[23]

Affixed to a bulkhead aboard *John D. McKean* is a large bronze plaque that contains the following inscription:

Named in memory of Marine Engineer
John D. McKean, who was burned
by live steam on Sept. 17, 1953
in an explosion on the "George B. McClellan."
Although fatally injured,
McKean heroically remained at his post
vainly trying to keep the vessel under control.
He died Sept. 22, 1953.

John D. McKean in her original black and white livery (with buff-colored stack). North River Pier 1, shown here, was the berth of Engine 57/Marine Company No. 1 for many years.

Even with the new and modern *John D. McKean* in service as Engine 57, the FDNY fleet was still composed largely of steam-powered fireboats from the early years of the twentieth century. On the day *McKean* tapped into service as Engine 57, the average age of the city's nine active fireboats was thirty-four years (exclude the brand new *McKean*, and the average shoots up to slightly more than thirty-eight years). The relatively new *John J. Harvey* was also starting to be seen as more and more of a problem since the practicality achieved by diesel propulsion in virtually all maritime applications made her status as a gasoline-fueled fireboat an unnecessary liability. "This boat is a bomb; some day it'll kill everybody," an anonymous Marine Division veteran was quoted as saying.[24]

What this led to was the largest single vessel-replacement program in FDNY history. Over a five-year period, five new diesel-powered fireboats would be built, *Harvey* would have her trouble-

On the day after she arrived from Camden, New Jersey, in 1958, *H. Sylvia A. H. G. Wilks* is tied up at the Marine Division's headquarters, then located at North River Pier 1.

some gasoline engines replaced with new diesels, and, eventually, all the steam-powered fireboats would be retired.

Four sister-ships were built, although it might be a trifle more precise to refer to them as "three sisters and one half-sister." Neither as big nor as powerful as *McKean* or *Fire Fighter*, they were 105 feet long and rated at a rather modest 8,000 GPM. Like *McKean*, though, they featured separate engines for pumping and propulsion.

In Camden, New Jersey, on January 16, 1958, at the same John H. Mathis Shipyard where *John D. McKean* had been built four years earlier, the first two of the new FDNY fireboats were launched into the Delaware River. First down the ways was *Harry M. Archer, M.D.*, sponsored by Mrs. Robert F. Wagner (who had also sponsored

H. Sylvia A. H. G. Wilks, the first of four diesel-powered fireboats that enabled FDNY to retire the last of its steam-powered vessels.

McKean). *Archer* was quickly followed by *H. Silvia A. H. G. Wilks*, sponsored by the wife of Fire Commissioner Edward F. Cavanaugh Jr. Four months later, *Wilks* headed north and became the first of the new boats to arrive in the harbor she would soon protect.[25]

Wilks, incidentally, was—and remains—the only FDNY fireboat to be named after a woman. Hetty Sylvia Ann Howland Green Wilks was a benefactor of the FDNY who established a private $3 million fund—separate from official civil service benefits and procedures—that firemen could use in times of medical and other emergencies. Harry Archer was a physician with a lifelong commitment to the Fire Department that eventually led to his being named an official FDNY medical officer. He was present at virtually every major fire in New York over a forty-year period, and his medical skills were responsible for saving the lives of many firemen injured in the line of duty. Ms. Wilks and Dr. Archer were two especially appropriate people to name fireboats after, and *The New York Times* remarked as much, editorially, at the time they were christened. "New York's two new fireboats have given the city an opportunity to honor two citizens who made notable contributions during their lifetime to the welfare of the city's firemen," said the newspaper.[26]

In addition to buying new 105-foot fireboats, the FDNY also did something about the vulnerability *John J. Harvey*'s gasoline engines represented. In 1957 they were replaced by five Fairbanks-Morse opposed-piston diesels, and *Harvey* emerged from its rebuilding as virtually a new boat. *Harvey* even took on a new external look during her reconditioning. When she was equipped with gasoline engines, she had a single funnel immediately abaft of the pilot house. After the diesels were retrofitted, a pair of additional funnel-like stacks were added amidships astern of the main stack.

Initially, the FDNY planned to build three 105-foot boats and a number of smaller vessels. Early experience with *Wilks* and *Archer* was quite favorable, though, so on April 30, 1960, another contract was signed with Mathis and a fourth boat was ordered. Plans for smaller fireboats were scaled back from "several" to "one." The third 105-foot fireboat was *Senator Robert F. Wagner*, delivered in 1959, about which more will be said shortly.

Governor Alfred E. Smith—the fourth 105-foot fireboat—is ever-so-slightly different from her ever-so-slightly older sisters. Where her monitor guns are operated manually, the earlier boats had hydraulically controlled ones; where the three other boats have stacks that are identical to each other, *Governor Alfred E. Smith* has a different shape to her stack housing. *Smith* was launched in Camden on May 26, 1961, and sailed into New York Harbor on October 4; her initial assignment was at the foot of 37th Street in Brooklyn.

As for *Senator Robert F. Wagner*, she was launched on July 8, 1959, and her advent marked a major change in fireboat livery. It is reported that in the nineteenth century, New York fireboats were painted red and white, with gold and black trim. By World War I, a rather handsome livery was developed that called for a black hull, white superstructure with black trim, and a buff-colored stack with a black band at the top. A vessel's name was rendered in black and gold at the bow and across the stern. As noted earlier, during World War II the boats were painted over in navy grey, but the black, white, and buff returned after VJ Day.

In the late 1950s, subtle changes began to appear. First, the fireboats were given Maltese Cross stack emblems that indicated the particular engine assignment the vessel was working: "57," "77," etc. Then, in 1959, the use of engine numbers was discontinued and the Marine Division adopted its own numerical identification scheme that was independent of land-based fire apparatus. Engine 57 became Marine Company No. 1, Engine 86 became Marine Company No. 2, and so forth.[27]

Next, many boats had their buff-colored stacks repainted fire-engine red. Finally, when the 105-foot *Senator Robert F. Wagner* was delivered in 1959, a completely new color scheme was unveiled: the white superstructure remained, but now not only the stack but also the entire hull and all the trim was painted bright red. This has remained the fleet's official color scheme ever since.

Then there was the day—July 13, 1965, to be precise—when *Wagner* left her berth at 90th Street and the East River to conduct some routine dock inspections; one fireman stayed behind in the shore station. He was soon on the radio, though, pleading with *Wagner*'s pilot to get back to the station as quickly as possible. The single-story frame structure by the side of the East River that was home to Marine Company No. 5 had itself caught fire. When *Wagner* returned, she was able to use her powerful monitor guns to bring the blaze under control—in all likelihood the only time ever, in New York or anywhere, when a fireboat helped put out a fire in her own firehouse.

A Tiny New Diesel and No More Steam

As for the smaller fireboat the FDNY purchased, it was named after the first American to orbit the earth, John Glenn. *John H. Glenn, Jr.* was seventy feet long, with a pumping capacity of 3,000 GPM. Designed by H. Newton Whittelsy, Inc., of New York and built in

John H. Glenn, Jr. was an FDNY effort to design a smaller fireboat. The vessel was later sold to the Washington (D.C.) Fire Department.

Jacksonville, Florida, by Diesel Shipbuilding, she had a novel propulsion system: *Glenn* was powered by three twelve-cylinder diesels, each linked to a separate screw propeller, and she could make 20 knots. When it came time to start the water, the two outboard diesels were disengaged from their propellers and hooked up to the pumping machinery. While the pumps were thus engaged, *Glenn* used only her center engine for propulsion.

Her initial assignment was Marine Company No. 4, a new fireboat station adjacent to Fort Totten, where she would be close to such areas as City Island and its many yacht basins. The idea of using a faster and smaller fireboat to protect large expanses of nonindustrial waterfront is an idea that makes all the sense in the world but that somehow or other never quite seems to work out in New York. The Fort Totten station was soon abandoned and the *Glenn* spent most of her days in New York filling in for more conventional fireboats, assignments where her reduced firepower was a distinct liability.

The *Glenn* was removed from service in 1978 and soon thereafter sold to the Washington (D.C.) Fire Department, where she has found a new home and continues to work as an active fireboat. One of her regular assignments is to take up station in the Potomac River whenever the President's helicopter makes a trip from the White House to Andrews Air Force Base—just in case *Marine One* has to make a forced landing.

A minor change that took place in 1961 is worth a brief mention. The FDNY moved the flagship berth from North River Pier 1 to North River Pier A, right next door. Soon afterward, the repair shop that keeps the fleet in tip-top condition was also moved to Pier A, and the older maintenance facility at Bloomfield Street and the Hudson River was closed, although the quarters of Marine Company No. 2 remained at Bloomfield Street. Bloomfield Street, incidentally, is a Manhattan thoroughfare that is well known to FDNY Marine Division personnel but can usually stump even the most veteran New York taxi driver. It runs inland from the Hudson River at Pier 53 but ends a couple of hundred feet after it begins.

Following the 1958–1962 fleet upgrade, it was at first thought that the steam-powered *John Purroy Mitchel* of 1922 could serve for several more years alongside the diesel fireboats. (Onward from 1961 and the retirement of the *William J. Gaynor*, the *Mitchel* was the only steam-powered fireboat left in the FDNY fleet; she was also the only steam fireboat to receive the new red-and-white color scheme the *Wagner* introduced in 1959.) In 1963 the *Mitchel* underwent an eight-month-long, $100,000 renovation that seemed to say she still had a definite role to play. But in early 1966, as part of a general FDNY economy move, the *Mitchel* was retired and the company she was covering—Marine No. 3, then based at North River Pier 80—was permanently disbanded.

As part of the shape of things to come in terms of relations between the municipal government and labor organizations representing city firefighters, the retirement of the *Mitchel* was heatedly criticized by various union officials as "false economy" and an example of "counting pennies instead of lives."[28] It was a theme that would be heard again and again in future years.

DOWNSIZING THE FLEET

What few realized when the pint-sized *John H. Glenn, Jr.* joined the ranks in 1962 is that it would be thirty years before the FDNY purchased another new fireboat. Instead, to borrow a piece of popular terminology from more recent times, the dynamic that soon became evident in the FDNY's fleet management policies was one of "downsizing."

The philosophy behind it all was basically this: patterns of waterborne commerce were changing radically. Never mind the diversion of passenger traffic away from Hudson River piers. From the perspective of fire fighting—and fire prevention—the more critical change was a shift away from break-bulk cargo handled on fire-prone wooden piers to containerized traffic flowing through spacious, open-air intermodal terminals. Items of rattan furniture, for instance, or drums of chemical solvent are less likely to become the start of a five-alarm fire if they are unloaded from a ship inside a steel container, and the container itself is swung directly onto a railroad flat car, than if they sit for two weeks inside a wooden pier and become a handy receptacle for carelessly tossed cigarette butts.

The general shift in freight movement to a greater reliance on containerization was prompted by larger economic issues than the cost of fire protection along the New York waterfront. But the

FDNY's outlays for keeping its fireboat fleet operational were able to be significantly reduced as this transformation took hold. The number of active fireboat companies was reduced as the 1960s became the 1970s, the 1970s became the 1980s, and fewer and fewer oceangoing vessels called at fewer and fewer New York piers.

With the retirement of the *John Purroy Mitchel* in 1966, the FDNY had an eight-boat fleet that was 100 percent dieselized. Soon afterward, though, cutbacks began:

- In 1972 the *H. Sylvia A. H. G. Wilks* had most of her firefighting equipment removed and she was sold off to the city's Department of Marine and Aviation for use as a general workboat; in later years, she was sold to a towboat operator on the Gulf Coast.
- As noted earlier, in 1978 the *John H. Glenn, Jr.* was removed from active service and, the next year, sold to the Washington (D.C.) Fire Department.
- By the mid-1980s, the FDNY was down to four active companies: Marine Company No. 1 at North River Pier A (the Battery), Marine 2 at North River Pier 54 (Bloomfield Street), Marine 9 at Saint George, Staten Island, and Marine 6 at Grand Street and the East River.

A primary fireboat was assigned to each of these companies: *John D. McKean* was Marine No. 1, *John J. Harvey* was No. 2, *Fire Fighter* held down No. 9, and *Harry M. Archer, M.D.* was No. 6. Both *Governor Alfred E. Smith* and *Senator Robert F. Wagner* served as "spare" boats for the primary vessels. Then, in early 1991, as part of yet another economy move, Marine Company No. 2 was disbanded and the FDNY dropped to three active fireboat companies. Again the cutback of firefighting capability in the City of New York drew criticism from organized labor. "The preservation of life is government's first responsibility. Everything else, including bond ratings, has to come in second," said James J. Boyle, the president of the Uniformed Firefighters Association.[29]

Before all this retrenchment assumed its ultimate dimension, two incidents that occurred in the waters of New York Harbor underscore a rather important point: Neither the peril of fire nor the need for powerful fireboats is going to disappear completely just because the city now has fewer wooden piers than it once did. Each incident is associated primarily with a single vessel—the *Alva Cape* and the *Sea Witch*. As long as there is a Marine Division in the FDNY, these are two names that will never be forgotten.

The first incident took place on the afternoon of Thursday, June 16, 1966. The day was clear, the sky was blue, the wind was moderate; there was nothing to portend the tragedy that was about to unfold.

The tanker *Texaco Massachusetts* had just cast off from that company's Bayonne Terminal at the southern end of Newark Bay and was outbound in ballast, en route to Port Arthur, Texas. She had just delivered a cargo of gasoline and was proceeding south, about to make a turn to port into the Kill Van Kull. Inbound on her way through the Kill Van Kull toward Newark Bay was the tanker *Alva Cape*; her cargo was 5.6 million gallons of naphtha from Karachi, Pakistan. At 2:12 P.M., as the two ships were passing each other about two hundred yards west of the Bayonne Bridge, *Texaco Massachusetts* knifed into *Alva Cape*.

There was a tugboat shadowing each tanker. The impact produced a grinding crunch, but only that; it was not until moments later, as the two ships moved back from each other, that naphtha began to spew out of a gash in *Alva Cape*'s hull. *Texaco Massachusetts* had ordered "full astern" prior to the impact, and the effect of this pulled the big ship away from *Alva Cape* after the crash. The highly flammable liquid flowed onto *Esso Vermont*, the tug that was traveling with *Alva Cape*. When it reached the engine room, a terrible series of explosions were set off; fire followed the blasts.

Thirty-four people lost their lives in this unfortunate incident. First on the scene from the FDNY was the fireboat *Governor Alfred E. Smith*, working that day as Marine Company No. 8 in Brooklyn; she was soon joined by *Fire Fighter*, *John D. McKean*, and *John J. Harvey*. *Fire Fighter* was technically out of service at her Saint George berth being repainted when the accident happened, and hence the *Smith* from Brooklyn was the first fireboat on the scene. But *Fighter* was fully staffed and available, if needed, so after the painting contractors were put ashore, she followed the *Smith* to Bayonne.

When the fire was eventually brought under control, *Alva Cape* had the appearance of a ship that had been attacked by enemy dive bombers. Hugh Greenan, Director of Public Safety for the City of Bayonne, described the incident in these words: "It looked like D-Day. Dozens of bodies were floating in the water. Flames were shooting up all over the place."[30]

Despite the explosion—and despite the fire that followed it—there were thousands of gallons of flammable naphtha still aboard the badly damaged *Alva Cape*. Several days later she was carefully towed to Gravesend Bay, and with the *Smith* standing by in case anything went wrong, efforts were begun to offload the remaining product. At 3:49 P.M. on Tuesday, June 28, another series of explosions tore through the unlucky ship, killing four more people and inflicting serious damage to the fireboat *Smith*.

Additional FDNY boats responded, and the fire that followed the explosions was brought under control in less than an hour. But authorities quickly decided that the *Alva Cape* was worth no further effort. The Coast Guard ordered that she be taken out to sea and sunk. Traffic both into and out of New York Harbor was halted while the tugboats *Kerry Moran* and *Nancy Moran* gently towed the badly damaged tanker away from Gravesend Bay, through Ambrose Channel, and out to a point in the Atlantic 140 miles due east of Cape May, New Jersey. There, on July 3, 1966, the Coast Guard cutter *Spencer* put thirty-seven five-inch shells into her hull and sent *Alva Cape* to the bottom.[31]

Seven years later, on June 2, 1973, there would be another tragic collision in New York Harbor. American Export Isbrandtsen's container ship *Sea Witch* had sailed at midnight; her destination was the island of Aruba in the Caribbean, with a stopover scheduled in Norfolk. Forty-five minutes later, as she was proceeding outbound through the Narrows, she collided with the tanker *Esso Brussels*, riding at anchor. The tanker's hold contained two million cubic feet of Nigerian crude oil.

The two ships became wedged into one T-shaped floating catastrophe. Oil leaking out of *Esso Brussels* caught fire; "the problem was how to control and extinguish a fire with flames, at times, ten stories high, three thousand yards long, and moving freely . . . influenced only by the tide and the wind."[32] Forget all the bad jokes about the Cuyahoga River in Cleveland catching fire. On June 2, 1973, in the City of New York, the Narrows was on fire.

The first fireboat on the scene was *Fire Fighter*, which had to use her powerful deck monitors at first not to *extinguish* any fire, but to *move* a free-floating inferno of burning oil away from the *Esso Brussels* so firefighters could see if there were crew members aboard the tanker in need of rescue. What they found as *Fire Fighter* worked her way through the blazing water was a second ship, the *Sea Witch*, and a group of men huddled on her fantail as they sought refuge from the flames. *Fire Fighter* would later be awarded the highest decoration any U.S. merchant ship can receive, for taking thirty men off the *Sea Witch* in the very midst of a sea of flaming oil and saving them from certain fiery death.[33]

What was happening aboard the *Sea Witch* was something that just wasn't supposed to be able to happen: 285 containers lashed to her deck were in flames, a fire that would continue for many days. Once it was extinguished and the *Sea Witch* moved to a Staten Island pier for examination, it was discovered that additional containers being hauled below deck had also caught fire and had been destroyed during the conflagration.

Five FDNY fireboats were called to the scene on the night the containership *Sea Witch* collided with the *Esso Brussels*: *Fire Fighter, John D. McKean, John J. Harvey, Harry M. Archer, M.D.,* and *Senator Robert F. Wagner*. The death toll on both vessels was sixteen.

The most chilling thing about the incidents involving the *Alva Cape* and the *Sea Witch* is that they involved tremendous fires and significant loss of life following collisions in port between precisely the kind of merchant ships that form the backbone of contemporary waterborne commerce in and out of New York Harbor—tankers and containerships.

THE FUTURE

The three active marine companies have continued to evolve. Both *Archer* and *Wagner* were sold; like *William L. Strong* four decades earlier—and their own sister-ship, *H. Sylvia A. H. G. Wilks*, in more recent years—the pair were purchased by Gulf Coast interests and have been converted into towboats. Indeed, all three former 105-

foot fireboats of the FDNY now work for Crescent Towing and Salvage of Mobile, Alabama, and are based in New Orleans.

Harvey has been deactivated, and while *McKean* remains Marine Company No. 1, the flagship post has recently been moved from Pier A at the Battery to North River Pier 54, *Harvey's* steady assignment since 1938. Pier A at the Battery—a New York Harbor landmark that had been the berth of Marine Company No. 1 since 1961—was to be converted into a restaurant and visitors' center.

Moving out of Pier A also required finding a new home for the FDNY shops, and these have been shifted to Pier G in the old Brooklyn Navy Yard. A sensible thing was then to have Marine Company No. 6—held down by *Smith*—move across the East River from Grand Street on the Manhattan side to the same Navy Yard location. *Fire Fighter* continues as Marine No. 9 at Saint George.

As the twentieth century entered its final decade, the FDNY made a concerted effort to upgrade its fireboat fleet. Though well-intentioned, the effort proved to be disappointing. That a fleet-modernization program was needed had become self-evident. In 1988, *Fire Fighter* celebrated the fiftieth anniversary of her launching; *McKean* was still the FDNY flagship, yet she had been delivered in the middle of Dwight Eisenhower's first term; people who were born in the year *Harvey* fought her first fire were starting to receive Social Security checks in the mail. The "newest" fireboat in the FDNY fleet was *Governor Alfred E. Smith*, and she joined the ranks in 1961.

The key feature the FDNY believed their next generation of fireboats needed was speed. Back in the days when ten fireboat companies were positioned throughout the city, it hardly mattered how fast a fireboat could travel; the key thing was pumping capacity, since most fire-prone locations were within sight of a fireboat's berth. But with fireboat stations in New York now down to three, getting to the scene quickly took on a new kind of importance. And so following the lead of the Tacoma (Washington) Fire Department, the FDNY ordered two high-performance fireboats from Textron Industries, vessels that were virtual twins of two units Tacoma put in service in the early 1980s. The reinforced plastic hulls of the new boats were built in Southampton, England, by Vosper Hovermarine and then sent to New Orleans—by ship—where Textron completed their fitting out. (From fireboat hulls made of wood to hulls made of iron to hulls made of steel . . . and now, hulls made of plastic.)

The two boats are fast—specifications called for 30-knot speed, and this was reportedly exceeded during tests. They managed such high-speed performance by the use of a marine technology known as "surface effect"; thus are they known as "surface effect ships," or SES. Basically, the two 70-foot fireboats are twin-hull catamarans with a fabric curtain enclosing the open space between the hulls. A powerful downward-facing fan forces air into this enclosure while the boats are underway, thus raising the boat and reducing draft from a normal 5'4" to 3'6". Propulsion is quite conventional—twin direct-drive diesels. But raising the hull almost two feet by "fan power," and thereby reducing drag while the boats are underway, is the key to achieving 30-knot speed with propulsion engines that are relatively modest in size and output.

In addition to speed, the two new fireboats feature far more in the way of automatic controls than do the older FDNY vessels. In theory, one person could comfortably operate all functions of the boat from a seated position in the wheelhouse, including the operation of the monitor guns. (In practice, FDNY assigned a crew of three marine ratings and two firefighters to each boat.) The new vessels have a pumping capacity of 7,075 GPM and cost the Fire Department a hefty $3.5 million each.[34]

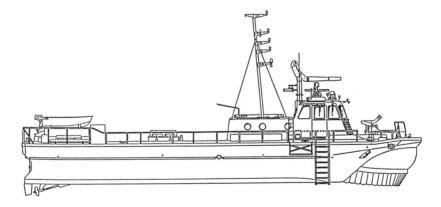

Outline drawing of one of the surface-effect ships that proved ineffective as FDNY fireboats.

Kevin C. Kane, a pint-sized fireboat whose monitor guns pack a potent punch.

The two SES fireboats were built, delivered, and accepted. *John P. Devaney* entered service on June 20, 1994, and *Alfred E. Ronaldson* two days later, on June 22. Both boats were named in honor of FDNY firemen recently killed in the line of duty.

Technical people from the Tacoma Fire Department traveled east to help train FDNY personnel in the operation of the new boats, but maintenance of the high-tech units proved to be much more than had been anticipated. Less than five months after they entered service, both *Devaney* and *Ronaldson* were officially stricken from the active roster and put up for sale. SES fireboats—at least in New York—proved to be a noble experiment that just didn't work.

During their short tenure with the FDNY fleet, neither the *Devaney* nor the *Ronaldson* worked any truly memorable fires. On August 23, 1994, the *Ronaldson*, serving as Marine Company No. 9, worked a pier fire across the Hudson River from Manhattan in Edgewater, New Jersey. (See chapter 4 for further information on a New York steamboat company that once had its home base in Edgewater, New Jersey.) Four days earlier, on August 19, 1994, the *Devaney*, as Marine Company No. 6, helped put out a minor fire aboard the cruise ship *Regal Empress* while it was docked at North River Pier 90. (See chapter 6 for a chance encounter with *Regal Empress* a year later, in August 1995.)

In addition to the two SES vessels, FDNY purchased a more conventional fireboat, albeit a rather small one, in 1993. After an earlier boat ordered from a yard in Arkansas failed to pass acceptance tests and was refused, the FDNY took delivery of a fast, 52-foot aluminum fireboat from a Massachusetts builder, and once she joined the fleet as the *Kevin C. Kane* on September 27, 1993, she

Originally designed as a tender to ferry Fire Department personnel, *Smoke II* was later equipped with a small monitor gun and converted into a mini-fireboat.

quickly earned very high marks throughout the Marine Division.[35] Thanks to improvements in pumping technology over the years, the diminutive *Kane* has a capacity of 6,500 GPM, which, coupled with the boat's 28-knot speed, has made her an excellent addition to the fleet. She began by serving primarily as a supplementary vessel, but more recently she has taken over as the principal fireboat assigned to Marine Company No. 6 in the Brooklyn Navy Yard. In July 1996, when a TWA 747 crashed in the Atlantic Ocean off the eastern end of Long Island, the *Kane* was among the vessels sent to the scene to assist in the recovery of victims and of wreckage.

The fireboats of the FDNY face an uncertain future. Throughout the country there has been a marked shift to smaller and faster vessels for harbor firefighting, although contemporary pumping technology can give a relatively small boat a pretty potent gallons-per-minute rating; the *Kane* herself is a perfect example of this.[36] In virtually all U.S. port cities, more-stringent building codes have drastically reduced the potential for fire in wharfs and piers, thus making yesterday's fireboats a ripe target for those charged with balancing municipal budgets today.

Eventually, though, *Fire Fighter*, *John D. McKean*, and *Governor Alfred E. Smith* will have to be replaced. When they are finally removed from service, perhaps we should hearken back to the launching of the fireboat *New Yorker* more than a century ago and recall the words of the Henry Wadsworth Longfellow poem, "The Building of the Ship," that Judge Gildersleeve recited that day.

We know what Master laid thy keel,
What Workman wrought thy ribs of steel,
Who made each mast, and sail, and rope,
What anvils rang, what hammers beat,
In what a forge and what a heat
Were shaped the anchors of thy hope.[37]

NOTES

1. The *Havemeyer* was the second municipally owned fireboat to enter service in an America city; the first was Boston's *William M. Flanders* in 1873. For further information about the overall development of fireboats in America, see Paul Ditzel, *Fireboats* (New Albany, IN: Fire Buff House, 1989); see also Clarence E. Meek, "Log of the Nation's Fireboat Fleet," *Fire Engineering* 110(8) (August 1957), 758–61, 867–69; 110(9) (September 1957), 938–41, 976. Ditzel's book, while devoting more attention to Los Angeles/Long Beach than to any other American city, is quite comprehensive and includes an extensive fireboat bibliography plus a roster of all U.S. fireboats. Meek was an honorary FDNY chief and that department's foremost historian; many of the articles he wrote for *Fire Engineering*, as well as for the FDNY house organ, *With New York Firemen* (*WNYF*), deserve republication for a broader audience. See especially Meek, "Fireboats through the Years," *WNYF* 25(3) (July 1954), 24–27; "F.D.N.Y. Flotilla," *WNYF* 30(1) (1969), 16–21.
2. FDNY fireboats were given numerical "engine" designations similar to conventional units in the department. In the earliest days, a boat retained its original engine number, no matter where it was assigned (for instance, the *Havemeyer* was Engine 43 for its entire service life). By the time of *The New Yorker*, engine numbers were assigned to fireboat berths, and whatever vessel was assigned to the berth assumed that engine number.

3. The gallons-per-minute rating of a fireboat can vary, depending on the water pressure being maintained. Most citations assume water pressure of 150 psi. For a technical discussion, see John Buursema, "Some Notes on Fireboat Design," *Marine Engineering/Log* 63(11) (November, 1958), 73–76, 106–107.

4. The firehouse at the Battery was not completed at the time *The New Yorker* entered service, and, when built, she included a deck cabin to house her crew. Once the firehouse was ready in 1895, the deck cabin was removed; this is likely when the original funnel was replaced with the larger one that is seen in most photographs of the vessel.

5. Quotations from *The New York Times*, March 12, 1905, pt. III, p. 7.

6. *The New York Times*, July 1, 1900, p. 2.

7. For a discussion of the Hoboken fire, see John Kenlon, *Fires and Fire-Fighters* (New York: George H. Doran, 1913), 267–72.

8. For further information on the *General Slocum* tragedy, see chap. 5, note 1. For an interesting account that emphasizes the FDNY role in the disaster, see Frank Cull, "*General Slocum* Afire! Hundreds Perish!!" *WNYF* 40(2) (1979), 8–13, 23.

9. Quoted in Meek, "Log of the Nation's Fireboat Fleet," 761. Henry deBerkely Parsons was the brother of another turn-of-the-century engineer who left an indelible mark on New York City. He was William Barclay Parsons, the man who designed the city's first subway system. The brothers began a consulting engineering firm in 1885 and together designed the water-supply systems for Vicksburg and Natchez, as well as the Fort Worth and Rio Grande Railroad in Texas, before going their separate ways. I have written of the New York subways, and of William Barclay Parsons, elsewhere (see *Under the Sidewalks of New York* [New York: Fordham University Press, 1995]).

10. For further information about the Parsons-designed *Hewitt*, see Meek, "New York Fireboat," *Marine Engineering* 8(3) (March 1903), 118–20.

11. Ibid.

12. See Kenlon, *Fires and Fire-Fighters*; Kenlon, *Fourteen Years a Sailor* (New York: George H. Doran, 1923).

13. For further information about *Mitchel*, see, I. C. G. Cooper, "Fireboat *John Purroy Mitchel*," *Marine Engineering and Shipping Age* 27(4) (April 1922), 229–31.

14. Several years ago I interviewed the late James McAllister and the subject of fireboat *John J. Harvey* came up. I don't have the exact quotation, but Captain McAllister said something to the effect that he thought it was downright silly to have built a gasoline-powered fireboat in the first place. For an interesting article on the *Harvey* written toward the end of her career, see Al Trojanowicz, "*John J. Harvey*; Sixty Years of Outstanding Service," *Steamboat Bill* 200 (Winter 1991), 285–91; for an earlier treatment, see "The World's Most Powerful Fireboat; *John J. Harvey*," *Marine Engineering and Shipping Age* 37(2) (January 1932), 30–32.

15. For an account of the 1932 Cunard pier fire, see John J. T. Waldron, "Cunard Pier Fire," *WNYF* 5(2) (April 1944), 24–26; see also *The New York Times*, May 7, 1932, pp. 1, 3.

16. For further technical information about *Fire Fighter*, see "World's Most Powerful Fireboat," *Marine Engineering and Shipping Review* 43(12) (December 1938), 566–70; see also George Geller, "A Day with the *Fire Fighter*," *WNYF* 3(3) (July 1942), 9–12.

17. *The New York Times*, August 29, 1938, p. 12.

18. *The New York Times*, August 31, 1936, p. 17.
19. For more information on FDNY fireboat operations during World War II, see William A. Sandin, "Harbor Guardians," *WNYF* 7(2) (April 1946), 16–19; see also Jeannette Edwards Rattray, *Perils of the Port of New York* (New York: Dodd, Mead, 1973), pp. 210–20.
20. For a popular account of this incident, see Stewart Sterling, "Unsung Heroes of New York's Worst Hour of Peril," *Readers Digest*, April 1955, 147–50; see also, Sandin, "Harbor Guardians," 18; Rattray, *Perils of the Port of New York*, pp. 217–18.
21. See, for example, Frank O. Braynard, *Picture History of the "Normandie"* (New York: Dover, 1987), pp. 82–126; John Maxtone-Graham, *The Only Way to Cross* (New York: Macmillan, 1972), pp. 361–92; an especially detailed recent article is Robert J. Russel's, "SS *Normandie*/USS *Lafayette*; Death and Dismantling," *Steamboat Bill* 213 (Spring 1995), 4–30. For a short article that deals particularly with the FDNY's role in the *Normandie* fire, see Robert P. Smith, "*Normandie* Burns; A Fifty-Year Retrospective," *The Housewatch* (September/October 1992), 1–4.
22. *The New Yorker* held down the flagship post as Engine 57 from February 1, 1891, until December 1, 1922, when she was reassigned to Engine 77. *McKean* broke this record in 1986 and, as of this writing (Fall 1996), is still serving as Marine Company No. 1, the flagship of the FDNY fleet.
23. For further information about *McKean*, see "New York's Fireboat *John D. McKean*," *Marine Engineering and Shipping Review* 59(12) (December 1954), 63, 93.
24. Quoted in Trojanowicz, "*John J. Harvey*; Sixty Years of Outstanding Service," 289.
25. The 105-foot fireboats are usually called the "*Wilks* class," even though *Archer* was the first launched. *Wilks*, on the other hand, was Mathis hull No. 211, whereas *Archer* was No. 212, suggesting the former was senior. For further information on these vessels, see Thomas E. Baker, "New York City's New Fireboats," *Marine Engineering Log* 63(8) (July 1958), 59–62, 131–33; see also Curt Elie, "The Pride of the Fleet," *Fire Apparatus Journal* 9(4) (July-August 1992), 26–27.
26. *The New York Times*, January 22, 1958, p. 26.
27. While the location of various fireboat companies changed over the years, the following table displays where Marine Division "engine companies" were quartered circa 1945; the second column shows the new notation that was adopted in 1959.

Old notation	Location	New notation
Engine 57	The Battery ("flagship")	Marine No. 1
Engine 86	Hudson River/Bloomfield St.	Marine No. 2
Engine 85	Hudson River/W. 35th St.	Marine No. 3
Engine 77	East River/Fulton St., Brooklyn	Marine No. 7
Engine 66	East River/Grand St., Manhattan	Marine No. 6
Engine 232	East River/Noble St., Brooklyn	—
Engine 78	East River/E. 90th St.	Marine No. 5
Engine 87	Harlem River	—
Engine 223	Upper NY Bay/37th St., Brooklyn	Marine No. 8
Engine 51	St. George, Staten Island	Marine No. 9
—	Fort Totten	Marine No. 4

28. *The New York Times*, February 12, 1966, p. 29.
29. *The New York Times*, January 8, 1991, p. 1.
30. *The New York Times*, June 17, 1966, p. 24.
31. USCGC *Spencer* expended every shell she had aboard in an effort to sink the *Alva Cape*. "She was tougher than we thought—a lot tougher," said the ship's gunnery officer (quoted in *The New York Times*, July 4, 1966, p. 1). For further information about this incident, see, Rattray, *Perils of the Port of New York*, pp. 136–40; U.S. Maritime Administration, *Marine Fire Prevention* (Washington, DC: Maritime Training Advisory Board, 1980), 51–54; Joseph F. O'Connor and F. P. Barry, "Marine Disaster . . . Naphtha Tanker Fire," *WNYF* 28(1) (1967), 4–9; Joseph F. O'Connor, "Marine Disaster . . . Sequel to Naphtha Tanker Fire," *WNYF* 29(1) (1968), 4–7.
32. Thomas P. Walsh, "The *Sea Witch* . . . and a Cauldron of Fire and Death," *WNYF* 34(4) (1973), 4.
33. *Fire Fighter* was awarded the "Gallant Ship" plaque, a federal designation established in 1928 for outstanding action during a marine disaster; the Maritime Administration also honored the crew of *Governor Alfred E. Smith* for their work in the *Alva Cape* incident.
34. For further information on *Devaney*, see "*John P. Devaney*," *Maritime Reporter and Engineering News* 54(11) (November 1992), 29.
35. For further information on *Kane*, see "Gladding-Hearn Begins Construction of New York City Fireboat," *Maritime Reporter and Engineering News* 54(10) (October 1992), 69.
36. See James Phyfe, "Fireboats of the '90s," *Professional Mariner* 7 (June/July 1994), 36–42, 44–50.
37. Eight brave men from the FDNY Marine Division have lost their lives in the line of duty. The Honor Roll includes the following:

Name	Fireboat	Date killed
Engineer John Bulger	*Havemeyer*	10/28/1890
Fireman Thomas J. Cooney	*Low**	3/19/1902
Fireman Brerton F. Johnson	*Hewitt*	8/13/1913
Fireman Edward J. Fox	*The New Yorker*	1/27/1927
Fireman John M. Grane	*The New Yorker*	1/27/1927
Pilot John J. Harvey	*Willett*	2/11/1930
Fireman Peter Engel	*Mitchel**	1/5/1950
Engineer John D. McKean	*McClellan*	9/17/1953

*Identity of fireboat not certain, merely assumed.

Cygnus, one of the steamboats that helped the Iron Steamboat Company inaugurate service to Coney Island in 1882.

4

Down the Bay to Coney Island: The Iron Steamboat Company

Captain William Van Schaick stood on the deck of the fifty-one-year-old steamboat *Cepheus—his Cepheus.* It was February 1, 1933, but on this winter Wednesday neither the aging 213-foot sidewheeler nor any of six fleetmates moored in adjacent slips had any place to go. Captain Van Schaick was wearing civilian clothes, not the blue serge uniform that had long marked his rank as a senior officer with a transportation agency known as the Iron Steamboat Company.

"Tell them you'll throw in the captain, too," Van Schaick shouted sarcastically to bankruptcy auctioneer David Williner when no vigorous bidding developed. Williner was conducting proceedings that would soon liquidate the tangible assets of a New York and New Jersey maritime institution that had reached the end of its corporate tether. Van Schaick was accompanied by two other veteran captains of the Iron Steamboat fleet, I. H. Gant and Nelson B. Allen. Like the steamboats, the old captains had no place to go, either.

The auction was being held in Edgewater, New Jersey, on the west bank of the Hudson River opposite upper Manhattan, long the place where vessels of the Iron Steamboat Company were quartered during winter months as they awaited the arrival of warm weather and their annual return to excursion boat service in and around New York Harbor. While a new company would be formed soon after the auction and most of the boats would actually steam again, the old company—and the old name—fell under auctioneer Williner's gavel on that February day in 1933. The boats sold for pitifully low prices: an average of $2,050.00 per vessel, with one going for a mere $550.00.[1]

Across the Atlantic Ocean in Berlin on the very same day (to give this event some historical context), Chancellor Adolf Hitler dissolved the Reichstag and called on the German people to give his National Socialist party a clear majority in the upcoming elections. In the United States, Franklin D. Roosevelt was just about a month away from inauguration as the country's thirty-second president. America's president-elect was born in 1882. The steamboat *Cepheus* and her sister-ships were launched in 1881.

In retrospect, if there is any one thing that can be said to characterize the Iron Steamboat Company for all of its years, it has to be the consistency of its service and operations for a half century that was otherwise a period of extraordinary and continual change, development, and growth in New York. A newly formed company entered the highly competitive excursion-boat trade with a fleet of brand new vessels in the summer of 1881, offering frequent seasonal day trips from points in Manhattan down New York Bay to Coney Island. In the summer of 1932, the company's last, the same vessels were offering the same service.

BEGINNINGS

The Iron Steamboat Company had its beginnings on Tuesday, September 28, 1880, at the Monmouth County courthouse in Freehold, New Jersey. Papers filed that day named thirteen distinguished citizens as incorporators of a new company whose purpose was set forth in official documents as "the building, furnishing, fitting, purchasing, chartering, managing, navigating, and owning of steam-boats and other vessels, to be used and employed for carrying and transporting passengers and freight on the Hudson River, New-York Bay, Long Island Sound and other waters."[2] More specifically, the company planned to operate seasonal excursion boats at frequent intervals between Manhattan and Coney Island, then in its early years as a summertime watering spot for city dwellers. In addition to Coney Island, the new company would also link New York with Long Branch, New Jersey, with plans for an even more extensive steamboat network. A World's Fair was being planned for New York in 1883—former president Ulysses S. Grant was serving as head of the commission that was attempting to organize the exposition—and the need for expanded waterborne transportation seemed immense.

A fleet of eight or nine new steamboats was to be designed and built in time for the next excursion season, 1881, less than a year away, and a total of thirty such vessels would be in service by the summer of 1883. Of $10 million in capital stock the new company was prepared to offer—a serious sum of money in that day—$800,000 was said to be already pledged at the time of incorporation.

But plans are just plans; facts often turn out to be something else again, and the Iron Steamboat Company's fleet never grew to anything even remotely approaching thirty vessels in size. (The World's Fair of 1883 never happened, either.) In fact, even the anticipated first order, announced as eight or nine boats on the day the firm was founded, turned out to be only seven. And with the exception of a few secondhand vessels acquired for short-term use over the years, these seven steamboats proved to be the backbone and full extent of the company's fleet for all of the fifty-two summers it would be in business.

Orders for the new vessels were quickly placed with two famous Delaware River shipyards, each of which had a family member among the new company's incorporators. William Cramp and Sons of Philadelphia turned out four boats, while the other three were built downriver in Chester, Pennsylvania, by John Roache and Son. Although the seven boats looked for all the world like typical excursion steamboats of the era—which is to say, built of wood—in fact, they had iron hulls that were divided into twelve separate watertight compartments, the decks were made of iron, and the cabin work was iron plated. *The New York Times* observed that "it would be impossible for a fire to make any serious headway even if one should originate."[3] A promotional slogan the company often used to describe its "iron steamboats" was "They Cannot Burn! They Cannot Sink!" Another piece of self-promotion Iron Steamboat once put forth was this: "The boats of this company are iron, palatial, first-class sea-going steamers, fitted with every convenience for safety and comfort of passengers, and officered by competent and experienced men."[4]

Twelve watertight compartments in a steamboat slightly more than two hundred feet long was rather unusual—three or four would have been normal. (RMS Titanic, launched thirty years later and in excess of 880 feet long, had only four more.) The design was dictated by the fact that the company's vessels would not restrict themselves to the calm waters of inland rivers and bays. To reach Coney Island they would sail around Norton's Point—then called Coney Island Point—and dock on the "ocean side" of the resort; and to reach Long Branch, they would sail outside Sandy Hook into even less sheltered waters, namely, the North Atlantic Ocean. Furthermore, the company envisioned sending its fleet south when the New York excursion season ended each fall, and the watertight compartments would mean additional protection during the exposed ocean voyage back and forth to winter service in Savannah, Jacksonville, or along the Gulf Coast.

While originally there was talk of more-modern compound engines, the new vessels were instead powered by single-cylinder vertical beam steam engines, the epitome of conventionality of the era. Undoubtedly, the need to have the boats built quickly was a factor in the choice. Some of the fleet had engines fabricated by W. & A. Fletcher, others were powered by engines from Cramp and Sons; all turned paddlewheels equipped with radial-style buckets, and the seven-boat fleet proved to be quite fast, easily maintaining speeds of 20 MPH or better.

SERVICE BEGINS

The first of the seven three-deck excursion boats arrived in New York in early May 1881; this was the Roache-built Cygnus, which bore a price tag of about $200,000. On Monday, May 23, the new steamboat took a shake-down cruise around the harbor from the foot of East Eighth Street and the East River, where final fitting out had been done. Company officials and the press were effusive in their praise of the new steamboat, harbor craft greeted the newcomer with lusty whistle salutes, and everyone was looking forward

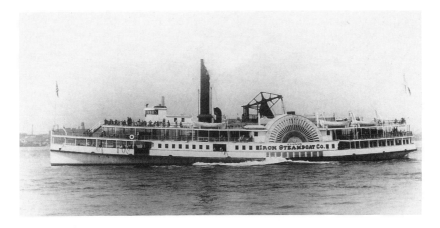

Cygnus steams down the Hudson, with passengers clustered forward on the third deck.

to the inauguration of regular steamboat service to Coney Island on the upcoming Saturday.

Two days later—Wednesday, May 25—*Cygnus* took the press and associated dignitaries on another pre-inaugural sail, this one a champagne cruise all the way to Coney Island. The next day, May 26, the company's second vessel, *Cetus*, left Cramp's Delaware River yard, but only after some frantic telegraphing back and forth between Philadelphia and Washington to secure the issuance of an "official number" by the federal government, a requirement for the vessel's formal enrollment as a documented U.S. merchant vessel.[5] *Cetus*, official number 125903, reached New York on the morning of Friday, May 27; and as she had been completely fitted out and tested before steaming north, she was ready to help *Cygnus* inaugurate the new company's service on Saturday, May 28, 1881. For the record, the first revenue trip from Manhattan to Coney Island that day carried a mere fifty-two paying customers—fifty-two people aboard a steamboat built to carry two thousand. Remaining units of the seven-boat fleet were completed and sent north during June and early July.

As to the names of the boats, this exchange on opening day says it all. "Where did you get those queer names for your boats?" a passenger asked the first mate on one of the afternoon trips. "I see there the *Cygnus*, and we are on the *Cetus*. What does it all mean?"

Instead of answering himself, the officer felt it would be better to demonstrate for his passenger how the new company's policies were infused throughout the ranks. So he called over a uniformed deckhand and said, "Tell this gentleman where we got those names, *Cygnus* and *Cetus*."

The deckhand replied promptly, "From astronomy, sir: the constellation of the heavens. Cygnus means a swan. Cetus a whale. We are now on a whale, sir," the deckhand concluded, and, tipping his cap, returned to his regular duties.[6]

Perhaps more interesting than the names themselves is the way they were downplayed in the style of decoration the company selected for its new vessels. Sidewheel steamboats of the era almost universally featured a vessel's name rendered in bold and unmistakable letters across the paddleboxes. But on each of the seven boats of the new company, the name of the individual vessel was completely overshadowed by the name of the firm, "Iron Steamboat Co." Clearly, the goal was to call public attention less to this boat or that one and more to an overall steamboat service. One might even suggest that the choice of vessel names—*Cetus, Cepheus,* and *Cygnus; Perseus* and *Pegasus*—were so like-sounding as

While the seven-boat fleet of the Iron Steamboat Company remained largely unchanged over the years, one area where modifications were made is in the length of the third deck. Note in this view of *Perseus* that the third deck ends immediately forward of the pilothouse; a later photograph (see below) shows the third deck extending further forward, with a staircase at its end. Other boats appear to have had their pilothouses raised a few feet in conjunction with the extension of the third deck, to afford ship's officers better visibility.

to blur further the identity of individual boats and thus emphasize the total operation. (The remaining two constellations in the new iron firmament were *Sirius* and *Taurus*.)

During that first season of 1881, Iron Steamboat Company service ran between Manhattan and Coney Island, where vessels docked at what was called the "iron pier," a structure built in 1879 by Coney Island restauranteur Charles Feltman near the spot where today's West Eighth Street meets the ocean. (Feltman is far more famous for a gastronomic innovation: the man is widely acknowledged to be the true inventor of the hot dog.)

The iron pier was not merely a landing stage for steamboats; it was also an attraction in its own right, featuring concessions and entertainment. People paid an admission charge to stroll its length and enjoy the ocean breezes, but passengers arriving aboard steamboats were welcomed on the pier as guests. The new company was not alone in serving the iron pier from Manhattan during its first season; steamboats of White's Regular Line also called at the facility, and, as a result, patronage levels on the new service never developed to a point that would justify the investment the company had made. That first year of 1881, in other words, was not terribly

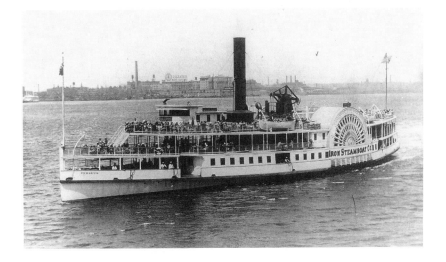

With a crowd of Coney Island-bound excursionists already aboard, the Iron Steamboat Company's *Perseus* is about to dock at North River Pier 1 in lower Manhattan.

successful for the Iron Steamboat Company. Officials even complained that free daily orchestra concerts they sponsored on Pier 1 in Manhattan, nominally to attract customers to the company's steamboats, were frequented more by the patrons of its competitors.

THE SECOND SEASON

Over the winter of 1881–1882, the Iron Steamboat Company took steps to better its position. First, it negotiated a contract with Feltman's Ocean Navigation and Pier Company, the owners of the iron pier at Coney Island, to be the exclusive steamboat line serving the facility from Manhattan. Next, Iron Steamboat executed a sim-

A fantail view of *Sirius* taken as the steamboat is leaving Pier 1. (Courtesy of the Mariners' Museum, Newport News, Virginia.)

ilar agreement with the owners of a second Coney Island iron pier that was ready to open for the 1882 season.

This second ocean pier was built—amid much controversy and litigation—by the Brighton Navigation and Pier Company, a subsidiary of Andrew Culver's Prospect Park and Coney Island Railroad, a firm whose excursion railway trains first reached Coney Island several years earlier, in 1875. The new pier's name might be a little misleading to those familiar with Coney Island and environs today. The second Coney Island ocean pier was not located in the area now called Brighton Beach. It was across from Culver Depot, roughly at the site of today's New York Aquarium, seven hundred feet or so to the east of the original iron pier. In the 1880s, much of what is today generally referred to as "Coney Island" was known as "West Brighton."

Finally, that winter, Iron Steamboat negotiated yet another exclusive landing contract, this one with the Ocean Pier Company, owners of an iron pier in Long Branch, New Jersey. Thus armed with agreements that shut out a good deal of competition from important steamboat landings, Iron Steamboat approached its second season, 1882, with greater confidence. Service to Coney Island was doubled over what the company provided in its first year, 1881. Departures were scheduled to leave Manhattan every thirty minutes during the summer, with this unusual twist: on odd days, boats leaving lower Manhattan on the hour operated to the older iron pier, and boats leaving on the half hour operated to the newer pier; on even days, on-the-hour departures served the new pier, and departures on the half hour landed at the older facility.

With these arrangements in place, and with a man named C. H. Longstreet serving as superintendent, the company was able to call itself "the only line having exclusive control of all the docks and piers at which it lands passengers, thus preventing annoying changes from boats to cars, laying out in a stream waiting to land, and other vexatious delays."[7] The company also tightened up its policy with respect to those concerts on Pier 1. Unless one could show a ticket to ride the company's vessels, attending a concert cost fifteen cents in 1882. Finally, Iron Steamboat and Culver's Prospect Park and Coney Island Railroad worked out an arrangement so passengers could travel one direction by land and the other by sea.

OTHER STEAMBOAT SERVICES

Over its years, Manhattan–Coney Island service would be the company's bread and butter. The great bulk of its scheduled departures were over this route, with fifteen to twenty round trips daily during high summer, sometimes more. But scheduled service was also operated to other places from time to time.

In 1883 a service was established between Coney Island and Long Branch, New Jersey, permitting patrons to combine a (short) visit to both Coney Island and Long Branch into a single day's outing. The following season, 1884, saw the addition of a direct Manhattan––Long Branch route with as many as four daily round trips and discontinuation of the Coney Island–Long Branch service. In 1906, after some earlier experimentation, regular service was established between Manhattan and Rockaway Beach, New York; two or three daily round trips were typical for this route. Once established in 1884, the Manhattan–Long Branch service ran through the summer of 1891. It then suffered an on-again/off-again fate until the end of the 1901 season, when it was permanently dropped. The company continued to serve Rockaway Beach until 1931, its next-to-last season.

Neither Rockaway nor Long Branch ever came close to rivaling Coney Island in terms of frequency of service, but each was run for many years. There were also other operations that ran for but a single season, like the one-year Coney Island–Long Branch service of 1883.

During the company's very first year, 1881, it supplemented its regular New York–Coney Island operation with a ferrylike service between lower Manhattan and Bay Ridge, where passengers could continue on to Coney Island aboard trains of the New York and Sea Beach Railroad.[8] In 1892, with Long Branch service temporarily discontinued, a route was established linking lower Manhattan and downtown Brooklyn with Belden Point, a resort on Long Island Sound.

Manhattan landing sites changed over the years; there was always service from the southern tip of Manhattan Island—North River Pier 1, almost exclusively—but at one time or another, Iron Steamboat vessels called at West 23rd Street, West 41st Street, West

129th Street, and *East* 31st Street; even Yonkers saw scheduled Iron Steamboat service from time to time.

The dual pier arrangement at Coney Island continued for a number of years, although with a good deal less complexity than the odd-days-here/even-days-there arrangement of 1882. By the mid-1890s, though, the company's boats were landing only at the new iron pier in Coney Island.

In certain early years, some boats en route to the iron pier(s) in Coney Island also paused at Coney Island Point before they got there. This was the only steamboat landing at Coney Island in the years before the first iron pier was built in 1879.

And so the Iron Steamboat Company became an ordinary part of New York's basic transportation network, albeit a seasonal part serving a largely recreational market. But the company's service had to meet certain standards of performance, and the city's press was ever alert to point out shortcomings—for instance, crowded vessels.

Sunday, June 30, 1901, was an exceptionally hot day in New York, and many city residents sought relief at Coney Island. The next morning's *New York Herald* contained this critique of the Iron Steamboat Company's role in the exodus: "All (boats) went down the bay crowded to suffocation, loaded to the guards, and some of them careening so heavily toward the shady side that the opposite paddle wheel barely caught the water, while its fellow was churning deep in the brine." The article continued: "When the *Sirius* started down the bay, a little after four o'clock, she was densely packed, and so listed to one side that her funnel leaned like a tree in a gale, at an angle of 8 or 10 degrees."[9]

Steamboat competition between Manhattan and Coney Island emerged from time to time when Iron Steamboat was unable to maintain exclusive landing rights at the resort. In 1895, with Iron Steamboat running only to the new iron pier, a competitor came on the scene and used the old iron pier. Another example occurred in 1904, when the steamboats *Dreamland*, *St. John*, *City of Lawrence*, and *Rosedale*, running as the Dreamland Line of Fast Steamers, jointly operated eleven daily round trips opposite the Iron Steamboat Company. They were off the run by 1905, as few steamboat operators had the resources to match the extremely frequent ser-

The World of the Iron Steamboat Company

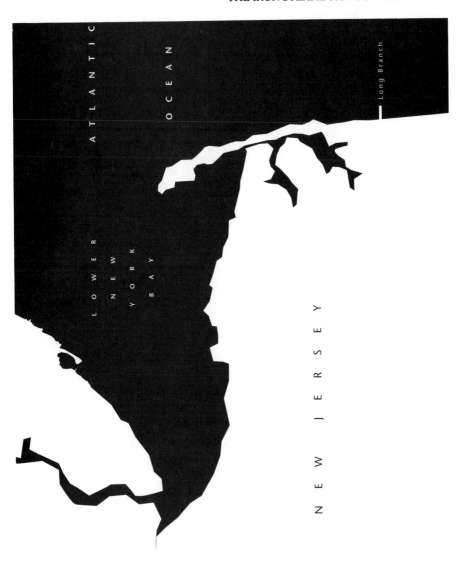

vice Iron Steamboat normally operated to Coney Island. On the company's Rockaway route, though, where only two, three, or, at most, four daily trips were the rule, smaller companies could give the larger firm a run for its money, and competition was more common. In the summer of 1913, Iron Steamboat took out an ad in the newspapers because it felt agents of another company were misleading potential Rockaway-bound passengers. It read: "Special Notice. Strs. *Rosedale* and *Sylvester* are NOT operated by this Co. Patrons at W. 129th St. Dock are cautioned to buy tickets only at Iron Steamboat Co.'s Box Office."[10]

"IRON STEAMBOATS" MADE OF WOOD

At least two additional vessels joined the original seven "iron steamboats" over the years: older and larger wooden-hulled boats that gave the company added carrying capacity. *Columbia*, a hog-frame sidewheeler built in 1877, was purchased from the Baltimore and Ohio Railroad at the start of the 1900 season and ran for two years before being sold to Delaware River interests. Primarily used on the restored Manhattan–Long Branch route, often with *Taurus* as her running mate, she was about forty feet longer (and seven hundred gross tons larger) than the seven sister-ships.

An additional vessel to join the fleet—probably the only other one—was *Grand Republic*, built in 1878 at the John Englis yard in Brooklyn. She was seventy feet longer (and one thousand gross tons larger) than the "iron steamboats." *Grand Republic*'s normal assignment with the company was the route from Manhattan to Rockaway Beach; wooden hulled, she became an "honorary iron steamboat" in 1906 and stayed with the fleet until 1917, when she was sold to the McAllister organization's Highlands Navigation Company.

(The McAllisters then ran *Grand Republic* up the Hudson between New York and Bear Mountain for several years, until the vessel was destroyed by fire in 1924. Interestingly, the McAllister people still operate a passenger-boat service in the New York area, the Long Island Sound ferry between Port Jefferson, New York, and Bridgeport, Connecticut. A new diesel-powered vessel that was built for the service in 1983 is called, in proud memory of the earlier boat, *Grand Republic*.)

Excursions. *13 Aug 01*

IRON STEAMBOAT CO.

THE ONLY ALL-WATER ROUTE TO
CONEY ISLAND.

Leave FOOT 22D ST., North River, 9.00, 10.00, 11.00
a. m., 12.00 m., 1.00, 1.45, 2.30, 3.15, 4.00, 5.00, 6.00, 7.00,
8.00, 9.00 p. m.

Leave Pier (New) No. 1,⎫
    North River,   ⎬ Half hour later.

Leave NEW IRON PIER, CONEY ISLAND, 10.40,
11.40 a. m., 12.40, 1.40, 2.40, 3.25, 4.10, 4.55, 5.40, 6.40,
7.40, 8.40, 9.40, 10.40 p. m.

ROUND TRIP TICKETS, 25 CENTS.

Ocean Route
to
LONG BRANCH.

PALATIAL 4-DECK OCEAN STEAMER
"COLUMBIA,"

Time Table for To-day:

Leave Foot 22d St., North River.	Leave Pier (New) No. 1, North River.	Leave Iron Pier, Long Branch.
9.30 A. M.	10.00 A. M.	12.30 P. M.
1.00 P. M.*	1.80 P. M.*	3.45 P. M.*
3.30 P. M.	4.00 P. M.	6.30 P. M.

*Iron Steamboat "Taurus."

ROUND TRIP TICKETS, 75 CENTS.
SINGLE TRIP TICKETS, 50 CENTS.

Newspaper advertisement from 1901.

Before joining the Iron Steamboat fleet, *Columbia* and *Grand Republic* had run together for a time between Manhattan and Rockaway Beach under the house flag first of White's Regular Line and later of Knickerbocker Steamboat Company. After *Columbia* joined the Iron Steamboat Company in 1900 and before she herself did, *Grand Republic* ran to Rockaway for a few seasons in tandem with *General Slocum*, an excursion boat that later, in 1904, caught fire near Hell Gate with a loss of 1,030 persons, the worst disaster in New York history, maritime or otherwise.[11]

Columbia and *Grand Republic*, while both running for White's Regular Line in 1881, were among the vessels that competed with the Iron Steamboat Company between New York and Coney Island during the latter's first season, pausing at the iron pier en route to Rockaway. Finally this about the pair: When they ran for Iron Steamboat, both were technically owned not by the company itself but by a subsidiary, the New Jersey Navigation Company.

The Iron Steamboat Company underwent management changes after about two decades of service. In the late 1890s the company's finances had grown shaky, and in 1902 a reorganization brought a change in the company's formal name. Gone was the Iron Steamboat Company of Long Branch, Incorporated, the firm that had been founded back in 1880; in its place was the Iron Steamboat Company of New Jersey, a name that would remain until the end. With this change, Frederick Bishop, a forty-one-year-old Brooklyn native, came on the scene and took over operation of the line, eventually advancing to the position of president. Bishop remained in that post until the liquidation of 1933.

Something interesting about Bishop, the man, that resulted in an unusual venture for Iron Steamboat, the company, was the fact that he was an ardent fisherman. In 1904 he took the steamboat *Taurus* off the Coney Island excursion run and operated her every day as an

Grand Republic, a wooden-hull steamboat that ran for the Iron Steamboat Company in the early years of the twentieth century. (Courtesy of the Mariners' Museum, Newport News, Virginia.)

off-shore fishing boat to give city residents an opportunity to experience the pleasures of Bishop's own favorite sport out on the ocean fishing banks.

A bit of contretemps developed over these off-shore fishing trips in late 1915. New federal safety legislation, passed in the aftermath of the *Titanic*, *Empress of Ireland*, and *Lusitania* disasters, specified the number and kind of lifeboats and how many able-bodied seamen each oceangoing merchant vessel must have aboard. The U.S. Steamboat Inspection Service decided that *Taurus* was to be regarded as "a merchant vessel carrying passengers in coastwise trade," and therefore a host of new rules and regulations had to be observed.

Bishop was livid; he threatened to discontinue the fishing trips entirely and spoke of assurances he felt he had received from federal officials in Washington that *Taurus* would not be treated as if she were a transatlantic mail boat. But the business of complicated federal regulation of, and intrusion into, all sorts of commercial activities was the wave of the future, not just a one-time aberration. When Bishop realized what he was up against, he backed off; and when *Taurus* headed out to the fishing banks in 1916, her capacity had been reduced to five hundred people, Captain Henry Beebe conducted mandatory lifeboat drills each day, and two able-bodied seamen and three boat handlers were aboard for each lifeboat, all of which had federally mandated stashes of biscuits to forestall starvation of the survivors of any mishap at sea.

A year later, in the wartime summer of 1917, off-shore fishing trips aboard *Taurus* took on another new dimension. Posted at the pier she sailed from each morning was this stern warning: "No alien can go aboard without a passport from his consulate, which must be shown at the gangway and all naturalized Americans must show their citizenship papers, which will be examined by a government official at the pier. No alien enemy can go aboard the *Taurus* at all."

Meet Me Tonight in Dreamland

With respect to Bishop's impact on the company's regular excursion services, in 1905 he developed a working relationship with one of the three principal amusement parks that had by then come to

They Cannot Burn!   **They Cannot Sink!**

All Tickets Include Admission to
DREAMLAND, CONEY ISLAND,
Greatest Amusement Enterprise in the World.

TIME TABLE (SUBJECT TO CHANGE).

Leave foot 129th St., North River, 9:45, 11:00 A. M.;
12:30, 2:00, 3:00, 4:50, 7:45 P. M.

Leave foot 22d st., North River, 9:00, 9:45, 10:30, 11:05,
11:45 A. M.; 12:30, 1:15, 2:00, 2:45, 3:30, 4:00, 4:45,
5:30, 6:15, 7:00, 7:45, 8:30, 9:00 P. M.

Leave Pier 1, North River, half hour later than at
22d st.

Returning—Leave Iron Pier, Coney Island, *10:40,
*11:25, 12:10, *12:45, 1:25, *2:10, 2:55, 3:40, 4:25,
*5:10, 5:40, *6:25, 7:10, 7:55, *8:40, 9:25, *10:10,
10:45. Returning from Coney Island trips marked
with a * go to 129th st., North River.

Round Trip Tickets, 35 Cents.
Round Trip Tickets, 129th St., 45 Cents.

STEAMER TAURUS makes trips EVERY DAY to
FISHING BANKS. Leave E. 31st St., 7:30 A. M.; Pier
(New), No. 1, N. R., 8:20 A. M. Bait and Tackle on
board. Fare: Gentlemen, 75c; Ladies, 50c.; Chil-
dren, 25c.

Early twentieth-century advertisement.

dominate the Coney Island scene, and as a result a round-trip ticket aboard his company's vessels gave the holder free admission to Dreamland Park.

Dreamland—opened in 1904 and, according to many with informed opinions on the subject, the grandest American amusement park of all time, subsequent developments in Anaheim and Orlando notwithstanding—burned to the ground at the start of the 1911 season. It was never rebuilt, and the original meaning of the popular song "Meet Me Tonight in Dreamland" would be lost on future generations.

Bishop quickly turned around and negotiated a new arrangement with George C. Tilyou, the chief factotum of rival Steeplechase Park, and on the day after the fire, with the ashes of Dreamland still smouldering, Bishop's boats deposited Coney Island-bound patrons at Tilyou's Steeplechase Pier, the third and last major ocean pier to be built at Coney Island. An Iron Steamboat ticket now included free admission to Steeplechase.[12]

Both the original iron pier of 1879 and the second one that was built in 1882 by a subsidiary of the Prospect Park and Coney Island Railroad, if not actually destroyed in the Dreamland fire, had their usefulness negated. Tilyou built Steeplechase Pier in 1907 and, after a fashion, it still stands. It was deeded over to the city at the time the municipal boardwalk was built in 1922, but thanks to both fire and weather damage over the years—not to mention routine maintenance and modernization—today's Steeplechase Pier is a completely different structure from the one that, in 1911, became the final Coney Island landing spot for the Iron Steamboat Company.

Frequent service throughout the day between Manhattan and Coney Island remained the bulk of the Iron Steamboat Company's service from 1881 through 1932. But there were frequent opportunities for charter and other special work that took boats to unusual places. The following list of examples is by no means exhaustive:

- *Taurus* carried a delegation of West Point cadets down the Hudson River to New York, where they participated in the welcome the port gave Admiral Dewey after his victory at Manila Bay in 1898.
- On Sunday, July 2, 1899, *Cepheus* ran a one-day excursion for the general public from New York to Bridgeport and Roton Point, Connecticut.
- On August 3, 1908, *Sirius* was involved in a slight accident while steaming west of Execution Rocks in Long Island Sound, perhaps on some kind of similar assignment.
- In 1894, when the ocean liner *Normania* could not clear Quarantine at the entrance to New York Harbor because of a cholera scare, *Cygnus* was chartered to take the vessel's first-class passengers to more hospitable isolation on Fire Island.
- *Taurus* was based in Boston Harbor for a short time in 1883, but whether by Iron Steamboat itself or under charter to a New England company is not known.

- In 1886, *Cygnus* was assigned to Hudson River excursions that were run by, or in conjunction with, the Pennsylvania Railroad.
- On Friday, September 13, 1907, *Sirius* took a group of 1,500 enthusiastic sightseers from lower Manhattan to Quarantine, there to greet Cunard Line's new express liner *RMS Lusitania* on the completion of her maiden voyage.
- In 1911—on Sunday, May 28, and Decoration Day, May 30, the same weekend as the Dreamland Park Fire—*Grand Republic* ran a pair of public excursions up the Hudson River to West Point and Newburgh.

Toward the end of, and sometimes even after, the regular excursion season, yacht races and exhibitions of various kinds were once popular in the waters off New York, and vessels of the Iron Steamboat Company were regularly among the spectator fleet. On September 14, 1905, for example, *Cygnus* was cited by the Revenue-Cutter Service, precursor of the U.S. Coast Guard, for failing to observe proper rules during something called the International Motor Boat Carnival.

An important one-time event in which the Iron Steamboat Company played a role was the Hudson–Fulton Celebration of 1909, perhaps the grandest pageant ever staged in New York Harbor. An almost-impossible-to-imagine armada of 742 vessels steamed up the Hudson one day as part of a huge maritime review; among them were *Grand Republic, Cygnus, Sirius, Pegasus, Cetus,* and *Perseus.*

As Iron Steamboat's second season, 1882, was nearing its end, *Sirius* ran a pair of interesting special trips: on two successive Sundays, September 10 and September 17, she left Manhattan early in the morning and steamed out into the ocean around Rockaway Point all the way to Fire Island. Here passengers enjoyed three hours ashore, including dinner at Sammis's Surf Hotel. Departure for Manhattan was scheduled for 8:00 P.M., and it had to be close to dawn on Monday morning before *Sirius* and her undoubtedly weary passengers finally got there.

Then there is the matter of the company's celebrity passengers: pugilist John L. Sullivan was reported to be especially enamored of *Cygnus*; New York Governor Alfred E. Smith often spoke of wonderful days sailing down to Coney Island aboard the company's steamboats for a day of fun at the beach; during his only visit to America in 1902, Sigmund Freud once rode to Coney Island aboard a company vessel.

During the early years, many of the fleet were sent south once the New York excursion season was over, to earn money in warm-water areas rather than sit idle through the northern winter. This was a common practice with many New York steamboat operators, at least through the turn of the century, although it seems to have been more common for the operators of smaller vessels, such as Iron Steamboat, than for companies whose fleets consisted of larger steamboats, such as the Hudson River Day Line. ("Smaller," in this case, means two hundred feet or so in length, and "larger" means something closer to three hundred feet.)

Although the full story of when and where Iron Steamboat vessels worked through the winter remains to be told, it is known that, in one instance, *Cygnus* ran in the Jacksonville area over the winter of 1883–1884, Captain Charles Foster in command.[13] As railroads expanded throughout Florida in the early years of the twentieth century, the basic inland and coastal transportation services provided by wintering New York excursion boats grew less important, and the annual trek south became less attractive, from an economic perspective. That's when the common cycle for such vessels became one of steaming in excursion service during a short summer season in New York and then going into a prolonged period of inactivity generally called "winter quarters" until the days grew long again.

THE SUMMER OF 1915

From the economic perspective of an excursion-boat operator, though, they never stayed long enough. A case in point: On Sunday, September 19, 1915, a week after the Coney Island service had shut down for the season, president Bishop welcomed the Iron Steamboat Company's employees aboard *Grand Republic* for the firm's annual outing. The big two-stack, hog-frame sidewheeler pulled away from North River Pier 1 early that morning for a sail up the Hudson River to Newburgh.

While largely a day of relaxation and entertainment, it was not merely that; an annual banquet gave Bishop a chance to talk to his workers about the state of the firm, its finances, and the recently concluded excursion season. His report this day was anything but upbeat. In fact, he was certain that 1915 was absolutely the worst business year the company had ever suffered through since it ran its first steamboat in 1881. "Reports show that rain fell on ten Sundays out of thirteen during June, July and August; there were eight rainy Saturdays, and it rained on fifty-three days in ninety-two," the president pointed out.[14]

Of course, any commercial venture seeking to turn a profit on the basis of a short summer season at Coney Island—then, now, or ever—is necessarily at the mercy of weather. At the beginning of the 1915 season, Iron Steamboat had planned to operate 3,556 summer trips between Manhattan and Coney Island. By the end of the summer, though, only 2,732 had actually been run. Given the frequency of its service, if a particular sailing had but a few passengers aboard, it was smart business to cancel the trip entirely and hold passengers over for the next boat, often less than an hour away.

As the company's employees headed back down the Hudson that Sunday in September 1915 aboard *Grand Republic*, listening to the steady syncopated slap of the steamer's paddlewheels, they could only look ahead to 1916 and hope the weather would prove to be more auspicious for the excursion-boat business than it had been in the season just concluded.[15]

Grand Republic herself had become a focus of unfavorable attention several weeks earlier in 1915. On Sunday, August 1, she had come out of Jamaica Bay en route back to Manhattan on her usual run from Rockaway Beach, and was off Coney Island; it was a few minutes before 7:00 P.M. It was also a mere eight days since a terrible steamboat tragedy had taken place in Chicago. There the excursion boat *Eastland* had quite improbably rolled over and capsized at her berth along the Chicago River, killing more than 800 persons. As *Grand Republic* was steaming past Coney Island, it was also less than three months since Cunard Line's *RMS Lusitania* had been torpedoed in the Irish Sea off the Old Head of Kinsale; that disaster recorded a death toll of 1,198. It would thus seem fair to suggest that a crowd of passengers aboard any vessel in August 1915 might well have been a little more skittish than usual over matters relating to shipboard safety.

Actually, when accounts were later compared, nothing really happened aboard *Grand Republic* that evening, and there were no casualties; but it was a close call and panic almost broke out. The culprit was probably a company employee who was being disciplined and began to shout in protest of the pending action. The man's shouting led to more shouting, and passengers, upon hearing such loud exchanges, immediately thought of either fire or sinking. There was a mad rush for life preservers; two passengers even tried to lower one of *Grand Republic*'s lifeboats, but they were restrained by one of the boat's officers, who brandished a revolver to emphasize his point.

Panic was imminent when the steamboat *Newark*, operating between Coney Island and her namesake city in New Jersey, passed off *Grand Republic*'s starboard and passengers rushed to that side of the boat; Captain Edward Carmen signaled *Newark* to stand by. But as quickly as it all began, calm began to restore itself and at 7:10 P.M., *Grand Republic* made a safe, if unscheduled, stop at Steeplechase Pier. A subsequent letter in *The New York Times* suggested that better order could be ensured if the sale of beer and liquor were prohibited on board excursion boats.

Prohibition and the Nickel Subway Ride

The entire nation was about to go this suggestion one better: in two and a half years, Congress would send the Eighteenth Amendment to the states for ratification, thereby outlawing alcoholic beverages entirely, on land, on sea, or in the air. By the time Prohibition was repealed in 1933, the Iron Steamboat Company was nothing but a memory.

If any single factor can be cited in the downfall of the New York institution that was called the Iron Steamboat Company, though, it was not Prohibition. It was another, equally New York phenomenon—the subway. In 1882, when *Cetus*, *Cygnus*, *Taurus*, and the others began steaming down the bay, the alternative "overland" journey to Coney Island was virtually primitive by comparison.

Depending on one's point of departure, it could involve a street-running horsecar or steam-powered elevated-train ride in Manhattan to South Ferry, then a ferryboat across the East River to Brooklyn, yet another horsecar out to the city limits of Brooklyn, and finally travel aboard what were known as excursion railways—steam-powered lines such as Andrew Culver's Prospect Park and Coney Island Railroad which catered to the largely seasonal traffic bound for the seashore at Coney Island, Brighton Beach, or Manhattan Beach.[16] A breezy trip aboard an Iron Steamboat Company vessel was direct, downright relaxing, far more convenient, and, in most cases, less expensive and faster.

Over the years, corporate consolidations, technical improvements, and fare reductions were effected on these once separate railways and streetcar companies. Onward from the time roughly of World War I, it was possible to board a subway train at Times Square in Manhattan and for only five cents be whisked to Coney Island in less than an hour aboard an electric-powered rapid-transit train that was as modern as tomorrow.[17]

By contrast, the Iron Steamboat Company may have offered a more pleasant trip, but it cost more money and the ride took considerably longer. The steamboat company's very name, once connoting the very latest in transportation technology, now conjured a bygone era, and the subway allowed more hours on the beach or in the various amusement parks during a one-day outing. Bishop found himself in the classic economic tailspin of having to raise prices to compensate for reduced patronage but then finding that the higher tariff only drove more passengers to the less costly subway system. Travel to Coney Island grew by leaps and bounds with the advent of subway service—a million visitors were not unusual on a sunny summer Sunday—but it was a growth in which the Iron Steamboat Company never shared.

At one time, the longer steamboat ride to Coney Island at least offered the opportunity to relax and imbibe during the trip down the bay, something definitely verboten aboard the subway. Prohibition took away this competitive edge, and moreover, the subway got people to Coney Island faster, where, rumor had it, beverages of various sorts and vintages could still be obtained here and there, Volstead Act or no.

By 1932, the Iron Steamboat Company's last season, its round-trip

Iron Steamboat Co.

TO BOARDWALK
C O N E Y   I S L A N D

Schedule ' for THURSDAY, JULY 1ST

Lv. W. 129 St.		Pier 1, N. R.		Coney Island	
9:40	4:15	10:25	5:00	11:30	6:00
10:40	5:15	11:25	6:00	12:30	7:30
11:40	6:30	12:25	7:15	1:30	8:30
12:40	7:40	1:25	8:25	2:30	9:40
2:00	8:40	2:45	9:35	3:45	10:40
3:00	—	3:45	—	5:00	—

ROCKAWAY BEACH
SEASON OPENS SATURDAY, JULY 3rd
Telephone WHITEHALL 1279

This advertisement from the early 1930s includes a telephone number for passengers requiring additional information.

fare between Manhattan and Coney Island stood at one dollar, although the company reduced this to fifty cents on Monday and Friday, both light-traffic days. But a round trip on the faster subway was only a dime, and those free amusement park admissions that steamboat passengers once enjoyed were long gone by 1932. In 1881, when Iron Steamboat first ran to Coney Island, it charged passengers twenty-five cents for a round trip.

NUMBERS

Other statistics fill in more details about the company's decline. The last year Iron Steamboat turned even a nominal profit was 1929, when it had receipts of $392,000 against expenses of $390,000. Two years later, in 1931, with the Great Depression at full impact, prudent management had reduced expenses to $320,000, but falling patronage dropped revenues to $257,000. In the early 1920s, annual patronage on the company's boats averaged more than 900,000 cash customers each summer; by 1931, this had fallen to a mere 369,040, a massive drop of 56%.

As late as 1931, all seven of the original fleet were still under steam, although *Taurus* was chartered to the Meseck Line for service to Rye Beach, New York, for all or part of that summer. During the final season, 1932, with no Rockaway Beach service on the schedule for the first time in decades, at least one boat, *Cetus*, and possibly another, were left in winter quarters, and Bishop ran with a reduced fleet. He was even compelled to negotiate a reduction in the docking fees he had earlier agreed to pay the City of New York for the use of by then municipally owned Steeplechase Pier. The Board of Estimate reluctantly agreed and, on May 3, 1932, reduced the annual charge from $15,000 to $12,000.

Still, on the Fourth of July weekend in its final season, the Iron Steamboat Company scheduled fourteen daily round trips between Manhattan and Coney Island, virtually the same frequency with which it had operated since the end of the Great War. The last day of service to Coney Island that year—or ever, as it turned out, for the Iron Steamboat Company—was Labor Day, Monday, September 5, 1932, when eleven round trips were advertised.

(A final summary statistic: Between 1881 and 1932, the Iron Steamboat Company carried more than 95 million passengers to and from Coney Island aboard something like 125,000 individual steamboat sailings.[18])

Once the company closed its books at the end of the season, there was only one option: on November 29, 1932, Bishop petitioned the U.S. District Court, District of New Jersey, to place the company under voluntary receivership, citing liabilities of $750,000 against assets of little more than seven fifty-year-old steamboats.

The court appointed a receiver, and on February 1, 1933, the company's assets were auctioned off at Edgewater Basin. The next day, George R. Beach, the referee in bankruptcy, confirmed the sale and entered matters in his records at the bankruptcy court, 75 Montgomery Street, Jersey City, New Jersey. Ironically, the court was located just a few minutes' walk from the site where Robert Fulton once assembled the steam engine he later installed in a boat everyone knows today as *Claremont.*

The New York Times took note, editorially, of the Iron Steamboat Company's demise by saying, rather curiously, that "only old people like to sit on a boat and catch the sea breezes—and hardly

The seven original "iron steamboats," tied up in winter quarters at Edgewater, New Jersey. This is the way the fleet looked on February 1, 1933, when the assets of the company were sold at auction.

anybody is old nowadays," but otherwise lamenting the end of steamboat service to Coney Island.[19]

THE RAINBOW FLEET

But it wasn't exactly the end. A postscript was added to the Iron Steamboat story when another firm, Union Navigation Company, bought five of the older firm's vessels, leased a sixth, obtained still another vessel that once steamed between New York and Shelter Island for a maritime subsidiary of the Long Island Railroad, and reinstituted service between Manhattan, Coney Island, and Rockaway Beach in the summer of 1933 under the banner of something called the Rainbow Fleet. While the service would last only two years (the excursion seasons of 1933 and 1934), it is a bona fide continuation of the story of the Iron Steamboat Company.

Union Navigation certainly gave it the old college try. The ex-Iron Steamboat vessels were renamed, and this time proper steamboat tradition was observed—only a vessel's name, and not that of the

Shamrock, a) *Cepheus.* When Union Navigation purchased a number of the old Iron Steamboat Company vessels, the boats were renamed and proper steamboat protocol was followed: the boat's name, not that of the company, adorned the paddle boxes.

company, adorned the paddleboxes. (See roster in the appendix.) For the inauguration of service in 1933, the company put out a call in the newspapers to find the New Yorker who could remember riding to Coney Island aboard a steamboat earlier than anyone else. The "winner" of the pseudo-contest was one Mrs. Robert Disbrow, 77, of Nostrand Avenue in Brooklyn, who claimed she rode a steamboat to Coney Island Point as a seven-year-old girl in the Civil War year of 1863.

Former Governor Al Smith was prevailed upon to help the company inaugurate its new service; the day was May 17, 1933, and the ex-L.I.R.R. boat—renamed *Empire State*, "the flagship of the Rainbow Fleet"—made the ceremonial first trip to Coney Island. I. H. Gant, one of the three veteran Iron Steamboat captains who had been present for the auction at Edgewater three months earlier, was back in uniform and in the wheelhouse.

In mid-August of that first year, Steeplechase Pier found itself decked out in bunting for a week in a rather contrived celebration of the anniversary of the arrival of the first steamboat at the first iron pier in Coney Island in 1879. The people who ran the Rainbow Fleet, in other words, were mindful of the need to generate what a later generation would call "photo opportunities."

The new service followed the same general schedule as had the Iron Steamboat Company for most of its latter years—that is to say,

Empire State was a sidewheel steamboat powered by an inclined compound engine that served as the flagship of Union Navigation's short-lived Rainbow Fleet. View from West 129th Street.

a dozen or so daily sailings from West 129th Street and North River Pier 1, Manhattan, to Coney Island, with two or three trips each day continuing beyond to Rockaway Beach. Union cut Iron Steamboat's latter-day Coney Island round-trip fare of one dollar in half, but even with the rigors of Prohibition a thing of the past, too few people came to the docks and too many boats steamed down the bay with too little revenue to make it worth the effort. The Great Depression was not kind to new business ventures of any sort.

As to subway competition, the excursion season of 1933 was also the first summer that the city's new Independent Subway System was in operation, and while it did not itself serve Coney Island, it gave passengers from upper Manhattan, who might otherwise have been inclined to head for a Coney Island-bound steamboat at the foot of West 129th Street, a fast connecting ride to other trains that did.

On Monday, April 29, 1935—following the two unsuccessful seasons and just a little over two years after the original Iron Steamboat Company was liquidated—another auction was held at Edgewater, this one under the aegis of a United States Marshal. Federal auc-

You are cordially invited to attend

THE OWNERS' RECEPTION

aboard

THE S. S. "EMPIRE STATE"

The Flagship of the Rainbow Fleet

AT PIER ONE, NORTH RIVER, (foot of Battery Place)

SATURDAY, MAY TWENTY-SEVENTH, 1933

From noon to four P. M. and continued with the inaugural trip to Coney Island

UNION NAVIGATION COMPANY, Inc.

PLEASE PRESENT THIS CARD FOR ADMISSION

Invitation to a reception to inaugurate Union Navigation's Rainbow Fleet
service to Coney Island.

tioneer J. J. Donnelly handled the proceedings, and while the
1897-built *Empire State* went for an almost respectable $12,000, the
five old "iron steamboats" brought an average of just $2,270 per
vessel on the block.

Empire State would still see active years. The one-time L.I.R.R.
sidewheeler *Shinnecock* eventually migrated to New England waters, and there, as *Town of Hull*, she ran between Boston and an
amusement park at Nantasket Beach until 1944, when she was
fatally damaged in a hurricane.

None of the seven vessels from 1881 ever carried passengers
again. While one or another of them might have been used on a
charter trip or two after the close of the regular excursion season in
September 1934, more than likely the very last day any of the
original "iron steamboats" carried revenue passengers was Sunday,
September 9, 1934, the last day of Rainbow Line service to Coney
Island. If published schedules were followed, the final trip left West

129th Street and the Hudson River at 6:30 P.M., landed at Pier 1 at 7:15, and tied up to Steeplechase Pier a little before 8:30. Then, after boarding whatever passengers were waiting, it was time to cast off into the night and steam away from the bright lights of Coney Island for one last time—around Norton's Point, up through the Narrows, across Upper New York Bay, and finally on into the Hudson River to Manhattan. One can only wonder about the identity of the steamboat that made that last trip. Was it the newer *Empire State*? Or was it one of the originals launched on the Delaware River in 1881?

OTHER MATTERS

Seven years later, on January 25, 1941, another link with the past was broken. Seventy-nine-year-old Frederick A. Bishop, the man who guided the Iron Steamboat company for half of its corporate life, passed away in Brooklyn's Caledonia Hospital. Educated in the

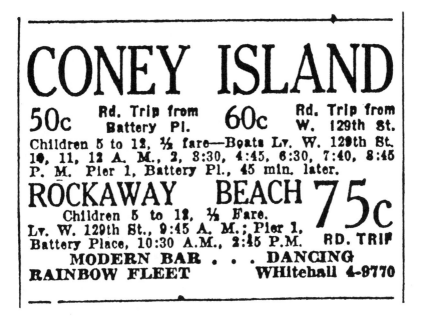

Newspaper advertisement for Union Navigation's Rainbow Fleet, the successor to the Iron Steamboat Company.

public schools of Brooklyn and associated with the Bridge Department of the City of New York in the heady years when that agency was following up the success of the Brooklyn Bridge with additional East River crossings, Bishop took over the Iron Steamboat Company in 1902 and saw it through the rest of its days.

There would be sporadic efforts to revive steamboat service to Coney Island in the years between 1934 and World War II, but never with the kind of strong corporate identity—much less the frequent service from morning through evening—that was the hallmark of the Iron Steamboat Company and, to a lesser extent, Union Navigation's Rainbow Fleet. Steamboats such as *Bear Mountain* tried to find a "market niche" on the Coney Island run, but with no lasting success. In 1935 and 1936, before she was sold to New England interests, *Empire State* ran a one-boat service between Hoboken (New Jersey), Battery Park, and Steeplechase Pier under the house flag of the Empire State Excursion Steamship Company of New Jersey.

(A personal note: I never rode to Coney Island on an excursion boat, but I have a vivid memory of returning to lower Manhattan with my parents from Roton Point one day aboard *Belle Island*—it was likely 1940 or 1941—and having someone point out *Bear Mountain* and identify her as "the boat that runs to Coney Island." As clearly as if it were yesterday, I can still see a uniformed officer standing behind the wheel in the pilothouse.)

The war years saw a general reduction of excursion boat operations in New York. Fuel was scarce, some boats were "conscripted" for military-related use, and while services like that of the Hudson River Day Line remained in operation throughout the duration, there was no chance—and no justification—for passenger steamboats to serve Coney Island while war was being waged. *Taurus* may have run to the off-shore fishing grounds during World War I, but there was too much convoy activity originating in New York Harbor during World War II to allow excursion boats to pick their way through the Narrows with curious civilians on board taking in all the details. Besides, the military was not about to open and close the harbor's submarine nets several times a day for an excursion-boat service whose schedules would be published in the newspapers.

Following VJ-Day, some efforts were made to return excursion-boat service to Coney Island, not via the ocean and Steeplechase Pier, but to the Gravesend Bay side of the island, not unlike service patterns that were run before the first iron pier was built in 1879 and steamboats landed inside what is now called Norton's Point. An ex-Delaware River excursion steamer named *Bojangles* is most associated with these postwar ventures, but the bayside docking area at Coney Island was so removed from the heart of the amusement area and the beach that such service was, for all intents and purposes, doomed from the outset. When excursion boats ran to Coney Island Point in the nineteenth century, they were met there by trains of Andrew Culver's Prospect Park and Coney Island Railroad for continuing service to the various resorts, hotels, and pavilions; passengers getting off *Bojangles* in the late 1940s had to walk.

In mid-July of 1956, what was undoubtedly the last scheduled excursion-boat service between Manhattan and Coney Island was begun; after five completely unsuccessful weeks, it was mercifully ended. A man by the name of Jeremiah Driscoll obtained a converted U.S. Navy LCI(L)-class landing craft bearing the improbable name *San Jacinto*—she had previously sailed Texas waters to the San Jacinto battlefield outside Houston—and inaugurated a route between the Battery and Gravesend Bay/West 23rd Street, Coney Island, on July 18, 1956. She was all decked out in bunting with the phrase "Coney Island Boat" painted amidships on the port side in letters much larger than her name. (This decoration was probably just a coincidence. Or did someone associated with Driscoll's Panorama Line remember an earlier fleet of Coney Island boats whose service was rendered across their paddleboxes in larger letters than their names?)

Few patrons rode *San Jacinto* to Coney Island in 1956; soon afterward, Driscoll put her into the around-Manhattan Island sightseeing trade after having her rebuilt with a lower wheelhouse to allow clear passage under Harlem River bridges.[20]

The following summer, 1957, Driscoll ran a one-round-trip-daily service between Newark, New Jersey, and the same Gravesend Bay side of Coney Island that *San Jacinto* had used the previous summer, but using a vessel called *Manhattan*. In the heyday of the Iron Steamboat Company, service between Newark and Coney Island, via the ocean piers, was commonplace. Driscoll's 1957 venture is mentioned for this reason: absent a better contender for the title, it will be here asserted that when Panorama Sightseeing Company's wooden-hulled—and by then diesel-powered—*Manhattan* pulled away from West 23rd Street in Coney Island during the early evening hours of Labor Day, September 2, 1957, the long and interesting history of scheduled excursion-boat service to Coney Island came to an end.

It just wasn't a good year for Brooklyn. Six weeks after the last excursion boat departed Coney Island, the borough's baseball team announced it was pulling out of Ebbets Field and heading for southern California.

NOTES

1. The low prices for which the seven boats sold had repercussions throughout the New York steamboat industry. When creditors of the Hudson River Navigation Company, better known as the "Night Line," sought to liquidate that company's assets in early 1933, a judge refused to allow a forced sale because of the Iron Steamboat experience. See Donald C. Ringwald, *Hudson River Day Line* (New York: Fordham University Press, 1990), p. 187.
2. The incorporators of the firm were: John Roache (ship builder); Charles H. Cramp and Joseph C. Ferguson, of Philadelphia; Nathan G. Miller, of Bridgeport, Connecticut; George S. Scott, James D. Smith, Washington E. Connor, and Charles E. Quinby (bankers), of New York; Samuel Carpenter (general eastern passenger agent, Pennsylvania Railroad); J. B. Houston (president, Pacific Mail Steamship Company); Alfred R. Whitney (iron merchant), of New York; Rufus Hatch, of New York. Quotations and information from *The New York Times*, September 28, 1880, p. 8.
3. *The New York Times*, May 24, 1881, p. 8.
4. *The New York Times*, July 4, 1885, p. 7.
5. A telegram sent to Washington from Philadelphia is included in the vessel's official documentation file in the National Archives, in Washington.
6. *The New York Times*, May 30, 1881, p. 8.
7. *The New York Times*, July 7, 1883, p. 7.
8. The New York and Sea Beach Railroad opened in 1879 between Coney Island and the foot of 61st Street, where patrons switched to steamboats to complete their trip to Manhattan. See note 16, below.
9. *New York Herald*, July 1, 1901, p. 4.
10. *The New York Times*, July 4, 1913, p. 8.
11. For additional information on the *General Slocum* disaster, see chap. 5, note 1.
12. For a general description of the early development of Coney Island and its amusement parks, see Edo McCullough, *Good Old Coney Island* (New York: Scribners, 1957).
13. For information on the migration of northern steamboats to southern waters during the northern off-season, see Edward A. Mueller, *St. John's River Steamboats* (Jacksonville, FL: the author, 1986), esp. pp. 196–99.

14. *The New York Times*, September 20, 1915, p. 5.
15. For a perspective on the following season, 1916, see Roger W. Mabie, "A Year in the Life of *Perseus*," *Steamboat Bill* 135 (Fall 1975), 151–53. Mabie obtained original log books from *Perseus* at the time the vessel was scrapped, and this article contains material from the 1916 operating season. See also Roger W. Mabie, "The *Perseus* at Twilight," *Steamboat Bill* 137 (Spring 1976), 21–23, for a similar account from the years 1929, 1930, and 1931.
16. Five excursion railways were built to Coney Island in the nineteenth century. Four later evolved into rapid-transit lines and remain in operation today as part of the city subway system; one was abandoned.

Railway	Date opened	Terminals	Current status
Brooklyn, Bath & West End R.R.	1864	Foot of 39th St. & West End Depot	B Line of Transit Authority
Prospect Park &Coney Island R.R.	1875	Greenwood Cemetery & Culver Depot	F Line of Transit Authority
New York & Manhattan Beach R.R.	1876	Long Island City & Manhattan Beach	Abandoned, 1941
Brooklyn, Flatbush & Coney Island R.R.	1878	Flatbush/Atlantic & Brighton Beach (later Culver Depot)	D & Q Lines of Transit Authority
New York & Sea Beach R.R.	1879	Foot of 61st St. & Sea Beach Palace (later West End Depot)	N Line of Transit Authority

For historical information on these early-nineteenth-century excursion railways, see the respective *Annual Report of the Board of Railroad Commissioners of the State of New York* (Albany: State Printer, 1882–   ).
17. I have written elsewhere of the New York subways. See *Under the Sidewalks of New York*, 2d rev. ed. (New York: Fordham University Press, 1995). A more comprehensive treatment of railway, streetcar, and rapid-transit service to and from Coney Island is needed.
18. Statistics from the *The New York Times*, April 20, 1932, p. 46.
19. *The New York Times*, February 3, 1933, p. 16.
20. For further information about *San Jacinto*'s later career as an around—Manhattan Island sightseeing boat—as well as information about her owner, Jeremiah Driscoll—see chap. 1.

Observation, the one-time New York sightseeing vessel that exploded enroute to Rikers Island on September 9, 1932, bringing death to 72 persons. (Courtesy of the Mariners' Museum, Newport News, Virginia.)

5

Another Disaster at Hell Gate: the Loss of the Steamboat *Observation*

That a body of water in New York Harbor bears the name Hell Gate certainly suggests it is a place where mariners would be well advised to exercise some degree of caution. Before the Army Corps of Engineers blasted away dangerous rock outcroppings in the area in 1876, hundreds of ships had sunk in the treacherous waters of Hell Gate. By far the worst tragedy associated with Hell Gate, though, happened long after the worst of the navigational hazards had been neutralized. On June 15, 1904, more than one thousand people perished when the excursion steamboat *General Slocum* caught fire as it steamed through Hell Gate with a church group from the lower East Side of Manhattan on their way to a picnic at Locust Grove on Long Island Sound.[1]

Measured by loss of human life, the fatal fire that destroyed the 1891-built *General Slocum* stands as by far the worst tragedy ever to befall metropolitan New York, on land, on the sea, or in the air. What is less well known, though, is that on Friday, September 9, 1932—28 years, 2 months, and 25 days after the *General Slocum* fire—another maritime disaster took place near Hell Gate and within mere yards of the spot where the *General Slocum* came to grief. It was an explosion, not a fire; the death toll was 72, not 1,030. But there are strange and eerie parallels between the two tragedies.

- Both involved wooden-hulled steamboats built in Brooklyn.
- In each case the work of federal inspectors whose responsi-

157

bilities were to ensure that passenger vessels met requisite safety standards was seriously faulted.

- In the year of the *General Slocum* fire, 1904, the City of New York opened the first leg of its very first subway line, the Interborough Rapid Transit. On the same day that 72 people died in the 1932 explosion, the first route of the city's new Independent Subway System carried its first revenue passengers.
- In the aftermath of the 1932 explosion, New York Police Commissioner Edward P. Mulrooney was on the scene, personally directing rescue efforts. In 1904, as a young detective with the NYPD, the man who would later become Commissioner Mulrooney was ordered by his superiors to go to Lincoln Hospital in the Bronx and there put William Van Schaick, the captain of the *General Slocum*, under arrest. (The captain of the vessel involved in the 1932 explosion was pronounced dead in Lincoln Hospital hours after the accident.)

In the depths of the Great Depression, the P. J. Carlin Construction Company regarded itself as fortunate when it was awarded a major contract to build a new $9 million penitentiary for the City of New York on Rikers Island in the East River. In addition to the usual kind of technical specifications associated with any construction project, the contract called for the company to provide waterborne transportation from the mainland out to the island each day for its workers. There was a municipal ferryboat line that operated to Rikers Island from the foot of East 134th Street in the Port Morris section of the Bronx. Construction workers, though, were required to use alternate transportation.

The Carlin Company retained a man by the name of George A. Forsyth, of Staten Island, to run such a service. The sixty-six-year-old Forsyth was born in Kingston, New York, and began his maritime career as a fourteen-year-old cabin boy aboard Hudson River steamboats. For most of his working life he owned and operated a fleet of tugs. In either 1930 or 1931, Forsyth purchased an old two-deck steam launch by the name of *Observation*; this was the boat he would use to ferry workers out to Rikers Island. Formal title to the vessel, though, was recorded in the name of Forsyth's

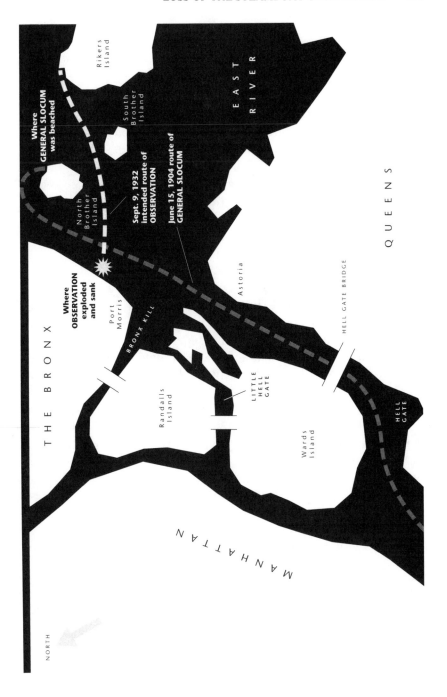

son, Alexander. This seemingly inconsequential matter would later prove to be very telling.

Observation, built in 1888 as the steam yacht Jean, was powered by a pair of two-cylinder compound steam engines (177″ x 34″ x 26″). In 1909 she was purchased at auction by Captain John P. Roberts of New York and sent to the T. J. Marvel yard in Newburgh for conversion into a sightseeing and tour boat; a new single-ended Scotch boiler was installed at this time. (See chapter 1 for further information about Captain Roberts and the early days of waterborne sightseeing service in New York.) Captain James P. McAllister owned Observation for a time in the early 1920s, and reportedly ran her in excursion service between New Rochelle and Rye Beach. A 1922 advertisement promotes cruises to Rye Beach aboard Observation from New York City.

Construction workers boarded Forsyth's Observation at a point in Port Morris north of the 134th Street municipal ferryslip.[2] Observation made three trips out to Rikers Island each morning and a similar number back to the mainland in the evening. On Friday, September 9, 1932, the 6:50 and 7:30 morning departures had gone routinely enough. At a minute or so after 8:00, Observation was preparing to cast off and head out to Rikers with the day's final boatload of workers.

On that day, the bulkhead area where Observation usually docked at the Bronx end of the run was crowded. As a result she was unable to make fast to any wharf proper and had to tie up outboard of the tug Montrose, owned by the Delaware, Lackawanna, and Western Railroad; construction workers boarding Observation thus had to walk across the deck of the tug before they could reach their Rikers Island boat. The lighter Gypsum, owned by United States Gypsum Corporation, was moored to the bulkhead astern of Montrose. To the rear of Gypsum, the 245-ton municipal ferryboat Greenwich Village was in a lay-up berth adjacent to the actual ferryslip at the foot of East 134th Street. Relief captain Robert Turnier had just taken over and was settling in for his day's shift.

By 1932, the 44-year-old Observation was well past her prime. It was later discovered that some of her timbers were so rotted that when she tied up with her port side adjacent to a wharf or pier, lines from the pier had to be run completely across the main deck to chocks and cleats on the vessel's starboard side because there was no longer any firm wood on the port side to which such hardware could be securely attached. The boiler was also in poor condition; several leaks had supposedly been repaired with sand and concrete, in complete violation of federal safety standards.

Up in the wheelhouse, Captain George Forsyth, who piloted the vessel himself, sounded a long blast on the whistle and began to back *Observation* away from her berth next to *Montrose*. It was 8:02 A.M. The weather in New York was fair and clear, and the temperature was in the mid-50s. Across town on the Hudson River at the same hour, Cunard Line's aging *Mauretania* should have just finished docking at Second Street in Hoboken after a transatlantic crossing, and at the foot of West 55th Street, Furness, Withy's new *Monarch of Bermuda* was completing a run from Hamilton, Bermuda. Another minute ticked off the clock. It was now 8:03 A.M. on Friday, September 9, 1932. *Observation* was several boat lengths away from her berth; Forsyth swung the wheel over to starboard and called for power ahead. At that very instant the vessel's boiler exploded.

Alexander Kanter was a motorman on the Third Avenue Railway's 138th Street trolley line. His car was on Locust Avenue between 135th and 136th Streets when the explosion occurred. "I saw a big cloud shoot up higher than the power house. I thought it was a Zeppelin splitting up, but later I saw it came from the river," Kanter said.[3]

Captain Leo Brennan of the lighter *Gypsum* was changing clothes in the pilothouse of his vessel. "I had turned for a moment to get a pair of trousers when the explosion came. All I could see . . . was a cloud of dust and smoke. When that cleared away, there was no *Observation* left, only wreckage."[4]

As was often the case when a marine boiler exploded, the force of the blast was focused in a single direction. In the case of *Observation*, that direction was forward. As a result, construction workers who were riding up front on either the main deck or the upper deck bore the brunt of the casualties. Bodies flew through the air like so many rag dolls. One unfortunate soul was thrown up against an exterior wall of the nearby United Light and Power Company generating station at a point fifty feet above street level; another was hurled onto the headhouse of the ferry terminal; five bodies came to rest on *Gypsum*'s main deck. One survivor told of flying through the air and being convinced while airborne that his own death was imminent, only to land in the water and be pulled to safety.[5]

Observation's single-ended Scotch boiler was located immediately abaft of the wheelhouse down in the hull. Forward of this position the hull was torn completely asunder, and water poured into what remained of the vessel; she sank in little more than a minute. The wheelhouse itself was flattened and found later in the day in Astoria, across the East River from the site of the explosion and on the far side of the Hell Gate Bridge. Captain George Forsyth was among the fatalities.

The spot where *Observation* exploded and sank—approximately one hundred feet out from the Bronx shoreline between East 134th and East 135th Streets—was only another three or four hundred feet inland from the route taken by the ill-fated *General Slocum* on June 15, 1904. Four blocks north, at the foot of East 138th Street, is where two units of the New York Fire Department—Engine Company No. 60 and Hook and Ladder Company No. 17—were waiting for the stricken *General Slocum* to turn in toward shore that tragic morning so its passengers might have a chance of escaping the awful conflagration; the fire companies hoped to hold the blaze at bay and permit such an evacuation.[6] But *General Slocum* never altered course; Captain Van Schaick steamed on, and the spot where she was eventually beached along the northeast shore of North Brother Island is about one thousand yards from the place where *Observation* exploded and sank.

It took several days for the extent of the death toll aboard *Observation* to be known fully. Some bodies were washed ashore miles away, but by the middle of the following week, it was established with certainty that seventy-two men had lost their lives in the incident.[7] The Carlin Construction Company operated under a "staggered work" plan, with certain crafts told to report at certain hours; as a result, the great bulk of the passengers on the 8:00 A.M. departure were iron workers. The International Association of Bridge, Structural, and Ornamental Ironworkers took an immediate hand in helping to identify victims and notify families. To reassure the loved ones of workers who had safely reached Rikers Island

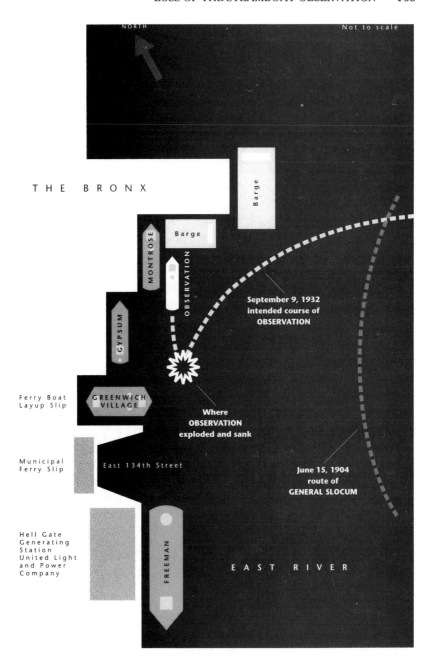

earlier that morning, construction of the new penitentiary was canceled for the day and employees sent home.

Because the man who was collecting fares as the workers boarded *Observation* was himself killed in the blast, no accurate count was immediately available of the total number of people who were aboard that morning, though it was later established as 127. While the Forsyth family operated *Observation* under contract to the Carlin company, each worker had to pay ten cents a ride to the boat owner. This fact would later result in Carlin arguing that it should bear no liability for death or injury, since each ride was a separate transaction between individual workers and the owners of *Observation*. The case went all the way to the United States Supreme Court, which held, in a 1936 decision written for the majority by Associate Justice McReynolds, that, indeed, Carlin did share liability.[8]

If seventy-two people were killed in the explosion, fifty-five were aboard *Observation* and lived to tell about it. Their survival can be credited principally to two circumstances. First, while there was no time for passengers to don life jackets, the explosion aboard *Observation* so disintegrated the old wooden steamboat that the water adjacent to the accident was filled with pieces of wreckage which survivors were able to cling to until help arrived. One eyewitness said that pieces of *Observation* were strewn across a circle two hundred yards in diameter.[9]

The second point is that *Observation* blew up not only close to shore but also close to other vessels whose crews were able to launch small boats and begin prompt rescue operations. Captain Brennan quickly launched *Gypsum*'s work boat, and Captain Turnier did the same aboard *Greenwich Village*. Another vessel that was able to put a boat into the water was the 3,350-ton bulk carrier *Freeman*, of the Pocohontas Steamship Company, which had arrived at the United Lighting and Power Company on September 6 with a load of coal from Norfolk.[10]

As survivors were brought ashore, their condition was initially assessed by physicians who had rushed to the scene and set up an emergency medical station in the municipal ferry station at the foot of East 134th Street. Injured passengers were sent to Lincoln Hospital, where many were admitted; to avoid overloading any single facility, though, some were retransported to other hospitals elsewhere in the city. Bodies were taken to the Bronx County morgue at Fordham Hospital.

Merritt, Chapman, and Scott raised the hulk of *Observation* after the explosion, but the vessel's boiler was never found, despite a week or more of intense underwater searching.[11] The safety valve was recovered, though, and in a test conducted at the nearby United Light and Power generating plant, it opened at just over 142 pounds of pressure. The safety valve was set to open at 150 pounds, and the test established that excess pressure was clearly not the cause of the explosion. Testimony from a number of individuals who had worked aboard *Observation* over the previous year soon allowed investigators to draw the conclusion that, in all likelihood, the boiler exploded because it had seriously deteriorated and was never properly repaired.[12]

Just as young Detective Mulrooney had put Captain Van Schaick of the *General Slocum* under arrest in Lincoln Hospital on the afternoon of the 1904 tragedy, so did members of Commissioner Mulrooney's department hold George Forsyth's son, Alexander, as a material witness following the 1932 incident. Alexander Forsyth was also a patient at Lincoln Hospital; he had been aboard *Observation* at the time of the explosion, working the coffee concession on the main deck abaft of the boiler.

Because he was technically listed as the owner of the ill-fated vessel, on September 30, 1932, a Bronx County grand jury indicted young Forsyth for manslaughter. The presentment of the grand jury was also harsh on the way U.S. steamboat inspectors had given *Observation* only a cursory once-over earlier in the year, and had even inserted letters in the file justifying their action in the days *after* the explosion. But no indictments were handed down against any federal inspectors or officials.

Forsyth was brought to trial in March of 1933; after a week of testimony, Judge James M. Barrett gave such exacting and detailed instructions to the jury concerning Forsyth's merely technical status as the vessel's owner that they had no other choice but to bring in a verdict of acquittal. Judge Barrett took sixty-five minutes to deliver his instructions; the jury needed less time than that to reach its verdict. While there were other civil trials associated with the disaster, Alexander Forsyth was the only person to be tried criminally.

A final irony brings forth a connection between Observation and another ill-fated American vessel—but not, oddly enough, the *General Slocum*. In the years after the accident, *Observation* continued to be listed as an officially enrolled vessel in several annual editions of *Merchant Vessels of the United States*. For one reason or another, her certificate of enrollment was not surrendered until November 17, 1934. (On the certificate, the date of the fatal explosion is incorrectly noted as September 7, 1932—two days earlier than it actually happened.)[13] Finally, in the 1935 edition of *Merchant Vessels of the United States*, matters were brought up to date and *Observation* was duly included among twenty-eight steam-powered vessels listed as "lost" and therefore no longer in documentation. Immediately ahead of a one-line notation telling of *Observation*'s tragic end was an equally brief report on another maritime tragedy. The accident that destroyed *Observation* took place mere yards from the spot where 1,025 people lost their lives in the *General Slocum* fire. Her final mention in *Merchant Vessels of the United States* is immediately below a listing telling of the loss of the *Morro Castle*.[14]

NOTES

1. For further discussion of the *General Slocum* disaster, see Irving Werstein, *The "General Slocum" Incident; Story of an Ill-Fated Ship* (New York: John Day, 1965); Claude Rust, *The Burning of the "General Slocum"* (New York: Elsevier, 1981). There have been many articles about the *General Slocum* disaster over the years in *Steamboat Bill*; see, for example, no. 53 (March 1955), no. 79 (Fall 1961), and no. 191 (Fall 1989).
2. During the summer of 1932, Forsyth ran moonlight cruises on Long Island Sound for the general public aboard *Observation* from the foot of East 134th Street. See *New York Daily News*, September 10, 1932, p. 3.
3. *The New York Times*, September 10, 1932, p. 3.
4. Ibid., p. 1.
5. *New York Herald Tribune*, September 10, 1932, p. 1.
6. The Fire Department's role in the *General Slocum* disaster is discussed in an article that appeared in the FDNY's house organ; see Frank Cull, "*General Slocum* Afire! Hundreds Perish!!," *WNYF* 40(2) (1979), 8–13, 23.
7. On the morning after the disaster, September 10, 1932, the *Times* coverage said that thirty-seven had died and sixty-four were injured; the *Herald Tribune* put the number of dead at thirty-nine and the injured at seventy-two; and the *Daily News* said thirty-eight had been killed and seventy-five injured. All coverage that day was cognizant of the fact that the ultimate toll would be considerably higher. The *Daily Worker* gave the tragedy front-page coverage, but not as the lead story: "Rotten Old Boat Blows Up, 37 Dead" was the headline.

8. See *The New York Times*, April 7, 1936, p. 18.

9. *Herald Tribune*, September 10, 1932, pp. 1, 3.

10. F. L. Collins, the second officer aboard the *Freeman*, described the explosion in these words: "There was one terrific blast. It sounded like the roar of a Big Bertha. I saw bodies hurtling in every direction, mingled with pieces of wreckage" (*Daily News*, September 10, 1932, p. 6).

11. *Observation*'s boiler may still be lodged in the muck and mud at the bottom of the East River off East 134th Street. One eyewitness claims the boiler was blown through the deck and into the air and disintegrated when it hit the water; see *Daily News*, September 10, 1932, p. 4.

12. For a summary of testimony detailing *Observation*'s shortcomings, see "*Observation* Disaster," *Marine Engineering and Shipping Age* 37(10) (October 1932), 413.

13. The certificate is on file in the National Archives, Washington, D.C.

14. *Merchant Vessels of the United States; 1935* (Washington, DC: 1936), p. 1028. For further information on the loss of the *Morro Castle*, see Chapter 6, note 7.

MONARCH OF BERMUDA

6

From *Ambrose* Light to Five Fathom Hole: New York to Bermuda by Sea

Bermuda. This properly British outpost in the middle of the Atlantic Ocean is 747 nautical miles east of Wilmington, North Carolina, 757 miles south of Halifax, Nova Scotia, and 697 miles southeast of New York. Bermuda is twenty-one square miles, hundreds of separate islands, and the northernmost coral reef on the face of the earth. If you find yourself in the vicinity of 32 degrees 18 minutes north latitude and 64 degrees 45 minutes west longitude, just relax and enjoy yourself—you're in Bermuda.

The first European ever to visit the place is thought to have been the Spanish navigator Juan de Bermudez, who arrived in the year 1515. All he left behind was his name, though, because the first settlers didn't arrive for almost another century. In 1609 a group led by Sir George Somers was en route from Plymouth, England, to the colony of Jamestown, in a new land called Virginia, when one of their ships, the *Sea Venture*, came to grief on underwater reefs surrounding the island chain in the midst of what was undoubtedly a hurricane. Undaunted, the shipwrecked travelers made their way ashore, and while some continued on to Jamestown the following spring, others remained behind in Bermuda. It is this incident that Shakespeare used as the basis of *The Tempest*.

Full fathom five thy father lies.
Of his bones are coral made.

Those are pearls that were his eyes.
Nothing of him that doth fade
But doth suffer a sea change
Into something rich and strange. [I:1]

Over the years, two things about Bermuda have remained more constant than not: ties between the island and Great Britain remain strong and unbroken, and commerce by sea linking Bermuda with the North American mainland—particularly New York—has always been very active. Actually there's probably a third constant: travel to and from Bermuda by sea remains vulnerable to disruption by seasonal Atlantic hurricanes.

Passing over the colorful era of sailing ships—which includes the roles Bermuda played, neither trivial nor without consequence, in the American Revolution, the War of 1812, and the Civil War—we come to the late nineteenth century when the development of modern oceangoing steamships began to give Bermuda's economy the early dimensions of its current shape and form.[1]

The Quebec Steamship Company

The first company to establish itself in any kind of major way on the ocean route between New York and Bermuda came on the scene thanks to an unusual turn of circumstance. The Quebec and Gulf Ports Steamship Company had been a principal link between Quebec City and what are today called Canada's maritime provinces, but in the years after the American Civil War, a newly constructed railroad between Quebec and Halifax began to erode the line's traffic. When approached by representatives of Bermuda about the possibility of establishing a New York–Hamilton service, the company was quick to seize the opportunity.

Simplifying its name to Quebec Steamship Company, the Canadian firm dispatched the 1,000-ton steamship *Canima* out of New York in January 1874 on the company's inaugural trip to Hamilton and beyond to the West Indies. Quebec Steamship would remain on the New York–Bermuda run for the next forty years or more, sailing primarily from North River Pier 47 in New York. In 1885 the company had a pair of 2,150-ton vessels built for the service,

Trinidad and *Orinoco*. Each had accommodations for thirty-five passengers, although in 1894 Trinidad was lengthened and her capacity increased to two hundred. Traffic grew during the final decades of the 1800s, but not, of course, to anything even remotely like the levels it would attain in the twentieth century. Almost 2,400 people traveled to Bermuda aboard Quebec Steamship vessels in the year 1900. By 1927 the annual passenger count would be closer to 24,000; it would be almost 56,000 in 1936; and today well over 100,000 people visit Bermuda annually by ship.

In 1904 Quebec Steamship took delivery of the first vessel ever to be specifically designed and built for luxury passenger service between New York and Hamilton, the 5,500-ton *Bermudian*, a handsome two-stack vessel with tall masts fore and aft and accommodations for 240 first-class passengers, 32 in second class, and 43 in third. (A preponderance of first-class space will remain a characteristic of vessels on the New York–Bermuda run until the advent of single-class ships in a later era.) *Bermudian* was built in Sunderland, England, by J. Laing and Sons. She was powered by a pair of triple-expansion steam engines whose cylinders measured 26, 43, and 71 inches in diameter, with a stroke of 48 inches.[2]

World War I took a toll on Quebec Steamship. *Bermudian* was recruited for government service on two separate occasions during

Bermudian, a) *Fort Hamilton*, is often regarded as the first luxury passenger ship to work the New York-to-Bermuda trade. (Bermuda Maritime Museum.)

the war, travel to the islands waned, and it took some years after armistice was declared in 1918 for stability to return to New York–Bermuda service. At one point toward war's end, a rebuilt cruiser from the Royal Navy—*HMS Charybdis* of 1896—was converted into a passenger vessel and put to work on the route, operated for the island government, under contract, by Quebec Steamship. The former warship left New York on her first commercial trip on March 8, 1918, but so deteriorated were her engines that she didn't reach Hamilton until March 12, four days later. *Charybdis* remained in service through 1920. That was when rather fundamental changes were effected in New York–Bermuda steamship operations.

Furness, Withy Ltd.

For corporate reasons of its own, Quebec Steamship was no longer interested in continuing to operate the New York–Hamilton run after the war. The company was by then affiliated with Canada Steamship Lines, and it saw its future as being in other areas. And so, in 1919, representatives of Bermuda negotiated an agreement with one of the largest steamship companies of all time. Furness, Withy, Ltd., of Great Britain, was not a force in the luxury passenger field, so its operations never achieved the kind of visibility that automatically accrued to companies engaged in, say, North Atlantic express mailboat service. Furness, Withy's forte was amalgamating fleets of largely freight-oriented steamships serving diverse and specialized markets, often under the house flags of subsidiary companies.[3] Furness, Withy would achieve its greatest visibility in North America as a result of the agreement it reached with the Bermuda government in 1919, even though Bermuda service would always remain a very small portion of the company's overall steamship operations. Except for the years of World War II, Furness would remain on the New York–Hamilton run for almost half a century, introduce some notable vessels to the route, and create a classic era of stylish travel. Bermuda's growth as a popular vacation spot in the period between the two world wars owes much to the strategic thinking of Furness, Withy.

Technically, Furness, Withy purchased the assets of the old Quebec Steamship Company, a transaction that included title to the fifteen-year-old *Bermudian*, by then back from wartime assignments. Furness created a new subsidiary to operate the service, the Bermuda & West Indies Steamship Company. In practice, though, under Furness, Withy, service between New York and Bermuda was popularly known as the Furness Bermuda Line.[4]

Bermudian was renamed *Fort Hamilton* and given a substantial reconditioning, her passenger accommodations were upgraded, she was converted from coal to oil fuel, and she first sailed out of New York for her new owners on December 8, 1919. As running-mates, Furness obtained a pair of steamers built in Scotland in 1912 for the Australian coastal trade, the sister-ships *Wandilla* and *Willochra*, and renamed them, respectively, *Fort St. George* and *Fort Victoria*. Both were powered by a pair of four-cylinder quadruple-expansion reciprocating steam engines. (See roster for further details.) All of the namesake fortresses figure prominently in Bermuda history, although some liberties were taken in the case of *Fort St. George*. She was named after a fortification in the town of St. George's that is called, in somewhat more secular fashion, Fort George. *Fort Hamilton*, on the other hand, was a doubly appropriate name for a New York–Bermuda vessel: a Fort Hamilton defended each end of the route.

During periods of light travel to Bermuda, *Fort St. George* and *Fort Victoria* would often be taken off the New York–Hamilton run and used in such operations as a Boston–Liverpool service operated by another Furness, Withy subsidiary, the Furness, Warren Line, as well as in New York–Trinidad operations of the Bermuda & West Indies Steamship Company.

Furness, Withy, though, was looking beyond merely running steamships to Bermuda; the company also had in mind the development of resort properties on the island, facilities that might then serve to increase demand for cabin space on its New York–Bermuda vessels. Furness thus became associated with the Bermudiana Hotel in Hamilton, the Mid-Ocean Golf Club, the Castle Harbour Hotel, and other tourist-oriented ventures.

Another factor that militated in favor of Americans booking passage aboard Furness vessels bound for Bermuda in the post-World War I era was the fact that the United States ratified the Eighteenth Amendment to its Constitution in 1919, barring the sale of alcoholic beverages during an era that was commonly known as

Bermuda

"Gem of Winter Playgrounds"

Sailings Twice Weekly

Only two days to these isles of delightful peace and quiet. Winter Temperature 60° to 70°. Golf and all other sports and recreations. Finest Hotels offer you every comfort. Luxurious transatlantic liners S. S. "FORT VICTORIA" and S. S. "FORT ST. GEORGE" leave New York every Wednesday and Saturday.

For Booklets and Further Particulars on Bermuda or St. George Hotel write

FURNESS BERMUDA LINE
34 Whitehall Street, New York
or any Local Tourist Agent

St. George Hotel, Bermuda—Unique location commanding wonderful views. Unsurpassed service. Magnificent, tiled, heated and covered swimming pool. Golf on adjoining course. *Lowest Rates*—$6.00 per day and up, including meals.

Furness Bermuda Line advertisement from the days when *Fort Victoria* and *Fort St. Geroge* held down the New York-to-Bermuda service.

Prohibition. Passengers aboard British-flag vessels, though, could belly up to the bar—and do so quite legally—as soon as a ship cleared U.S. territorial waters, often with the bright lights of Coney Island still visible on the horizon.

Because all of this added up to a potential for serious traffic growth, Furness began to think about new ships for the route. First came the 19,086-ton *Bermuda*, a two-stack motorship that was built in Belfast in 1927 by Workman Clark and Company and powered by a pair of eight-cylinder opposed-piston Doxford diesels driving quadruple screws. (In the 1920s the now common word *diesel* was inevitably capitalized.) Originally this vessel was to have been called *Mid-Ocean*, but she was launched as *Bermuda* and was one of the world's very first large oceangoing passenger ships to be powered by internal combustion engines.

Bermuda was 525.9 feet long and 74.1 feet wide and had a loaded draft of 26 feet, 9 inches—dimensions that were thought to be the maximum that Hamilton Harbor could tolerate. She featured accommodations for 616 first-class passengers, 75 in second, and no third class at all, and she introduced new standards of luxury to the service. She also pioneered a distinctive color scheme that would soon become a Furness trademark for its Bermuda vessels: white superstructure over a French-grey hull, green and white boot-topping, red funnels with black stripes, and lifeboats finished in natural mahogany. It was an altogether marvelous livery for a passenger vessel.

Once *Bermuda* entered service—she first sailed out of New York for Hamilton on January 14, 1928, after arriving from Belfast on January 11—the need for a suitable running-mate quickly became apparent. The aging *Fort Hamilton*, a) *Bermudian*, had been sold to Italy's Cosulich Line in 1926. (Renamed *Stella d'Italia*, she remained active until 1953.) Then, on December 18, 1929, unexpected tragedy occurred: *Fort Victoria*, outbound for Hamilton with 206 passengers and a crew of 165 aboard, was struck by the Clyde, Mallory steamer *Algonquin* in cold and heavy fog at the pilot station near *Ambrose* lightship outside New York Harbor.

In the words of *The New York Times*: "The fog had come down heavier than at any time during the last six days, during which the treacherous mists have been virtual masters of shipping at this port. The moan of sirens, the timed beat of melancholy bells and the sobbing blasts of whistle markers sounded on all sides.

"Suddenly out of the grey clouds of fog a tall, sharp prow appeared. The Clyde liner Algonquin, equally blind in the sea's great menace, was steaming out for Galveston. Unable to avoid the ship ahead, the Algonquin cut a deep hole in the Fort Victoria, amidships on the port side."[5] The accident happened at 4:00 P.M. while *Fort Victoria* was stopped to let off the Sandy Hook Harbor pilot, Captain Fred W. Fendt, who had guided her outbound from Pier 95 on the Hudson River.

Water poured into *Fort Victoria*. Her passengers and all but the captain and a skeleton crew of a dozen men were safely evacuated to the nearby pilot boat *Sandy Hook*, and, miraculously, there was no panic and not a single casualty. Captain Arthur R. Francis and a small crew attempted to save their stricken vessel, but the damage

Furness, Withy's *Fort Victoria*, which sunk near Ambrose lightship in 1928. (Bermuda Maritime Museum.)

was much too severe. The Coast Guard cutter *Columbine* eventually took Francis off the doomed vessel and at 7:30 P.M. *Fort Victoria* rolled over on her side and sank in fifty-odd feet of water. Salvage was out of the question; the hulk represented a menace to navigation and thus had to be blown up.

On an interim basis, the Furness Bermuda Line chartered Holland American Line's *Veendam* to run in conjunction with *Bermuda*, but obtaining new tonnage now took on a genuine sense of urgency. Out of this need would emerge the *Monarch of Bermuda*.

First a Monarch, Then a Queen

Laid down at the Newcastle yard of Vickers-Armstrong, Ltd., and launched on March 17, 1931, another tragedy would keep the new *Monarch of Bermuda* from ever becoming a running-mate of *Bermuda*. The latter caught fire in Hamilton in June of 1931—while *Monarch of Bermuda* was still being fitted out in England—and although damage was confined to upper works and her machinery was sufficiency unscathed to permit a return to Belfast under her own power for rebuilding, on November 20 of that same year, with reconstruction just about complete, *Bermuda* caught fire again; this time the vessel was a total loss.[6] *Monarch of Bermuda* made her maiden voyage to Hamilton from New York eight days later on

The *Monarch of Bermuda* at Hamilton before the Second World War. (Bermuda Maritime Museum.)

November 28, 1931, Captain H. Jeffries Davis in command. Furness, Withy was again forced to charter a vessel from another company to compensate for a lost ocean liner; this time it was Cunard's 1923-built *Franconia*, a ship whose single tall funnel amidships was repainted in Furness colors for the assignment.

Within days—possibly hours—of the destruction of *Bermuda*, Furness announced that it had contracted with Vickers-Armstrong to build another new vessel, a ship that would be a twin of the $8 million *Monarch of Bermuda*. This ship was to be called *Queen of Bermuda*, and few will contest the claim that she was to become the best known and most beloved vessel ever to sail between New York and Hamilton.

Queen of Bermuda was built not in Newcastle but at Vickers's Barrow yard. Her keel was laid on December 19, 1931—less than a month after the loss of *Bermuda*—and she was launched on September 1, 1932. Some claim she was more luxurious in interior appointments than her predecessor, but externally the two vessels were just about as identical as two ships can be. (Purists may note that the location of the main mast was slightly different on each

Low Cost October Trips to Bermuda

MONARCH *of* BERMUDA
FRANCONIA $50 *up*

Summer activities are still in full swing in Bermuda! Sail on the 22,424 ton "MONARCH OF BERMUDA", with a private bath in every room . . . two pools, three cafes, $250,000 dance deck, ship-to-shore 'phone etc. Or enjoy millionaire world cruise facilities on the "FRANCONIA".

For Round Trip on "FRANCONIA"

SAILINGS TWICE WEEKLY

Apply local tourist agent or Furness Bermuda Line, 34 Whitehall St. (where Broadway begins); 565 Fifth Ave., N. Y. C.

$60 up For Round Trip on "MONARCH of BERMUDA"

$55 for COMBINATION ROUND TRIP

FURNESS *Leads the Way to Bermuda*

With the loss of the motorship *Bermuda* in 1931, Furness, Withy chartered Cunard's *Franconia* to run with the new *Monarch of Bermuda.*

vessel.) Construction proceeded with dispatch and *Queen of Bermuda* sailed into Hamilton Harbor from New York—the first of more than 1,200 visits, as it would turn out—on March 9, 1933. Ten thousand people lined the shores to greet the newcomer when she reached Bermuda, despite the fact she was three hours late because of hurricane-force winds she had encountered en route. Thanks to the heavy weather, few of the 450 passengers who were aboard had much of a chance to enjoy the vessel's fine public rooms during the stormy trip, and some veteran travelers even said it was the roughest ocean voyage they had ever made. (The storm in March 1933 was an indication of things to come, as the summer and fall of that year turned out to be the most active hurricane season ever, a record that would be threatened—but not surpassed—in 1995. We will hear a little more about Bermuda and the hurricanes of 1995 anon.)

Queen of Bermuda's arrival in New York from Britain before departing on that first storm-tossed trip to Hamilton was also interesting. It was interesting from a maritime perspective, but it was also interesting because of larger developments in the city, the nation, and the world. She sailed out of Glasgow on February 21,

Meseck tugs guide *Queen of Bermuda* into North River Pier 95.

1933, and reached the New York quarantine station on the evening of Thursday, March 2, nine days later; there she anchored for the night. On Friday morning, March 3—escorted by *Monarch of Bermuda* inbound on a regular trip from Hamilton—the new vessel steamed up the Hudson River in a festive procession, with fireboats throwing streams of water skyward and airplanes circling overhead.

At a point off North River Pier 95, *Queen of Bermuda* again dropped anchor. The inbound *Monarch of Bermuda* was able to dock immediately, but *Queen* had to wait in mid-river until Grace Line's *Santa Paula* sailed from Pier 95 later in the afternoon before she was able to tie up. Commanding the whole operation from the bridge of the new vessel was Captain H. Jeffries Davis, the same man who had put *Monarch* into service two years earlier and who had also been in command of the motorship *Bermuda* when she entered service in 1928.

The air of celebration that surrounded the arrival of *Queen of Bermuda* in the port of New York was in contrast to the general mood of the city and the country. A "bank holiday" had recently been declared, and the Great Depression was grinding down the nation's optimism at a most alarming rate. Passengers who could afford to travel to Bermuda in March of 1933, for instance, found themselves unable to convert American money into Sterling once they got there. Cable dispatches from overseas were ominous in a different way. They told of rallies and torchlight processions being held in Germany in anticipation of an upcoming election that, it was predicted, would entrench the National Socialist party into a position of power it had not previously enjoyed.

When *Queen of Bermuda* arrived in New York from Glasgow on March 3, 1933, Herbert Hoover was president of the United States. When she sailed for Hamilton five days later on March 7, Franklin D. Roosevelt had been inaugurated as the nation's thirty-second president.

From a mechanical perspective, the two Furness, Withy sistership s were different from the earlier *Bermuda*. Rather than diesel engines, each of the two new vessels was powered by a pair of Fraser & Chalmers steam turbines, although these did not directly drive the quadruple screws with which each ship was equipped. They were linked, instead, to electric generators, and the propellers, in turn, were driven by electric motors manufactured in England by General Electric, Ltd. Such a turbo-electric propulsion system was selected in order to give the vessels the ability to respond quickly to engine commands, something that was felt to be especially necessary for safe maneuvering in the close confines of Hamilton Harbor. *Bermuda*'s pioneering use of diesel engines for propulsion would eventually become the epitome of conventionality on vessels running between New York and Bermuda. Furness, Withy, though, did not see fit to emulate *Bermuda*'s diesels in their two new ships; they opted instead for more-traditional steam turbines. (It was reported in some quarters that the company felt *Bermuda* was given to excessive vibration.) The limits of Hamilton Harbor again dictated statutory dimensions, although experience with *Bermuda* was such that the two new vessels were twenty-eight feet longer than the earlier motorship.

Finally, as if to underscore the claim that *Monarch of Bermuda* and *Queen of Bermuda* were to be regarded as true luxury ocean liners, Furness topped off the new ships with three black and red funnels (granted that one of the trio was a dummy unit included for aesthetic purposes only). In the history of seafaring, only two more classic ocean liners would ever be built with three stacks: French Line's *Normandie* and Cunard-White Star's *Queen Mary*. (*Normandie*—but not *Queen Mary*—also featured a turbo-electric propulsion system similar to the Furness Bermuda sister-ships.)

Once *Queen of Bermuda* entered service in 1933, she and *Monarch of Bermuda* then settled down to provide the kind of tandem luxury service between New York and Hamilton that Furness, Withy had long intended. Each ship generally managed a single round trip a week, with *Monarch of Bermuda* regularly leaving New York on Saturday and sailing out of Hamilton on Wednesday, *Queen of Bermuda* departing New York on Tuesday and Hamilton on Friday. Variations in this schedule, however, were not unusual, and either vessel could manage a New York–Hamilton round trip in a little more than eighty hours, if necessary. When *Queen of Bermuda* sailed from New York on Tuesday, April 4, 1933, Captain Davis told his chief engineer to crank things up a bit, and she made the run from *Ambrose* lightship to Five Fathom Hole off St. David's Light, Bermuda, in 32 hours and 48 minutes at an average speed of 20.33 knots, eclipsing the previous record of 33 hours and 35 minutes that *Monarch of Bermuda* had set on her maiden voyage in 1931. Normally the run took in excess of 36 hours; *Queen of Bermuda*'s 1933 speed record still stands.

Monarch of Bermuda accommodated 821 first-class passengers; because her staterooms tended to be a bit larger, *Queen of Bermuda* could handle only 733. Each vessel was able to convert a small number of its first-class cabins into a temporary second-class section whenever the need arose. The two liners sailed together during the peak season of Bermuda travel each year, which in those days was December through April. In the Bermuda off-season, one or another vessel might make a few Caribbean cruises out of New York, and each ship would also be withdrawn, in turn, for dry docking and other maintenance, usually back in England.

One out-of-the-ordinary event that should be noted involved *Monarch of Bermuda*. In the early morning hours of September 8, 1934, while approaching New York on a routine trip from Bermuda, she responded to an S.O.S. call sent out when the Ward Line's *Morro Castle* caught fire off the New Jersey coast on a regular trip from

From almost all angles, the *Queen of Bermuda* and the *Monarch of Bermuda* were look-alike sister ships. Here are two views, though, that point up the principal differences between the two. On the *Queen* (above), the mainmast is immediately abaft the cabin, while on the *Monarch* (below) it's farther abaft, and thus not seen in this view. (Bermuda Maritime Museum.)

Ticket envelope and luggage tag for round trip between New York and Bermuda, March 1935. "Down on the *Monarch*, back on the *Queen*."

Havana. The *Monarch* rescued seventy-one survivors from the *Morro Castle* and brought them safely to New York. Many passengers aboard the Furness Bermuda vessel later remarked that they could feel the heat of the fire aboard *Morro Castle* as Captain Albert R. Francis maneuvered his ship in close for the rescue.[7]

Francis, incidentally, was also the captain of the *Fort Victoria* on the December day in 1929 when she sank outside New York after a collision. In fact, as *Monarch of Bermuda* received the distress call from the *Morro Castle*, the Furness liner was taking on a Sandy Hook Harbor pilot adjacent to *Ambrose* lightship, the very spot where *Fort Victoria* had gone down almost five years earlier. On both occasions, Captain Francis displayed admirable courage and excellent seamanship.

The Furness Bermuda Line remained the principal steamship company operating on the New York–Bermuda run for the entire period between the two world wars. Competition, though, did emerge from time to time. The Royal Mail Line, for one, Canadian Pacific, for another, and Munson Line, for a third, entered the market at various times. Furness survived such challenges, though, and remained the dominant carrier. Over and above direct New York–Hamilton service, of course, ocean liners of many companies would call at Bermuda from time to time as part of a longer cruise itinerary.

WORLD WAR II

With the approach of World War II, both *Queen of Bermuda* and *Monarch of Bermuda* were taken off the New York–Hamilton run and conscripted by the Royal Navy. The Bermuda government made arrangements for United States Lines to put its 13,869-ton *President Roosevelt* into service between New York and Hamilton between late 1939 and October of 1940, but as the war expanded, this service was also canceled.[8]

Monarch of Bermuda served as a troopship for the entire duration, but *Queen of Bermuda* was fitted out as an armed cruiser during the war's early years, when Britain lacked warships in proper numbers. Equipped with armor plating and seven six-inch guns, she patrolled the South Atlantic and is reported to have fired only a single shot in anger during this period—and that was placed over the bow of a misidentified American merchant ship that somehow or other failed to heed an order to stop. In 1942–1943, with newly built warships in service for the Royal Navy but adequate transport tonnage still a strategic priority, *Queen of Bermuda* was converted into a troopship. By war's end she had steamed 178,000 miles as an armed merchant cruiser and 192,000 miles in

In the late 1930s, the *Queen* and the *Monarch* were holding down the New York-Bermuda service.

troop transport service. *Monarch of Bermuda*, whose wartime assignments involved only troopship work, steamed more than 450,000 miles. Between them, then, the two Furness Bermuda ships contributed 820,000 miles to the Allied cause, the equivalent of 135 round trips between New York and Britain.[9]

Both *Queen of Bermuda* and *Monarch of Bermuda* were conveyed back to Furness, Withy to resume service between New York and Bermuda after the war. But in an incident that recalled the earlier fate of the motorship *Bermuda*, on March 24, 1947, the *Monarch* caught fire while being reconverted at Tyneside. The British Government purchased the damaged vessel and rebuilt her into a single-class (and single-stack) emigrant ship that was put to work between England and Australia and christened, fittingly enough, *New Australia*. She was operated in this service, under contract, by the Shaw, Savill Company, yet another subsidiary of Furness, Withy. The ex-*Monarch of Bermuda* will make yet one more appearance in our story, another decade or so hence.

Queen of Bermuda, on the other hand, was successfully restored for New York–Hamilton service, but with these subtle differences from her prewar appearance. Originally, the exterior of her wheelhouse was finished in polished mahogany; after the war it was rendered in the same basic white as the rest of the cabinwork. And while her third and dummy funnel that was removed during the war was restored during the reconversion, now the three funnels were slightly stepped, the forward funnel being ever so slightly higher, and the aft funnel ever so slightly lower, than the middle one, a feature that imitated *RMS Queen Mary*. In prewar configuration, all three of *Queen of Bermuda*'s stacks were exactly the same height. *Monarch of Bermuda*, incidentally, operated throughout the war with all three of her stacks in place.

Queen of Bermuda steamed through Twin Rocks Passage into Hamilton Harbor on February 14, 1949, her first postwar visit. For

Queen of Bermuda entering a shipyard in Brooklyn for some maintenance and repairs. The all-white pilothouse marks this as a postwar photo.

residents of the island, who turned out in force to stage a spirited welcome, this was the signal that the years of wartime austerity were over and Bermuda was about to resume its role as a relaxing island vacation spot. Between war's end in 1945 and the return of *Queen of Bermuda* in 1949, Furness ran the passenger-cargo liners *Fort Townshend* and *Fort Amherst* on the New York–Hamilton run. The two vessels had been built in 1936 for Furness, Withy's Red Cross Line service between New York, Boston, Halifax, and St.

The year is 1949, and few people were traveling between New York and Bermuda. Furness service was limited to the passenger-cargo liners *Fort Townshend* and *Fort Amherst*, which maintained a Bermuda-New York-Nova Scotia-Newfoundland service.

John's, Newfoundland, and had occasionally been used in Bermuda service before the war. Each vessel featured accommodations for just over one hundred passengers, and because New York–Bermuda service saw only modest passenger levels in the immediate postwar years—people with urgent business, rather than vacationers—Furness, Withy was able to operate the two vessels over a combined Halifax/New York/Bermuda route. The parent company, in other words, operated its Furness Bermuda subsidiary and its Red Cross Line as if they were a single service. And finally, something else that happened between the end of the war and the return of *Queen of Bermuda* in 1949 was that Furness, Withy began to divest itself of the various tourist properties it had developed in Bermuda back in the 1920s.

A New Monarch Replaces the Old

With *Monarch of Bermuda* no longer available, Furness, Withy needed a proper luxury passenger vessel to run with *Queen of Bermuda* once traditional tourist traffic began to redevelop. The ship they designed and built, the 1951 *Ocean Monarch*, presaged the future of passenger travel by sea; it did not attempt to recreate the past. Slightly smaller than *Queen of Bermuda*, *Ocean Monarch* was of such a size as to allow her to call at Bermuda's other port city, St. George's, a harbor that was off limits to *Queen of Bermuda* because she was too big. *Ocean Monarch* was 516 feet long (versus *Queen of Bermuda*'s 553) and 13,654 gross tons (versus 22,575), but most importantly as far as ability to call at St. George's is concerned, *Ocean Monarch* had a draft of 24 feet to *Queen of Bermuda*'s 39. The twin-screw *Ocean Monarch* was powered by four Vickers-Armstrong steam turbines, had but one stack, and could carry 430 single-class passengers.

The fact that the new ship's name included no reference at all to Bermuda, as all previous Furness, Withy vessels built for the service did, was a clear signal that the company intended to use *Ocean Monarch* in more general cruiselike service to other warm-water ports, particularly during times when traffic between New York and Bermuda was traditionally low. This is exactly what happened, and a good case can even be advanced that *Ocean Monarch* was the

Excorted by several tugboats and a New York police boat, Furness, Withy's new *Ocean Monarch* steams into New York Harbor.

very first vessel to be purposefully built for precisely the kind of small-island cruising out of U.S. ports that has today become so popular. The name *Ocean Monarch* was one that evoked *Queen of Bermuda*'s prewar running mate, but it was also sufficiently different from the older vessel to indicate that one chapter was over and a new one was beginning.

Ocean Monarch was built by Vickers-Armstrong at Newcastle; she set sail from Tilbury, London, under the command of Captain Leslie F. Banyard on April 17, 1951, for a leisurely ten-day crossing to New York with a group of company officials her only passengers. She arrived early on Friday, April 27, and was greeted by *Queen of Bermuda*, inbound from Hamilton, in a manner similar to the way *Queen* was herself greeted by *Ocean Monarch*'s predecessor in 1933. A typical harbor welcome was laid out for the newcomer, with city officials and representatives of the news media boarding the new liner at quarantine from the tugboat *C. Hayward Meseck*. (Meseck Towing and Transport long held the contract for docking Furness Bermuda vessels.)

Ocean Monarch left New York on her maiden voyage on May 3, 1951, and sailed into Hamilton for the first time on May 5. But as if to underscore the fact her role would not be limited to New York–Bermuda service, she then continued beyond Bermuda to Nassau. Captain Banyard returned to his usual command, *Queen of Bermuda*, and Captain C. R. V. Dunford, who had previously been staff captain aboard *Queen*, took over as master of the new vessel. Later that summer, *Ocean Monarch* ran a series of cruises out of New York to the Saguenay River in Canada.

Monarch of Bermuda and *Queen of Bermuda* sailed together between New York and Hamilton for the better part of six years, from 1933 through 1939. *Queen of Bermuda* and *Ocean Monarch* sailed together on the same route for more than fifteen years, from 1951 through 1966.

In 1961, Furness, Withy invested $4.2 million in *Queen of Bermuda* and had her substantially rebuilt, clearly envisioning another ten years or more of service. Her original boilers—eight Babcock & Wilcox watertube models—were replaced by three newer and more efficient D-type Foster Wheeler units. This did two things: it freed up sufficient space below decks for the installation of a complete ship's air-conditioning plant, and it obviated the need for two working funnels (recall, of course, that the third stack had always been a dummy). Thus, once refitted, *Queen of Bermuda* emerged from the Harlan & Wolff yard in Belfast with a single streamlined stack positioned where the center funnel once stood. Her bow was also given an ever-so-slightly increased rake to compliment the new funnel, and the distinctive natural mahogany lifeboats gave way to perfectly ordinary white fiberglass models.

Many thought this change in the vessel's profile was nothing short of sacrilegious. One maritime historian said the vessel had been "tarted up" and suggested the changes made "the grand old dame more of a painted lady."[10] While understandable, this assessment was perhaps a bit on the severe side. Interestingly enough, *Queen of Bermuda*'s former running-mate, *Monarch of Bermuda*, had earlier undergone a similar transformation. When she was converted into the single-stack emigrant ship *New Australia* in 1950, no effort was made to create a particularly handsome vessel, and *New Australia* certainly won no awards for her appearance. But when the Greek Line took title to *New Australia* in 1958 and rebuilt her as *Arkadia* for its Mediterranean–St. Lawrence service, the ugly duckling emigrant ship was turned into, if not a beautiful swan, at least a nicely balanced ocean liner.

And so in their final years, the two prewar sister-ships of the Furness Bermuda Line once again bore a striking resemblance to each other: a classic ocean liner profile topped off by a single large stack amidships. Some have even wondered if the handsome appearance of *Arkadia* was instrumental in Furness, Withy's decision to alter her one-time running mate in a similar fashion.

FURNESS, WITHY BOWS OUT

The strangest aspect of the millions of dollars Furness invested in the *Queen of Bermuda* in 1961 was the fact that a mere five years later the company informed the Bermuda government that it planned to withdraw from the New York–Hamilton run. Jet airplanes could fly from Bermuda to New York in less time than it took *Queen of Bermuda* or *Ocean Monarch* to clear Five Fathom Hole beyond Pilot Station Bermuda and set a course for New York after departing Hamilton Harbor. Despite a modest subsidy the company received from the Bermuda government for operating the New York–Hamilton service—less than $150,000 a year—Furness, Withy was taking itself out of the luxury passenger business. "Our ships are no longer the essential means of communication they were when they were built," W. F. G. Harris, the New York general manager for Furness Bermuda Line, said.[11]

On November 23, 1966, *Queen of Bermuda*—with 594 customers aboard—sailed out of Hamilton for the very last time. She reached New York on the morning of Friday, November 25, and put her passengers ashore at North River Pier 88. (Just months earlier, Furness Bermuda Line had shifted its New York operations from Pier 95, where its vessels had docked for more than forty years, to Pier 88, a berth best known as the New York terminal of the French Line.) All that was left was a final trip across the North Atlantic to a ship breaker in Faslane, Scotland. By the following spring, *Queen of Bermuda* had been reduced to scrap. Back in Hamilton, her final days were dutifully recorded by wire stories in the island newspaper, the *Royal Gazette*. And in a most curious twist of fate, Greek

In its final months of operation, Furness Bermuda Line shifted its New York terminal from Pier 95 to Pier 88.

Line's *Arkadia*—the ex-*Monarch of Bermuda*—arrived in Valencia for her denouement a mere twelve days after *Queen of Bermuda* reached Faslane.[12]

The newer *Ocean Monarch* had been withdrawn even earlier, despite the rather complete renovation she had undergone at Belfast in 1963. She returned to England in September 1966 and was laid up, although she would later see additional years of work as the cruise ship *Varna*, flying the Bulgarian flag. Her end would come in 1981.

Once Furness, Withy announced its intention to withdraw from the New York-Hamilton service, the Bermuda government negotiated a contract with Cunard that called for a single vessel to operate a weekly service between New York and Bermuda, but only for six months out of each year. The vessel Cunard selected for Bermuda service, *Franconia*, was built in 1955 as *Ivernia*, one of a quartet of smaller vessels (600 feet long, 22,000 gross tons) that Cunard saw as being able to work Liverpool–Montreal in summer and handle Caribbean cruise work in winter. No sooner had *Franconia* established herself on the New York–Hamilton route than the Greek Line decided to shift its flagship, *Olympia*, to New York–Bermuda service in competition with Cunard. *Olympia* was built for the Greek Line in Glasgow in 1953 and was used primarily on a route between Piraeus and New York, although she, too, was designed with the Caribbean in mind.

But the very nature of New York–Bermuda service was also evolving. By the time *Franconia* and *Olympia* became regulars on the route, the typical passenger no longer traveled with steamer trunks stored below decks during the voyage, porters dutifully hauling them from dockside in Hamilton to the lobby of places like the Bermudiana Hotel. People now treated the voyage as a cruise and lived aboard the ship during its stay in port.

(Furness Bermuda Line first advertised "live-aboard" cruises in 1938, with *Monarch of Bermuda* and *Queen of Bermuda* departing New York together on July 16 that year to inaugurate the new option, offering a four-day and a six-day cruise, respectively. But it took some years—decades, actually—before it grew from a mere option into the standard way people would visit Bermuda by ship. Some trend-setting passengers began booking live-aboard cruises on their own even before Furness Bermuda Line formally advertised them in 1938.)

There was also an important change developing in what was regarded as Bermuda's peak season and what was the off-season. Jet airplanes—and to a lesser extent, air conditioning—are responsible for the shift. In the early days of the Furness Bermuda Line, travel between New York and Hamilton was heaviest in winter, when the islands provided a modest but accessible respite from the chills of a northern winter. It didn't take an ocean liner all that much more time to get to Bermuda from the Hudson River docks in New York than it took an efficient train to reach Miami from Penn Station.[13] Traffic was lowest in the summer when Bermuda's climate was more like that of the mainland.

More recently, though, with the entire Caribbean but a few hours away from wintertime New York by jet, and the cooler climate of Bermuda less desirable in winter, the island's peak vacation season has become the summer—with air-conditioned hotels and restaurants throughout the islands compensating for any minimal discomfort that summer weather might generate. This is also why cruise ships—air-conditioned cruise ships—that call at Bermuda in the post-Furness era do so almost entirely during the summertime.

In any event, after *Franconia* (and *Olympia*) worked New York–Hamilton for a number of seasons, a variety of other cruise lines took a turn at the service: Flagship Cruises, Holland-America Line, Home Lines. The cruise business itself was evolving and seeking new levels of stability; old companies faded away or shifted their focus into different kinds of markets, and new ones emerged to take their place. One entry into the Bermuda market that caused a good deal of confusion came along toward the end of the 1980s, when the Bermuda Star Line, a subsidiary of Effjohn International, put two 1958-built ex-Moore-McCormack passenger vessels on the run. Calling a vessel that was built as *Argentina* the *Bermuda Star* seemed inoffensive enough. But when the company turned around and bestowed the hallowed name *Queen of Bermuda* on a ship that began life as *Brasil*, it set off the same kind of hue and cry that would be heard a decade later when some dared suggest that it might be a good idea if American fast-food restaurants be allowed to open a few establishments throughout the islands.

Bermuda Star Line faded from the scene after a few years. The "royal pretender" that began life as *Brasil* was rechristened *Enchanted Seas* and transferred to Effjohn's Commodore Cruise Lines, occasionally to return to Bermuda waters in her new identity as part of a longer cruise. More recently, Effjohn has divested itself of its various cruise enterprises to concentrate on other business.

As dawn rose on the final decade of the twentieth century, established cruise ship operators with considerable experience on various Caribbean routes moved in to provide service between New York and Bermuda. Brand new vessels were designed and built for the service, and just as had happened in the past—once under Quebec Steamship and later under Furness, Withy—an era of stability and growth for ocean liner service to Bermuda seemed to be at hand.

The Contemporary Scene

The number of ships that call at Bermuda today is carefully controlled by the island government, especially in high summer. While the dollars cruise ship passengers spend in port make an important contribution to the Bermuda economy, great pains are taken to avoid letting this activity escalate into a situation that could be regarded as overcrowding. By the mid-1990s, five ships—flying the house flags of four different cruise lines—sailed regularly out of east-coast ports and maintained an interesting weekly service pattern to Bermuda. Other vessels call at Bermuda from time to time, but in a more random fashion, usually as part of a longer cruise itinerary. The pattern that prevailed in the mid-1990s will surely evolve in future years. But it can serve as an appropriate finale—at least for the time being—in the story of travel to Bermuda by sea.

Four of the five regular ships sail out of New York, and the fifth, Majesty Cruise Line's 1992-built *Royal Majesty*, works a Boston-Bermuda service. In 1995, *Royal Majesty* had the worst luck of the five Bermuda ships when she ran aground on Rose and Crown Shoal off Nantucket Island en route back to Boston in the early-morning hours of June 11. It took local tugboats almost a day to free *Royal Majesty*, and while there was only minimal damage to the vessel, she limped into Boston a day late and had to cancel her next round trip.[14] In August of the same year, when a Bermuda pilot was heading out to board *Royal Majesty*, he saw something that none of the ship's crew had been able to notice on the voyage from Boston: the carcass of an extremely dead whale had become lodged on the vessel's bulbous bow. It took some determined work with the bow thrusters to shake the unfortunate sea creature from the ship before *Royal Majesty* continued into port.

(In the summer of 1996, *Royal Majesty* again missed one of her weekly Boston–Bermuda trips, but this time for an entirely different reason. On Sunday, August 25, she set sail from Boston to a point in the North Atlantic five hundred miles east of Newfoundland and there afforded a specially invited group of passengers the opportunity to witness an attempt to raise from the ocean floor a section of the hull of *RMS Titanic*. The event, though unsuccessful, was widely covered in the press and on television.)

Royal Majesty docks only at the smaller port of St. George's during

Majesty Cruise Line's *Royal Majesty* holds down a Boston-Bermuda run each summer.

a typical seventy-six-hour stay in Bermuda. Depending on whether one measures as the crow flies or over winding Bermuda roads, St. George's is either nine or twelve miles from Hamilton, Bermuda's capital and principal city, a distance that can be traveled by bus in about an hour.

Celebrity Cruise Lines operates two ships between New York and Bermuda. Celebrity's *Meridian*—a vessel built in 1963 as *Galileo Galilei* for Lloyd Triestino's Italy–Australia service—is the only steam-powered vessel regularly calling at Bermuda. She ties up in Bermuda at a place called King's Wharf at the entrance to Hamilton Harbor, the newest island berth for passenger ships and one that can accommodate vessels with a little more draft than Hamilton Harbor itself. Once a facility of the Royal Navy, King's Wharf has more recently been transformed into an interesting historic site. It is also adjacent to the Bermuda Maritime Museum, a totally delightful attraction in its own right. (The world's most definitive collection of material on Furness, Withy steamship operations between New

Celebrity's *Meridian* docks outside Hamilton proper at a former Royal Navy facility.

York and Bermuda is safely housed behind the fortresslike walls of the Bermuda Maritime Museum, including a marvelous model of *Queen of Bermuda* that for many years was a fixture in the Furness Bermuda Line's New York offices.)

King's Wharf is a thirty-minute express ferry ride from downtown Hamilton, longer if one happens to catch a local ferry that makes a number of stops along the way. (Of course, the local ferry provides a nice close-up look at some otherwise inaccessible nooks and crannies of Bermuda and should not be avoided simply because it takes longer.) There is also regular bus service between Hamilton and King's Wharf; both buses and ferries honor the same all-day and multiday tickets.

Depending on one's point of view, the remove of King's Wharf from downtown Hamilton can be either an advantage or a disadvantage for the visiting cruise passenger. King's Wharf is the only cruise ship landing in Bermuda that's within easy walking distance of an ocean beach, for instance. (The beach, while not the island's largest, is on the far side of the Maritime Museum.) Hamilton, on the other hand, is the commercial and cultural center of Bermuda, and cruise ships that tie up along Front Street there afford passengers excellent access to everything the city has to offer.

Before and after operating out of New York during high summer, *Meridian* usually schedules a dozen or so Bermuda sailings from such other east coast ports as Charleston, Norfolk, Baltimore, and Philadelphia in the spring and fall. This underscores another point:

None of the five ships works Bermuda service the year round; all shift to Caribbean routes out of southern ports once the days grow short in the fall.

Even if restricted to six months out of the year, this is a large volume of service. The four ships sailing out of New York, among them, make about eighty-five round trips a year between early April and late October. *Royal Majesty's* schedule calls for twenty-five or twenty-six sailings between Boston and Bermuda each season. Add in *Meridian's* departures from various mainland ports in the spring and fall, plus occasional departures out of New York by other cruise ships, and it adds up to more than one hundred thirty annual sailings. In the glory days of the Furness Bermuda Line, *Monarch of Bermuda* and *Queen of Bermuda* between them would never make one hundred trips in a full year's time. Today's cruise ships do more than that in six months.

Through the season of 1995, Celebrity's second Bermuda vessel was the 1990-built *Horizon*. In 1996 *Horizon* was assigned to Alaska service, and her place on the Bermuda run was taken over by her slightly newer sister-ship, *Zenith*. *Zenith* (and before her, *Horizon*) is

Celebrity Cruise Line's *Zenith*, sister ship of the *Horizon*.

one of three vessels that call at two different ports during a typical stay in Bermuda: the capital city of Hamilton and the smaller port of St. George's. The others are Royal Caribbean's *Song of America* and Norwegian Cruise Line's *Dreamward*. Of the two vessels, *Dreamward*—built in 1992—is the newer by a decade.[15]

Per edict of the Bermuda government, all regular cruise ships must call during the week, not over the weekend; thus, vessels clear the island by Friday afternoon, with mainland departures scheduled for either Saturday or Sunday. This is just fine with the cruise lines, incidentally, who generally prefer to have seven-day cruises begin and end on a weekend, since to do otherwise is to be out of sync with the popular concept of passengers' taking off a single week from work to book a seven-day cruise.

Norwegian's *Dreamward* and Celebrity's *Zenith* both leave New York on Saturday afternoon, spend Sunday at sea—usually within sight of each other—and reach Bermuda Monday morning; Royal

Royal Caribbean's *Song of America* docked along Front Street in Hamilton.

Caribbean's *Song of America* leaves New York on Sunday, along with Celebrity's *Meridian*, and both tie up in Bermuda early on Tuesday; *Royal Majesty* departs Boston on Sunday and also arrives on Tuesday.

Only two ships can dock in either Bermuda port at the same time—although, if necessary, a third, and possibly even a fourth, could be squeezed into Hamilton at what is normally a freight facility.[16] As to how the vessels split their time between the two Bermuda ports, *Dreamward* first spends twenty-four hours in St. George's, then moves around for two days in Hamilton; *Zenith* does two days in Hamilton first before shifting to St. George's for its last day at Bermuda; *Song of America* hits St. George's for a day, then follows up with two in Hamilton.

Besides the five regular vessels that spend the entire summer steaming back and forth between the island and east-coast ports, other ships will call at Bermuda from time to time, often as part of a longer cruise. Such vessels are more common in summer but not completely unknown the year round. In both 1993 and 1994—but not in 1995, and not likely again soon—Crown Cruise Line ran a series of late-summer trips between Alexandria, Virginia, and Bermuda. Even the mighty *Queen Elizabeth 2* sails into Bermuda now and again each year, maintaining a long and venerable Cunard presence in what remains an outpost of the British Empire. (In 1995, Bermuda voters went to the polls and soundly defeated a referendum that would have led to the island's cutting its ties with Great Britain.)

Because of her size—length as well as draft—the *QE2* must anchor in Great Sound during her Bermuda visits, with passengers tendered to and from Hamilton. The fleet of government-operated passenger ferries that work out of Hamilton is large enough to deploy vessels for tendering duty without compromising routine ferry schedules.[17]

To Bermuda aboard *MS Dreamward*

On Saturday, August 19, 1995, Norwegian Cruise Line's *MS Dreamward* was tied up to the north side of Pier 90 on the Hudson River. Celebrity Cruise Line's *Horizon* was on the north side of Pier 88, the very berth where, in 1942, what was then the troopship *USS Lafa-*

yette, but is better known as the French superliner *Normandie*, caught fire and capsized. Interestingly, *Dreamward* also has a symbolic connection with *Normandie*. Both she and the ill-fated French Line vessel were built in St. Nazaire, France, at the Chantiers de l'Atlantique shipyard there. *Horizon* and *Dreamward* each have a white hull, white superstructure, and a large dark blue funnel positioned well toward the back of the ship, Celebrity's blue being several shades darker than Norwegian's.

On this beautiful and clear summer day, though, while eager passengers who were boarding the two ships had all purchased tickets for a seven-day cruise to Bermuda, the question uppermost in everyone's mind was this: Where are we going?

The question was as pertinent as it was unusual. Because while both ships regularly sail out of New York for Bermuda each Saturday from spring until fall, a week earlier neither of them was able to get there. Hurricane Felix had come along, and Felix was still out there in the Atlantic churning things up and generating uncertainty. (*Dreamward* headed north the previous week and treated her passengers to a delightful Canadian/New England cruise. When she made port at Bar Harbor, Maine, enterprising shopkeepers there erected a sign that read "Welcome to Bermuda." *Horizon* cruised south to the Bahamas.)

Embarkation proceeded normally on both vessels. Passengers boarding *Dreamward* (including my spouse and me) made their way to their staterooms, picked up their keys, and wandered around to familiarize themselves with the ship's layout as they waited for stewards to deliver luggage to their cabins. Lunch was being served in both the Four Seasons dining room on the International deck and the less formal Sports Bar on the appropriately named Sports deck. Down below there was frantic activity of all kinds; longshoremen were moving steel cages filled with suitcases, garment bags, and golf clubs onto the ship, members of *Dreamward*'s crew were hurrying back aboard after a few hours ashore in New York, and trucks bearing the names of wholesale grocers from all over the metropolitan area moved on and off Pier 90 in a kind of orderly chaos, delivering the provisions that would be needed over the next seven days—14,000 pounds of beef, 900 gallons of milk, 9,000 pounds of fresh vegetables, 3,500 pounds of flour, and on and on.

But still, as people struck up conversations with their new shipmates, the continual question remained: Where do you think we'll wind up going?

At 3:30 P.M., an hour before *Dreamward*'s scheduled departure, the mandatory lifeboat drill was held. Passengers all appeared on the Promenade deck at assigned stations and listened while a crew member explained how life jackets are properly fastened and what it takes to activate the little signal light attached to each life jacket. (Touch the same finger to each of two brass buttons on the life jacket, thus completing a circuit, and presto—a dim red light appears.) It was a somewhat underwhelming experience.

The deck where the lifeboat stations are located also contains *Dreamward*'s around-the-ship outdoor promenade. Fewer shipboard facilities see more diversity of use during a typical cruise than such a promenade, from frenetic exercise buffs busily going through their early morning rituals to moonlight strolls by romantic couples on into the night.

After the lifeboat drill, Captain Einar Lindrupsen made his initial announcement over the ship's public address system. Hurricane Felix was still out there, he said, but according to the latest weather information just received from the Naval Atlantic Meteorology and Oceanography Center in Norfolk, if we headed south along the Atlantic Coast for a few hundred miles before turning east toward Bermuda, we'd stay reasonably clear of the storm. It might take us a few extra hours to reach St. George's, the captain explained—and for that matter he couldn't be absolutely certain we'd be able to dock in St. George's at all until he got a better read on conditions there—but we were going to Bermuda. Period. Lindrupsen, I later learned, was not *Dreamward*'s regular master; he was a relief captain filling in while the permanent skipper enjoyed some time off.

As 4:30 drew near, *Dreamward* made preparations for departure. Visitors were told to get themselves ashore; the last of the luggage was brought aboard; a Sandy Hook Harbor pilot made his way to the bridge and joined Captain Lindrupsen and the other ship's officers. At 4:10 the pilot made a radio announcement over marine channel 16 to any and all interested parties in the harbor to the effect that *Dreamward* would soon be departing North River Pier 90 and she was "headed for sea."

About 4:20, things started to happen. Seamen aboard *Dreamward* loosened tension on some of the lines, and they were removed from chocks on the pier by dock workers and pulled back aboard ship; the sound of powerful winches at work could be heard at both the bow and the stern of the ship. Up on the bridge, a crew member had removed a blue canvas covering from the control console on the starboard bridge wing that would be used during departure, and Staff Captain Jostein Kalvoy checked three important readings: circuits were energized, allowing electrical current to be directed to motors that powered the two bow thrusters; the ship's twin rudders were set for nonsynchronized operation, meaning either could be activated independently of the other; and the two variable-pitch propellers were showing zero degrees of deflection, the engines turning them over.

During maneuvering in close quarters, *Dreamward*'s engines run at a steady rate, and both the vessel's speed and whether it proceeds forward or astern are controlled by adjusting not the engines but the pitch of the propellers. And it is the person on the bridge who actually does the controlling, who directly changes the pitch of the propellers. No precious seconds are wasted while an engine room telegraph transmits a command to the chief engineer down below who, in turn, actually executes the commands.

At a few minutes before 4:30, the last gangway is pulled back onto the pier, final lines are let loose, and the big vessel begins to move (unassisted by any tugs, incidentally). First the stern moves a few feet away from the pier; then *Dreamward* backs slowly out into the Hudson River.

(How many times had I stood on Twelfth Avenue and watched at this very same pier while a ship like Cunard's second *Mauritania*—similar to *Dreamward* in length and tonnage—required three or more tugboats to assist in her departure?)

It took less than fifteen minutes for the 623-foot *Dreamward* to clear Pier 90, turn her bow down river, and begin the voyage to Bermuda. Once away from the pier, the twin rudders are linked for synchronous operation, and the Sandy Hook pilot assumes a more dominant role; he—and not any ship's officer—calls out compass headings for the quartermaster to steer.

A harbor pilot's role, incidentally, is merely advisory. The captain can countermand any "order" given by the pilot, as he alone bears ultimate responsibility for the safety of the ship. In practice, though, the pilot functions as a kind of *de facto* captain, and his suggested headings are routinely accepted. In certain unusual navigational situations such as the Panama Canal, the role of the local pilot is more than merely advisory, and a ship's captain must defer to the pilot's judgment or not use the facility.

As we headed down the Hudson, virtually every passenger was out on deck taking in the sights. Captain Lindrupsen, a taciturn man from the land of the fjords who would later restrict his use of the PA system to little more than noon position announcements, was as talkative as any Circle Line cruise narrator in pointing out the Empire State Building, the World Trade Center, Battery Park, Ellis Island, the Statue of Liberty, and all the rest. When we were off West 23rd Street, a glance northward revealed that Celebrity's *Horizon* was clear of Pier 88 and was turning to follow us out to sea. But also this: As *Dreamward* headed down the Hudson River, *Horizon* was the only other seagoing vessel anywhere in sight. No freighters tied up at piers all along the Manhattan waterfront; no other ocean liners; no ships from strange lands being loaded or unloaded in Hoboken or Jersey City. I would venture to say that when *Monarch of Bermuda* left New York on any of her many voyages to Hamilton, there were always two or three dozen oceangoing vessels docked here and there along the Hudson River as she proceeded out to sea. On August 19, 1995, the only such vessel that could be seen from the decks of *Dreamward* was *Horizon*.

South of Liberty Island, the Whitehall Street-bound ferryboat

Dreamward heads down the Hudson enroute to Bermuda.

American Legion gave *Dreamward* a three-whistle salute, which we dutifully returned. Lindrupsen was quickly on the PA, telling us all that a captain from the municipal fleet was a passenger aboard *Dreamward* this trip and that his fellow workers were wishing him well. I wonder what the vacationing Staten Island captain felt when we didn't take a starboard turn at Robbins Reef just before St. George but instead assumed a course of about 155 degrees and headed toward the Verrazano Narrows Bridge and the open sea? (A stylistic precision: The place where the ferryboats land in Staten Island is called St. George; our destination in Bermuda is St. George's.)

There are two principal channels linking open water with New York Harbor. Ambrose Channel is the primary route, and it leads directly into the Narrows; there is also something called Sandy Hook Channel, and it finds its principal traffic among vessels heading into the Arthur Kill at the southern end of Staten Island. Ambrose light station—a Texas Tower-style structure that replaced *Ambrose* lightship some years ago—is approximately three nautical miles beyond the entrance to Ambrose Channel.[18] At one time, *Scotland* lightship was on station at the entrance to Sandy Hook Channel; today, only buoys tell mariners where this channel begins.

Immediately beyond the entrance to each channel is the area

where vessels either drop off or pick up their harbor pilots. In many world ports, harbor pilots ride directly between shore stations and the vessels they pilot aboard small (i.e., 40-foot) power launches. Because of the volume of traffic coming in and out of New York, plus the fact that the pilot station is relatively far from the shore base, a larger "station boat" patrols the area near Ambrose light and serves as a lounge, or even a dormitory, where pilots stay between outbound and inbound assignments. They ride from the station boat to and from their assignments aboard more-conventional pilot launches; the station boat drifts within a triangular area of approximately five square miles that is defined by the entrances to each channel and Ambrose light.

As *Dreamward* was slowing to drop off our outbound pilot, it was obvious that both high winds and heavy seas—remnants of Hurricane Felix—were going to make it difficult for the launch to come alongside. (Ocean beaches from Atlantic City to Montauk Point were closed to swimmers for the day, and heavy surf was breaking over Romer Shoal several minutes earlier as we approached the pilot station.) Consequently, the station boat *New Jersey* moved in to create a lee between herself and the outbound cruise ship, and the pilot disembarked with comparative ease. *Horizon* had by this time closed in behind us, and when her pilot disembarked, the same procedure was followed. The pilots who took *Dreamward* and *Horizon* out on Saturday afternoon were scheduled to remain on the station boat overnight and bring in *Song of America* and *Meridian* the next morning.[19]

(An earlier sailing from New York to Bermuda: December 18, 1929. While the harbor pilot was disembarking, Furness, Withy's *Fort Victoria* was rammed in heavy fog by the *SS Algonquin* and sent to the bottom.)

Further out to sea beyond the pilot station, three traffic lanes have been established to ensure predictability and order for vessels sailing in and out of New York. Each consists of both inbound and outbound lanes with a separation zone in between. To the northeast, one set of lanes heads toward Nantucket and the "great circle" route to Europe; the second runs to the southeast and links Ambrose with the fishing grounds of Hudson Canyon; the final set proceeds more or less due south and is called the Ambrose–Barnegat traffic lanes. Vessels heading for Bermuda normally get away from New

The sky was clear, but surf breaking over Romer Shoals was a tell-tale sign that the sea was anything but calm as *Dreamward* heads out Ambrose Channel.

York via Ambrose–Barnegat and then turn to the southeast and take a direct bearing on Bermuda an hour or so later. Both the Ambrose–Nantucket and the Ambrose–Barnegat traffic lanes begin at a sea buoy six-and-a-half miles beyond Ambrose light. The territory between the end of the two channels, Ambrose and Sandy Hook, and the start of the three traffic lanes is called a "precautionary area." "Traffic within the Precautionary Area may consist of vessels making the transition between operating in Ambrose or Sandy Hook Channels and one of the traffic lanes. Mariners are advised to exercise extreme care in navigating within this area."[20]

Because Hurricane Felix was still out there in the Atlantic, *Dreamward* didn't assume the usual direct course for Bermuda after transiting the Ambrose-Barnegat traffic lanes; instead we stayed on a more southerly heading until well after midnight. While we obviously avoided the worst of Hurricane Felix, we did encounter some weather on the fringe of the storm during our first night at sea. Thanks to her two Blohm and Voss stabilizers, *Dreamward* was able to remain rock solid as far as side-to-side rolling was concerned. Any irregular motion we experienced was more of a pitching sort, but it was minimal, and served as a nice reminder that travel to Bermuda by sea, from John Sommer's *Sea Venture* in 1609 to the maiden voyage of the *Queen of Bermuda* in 1933, has always been vulnerable to disruption from Atlantic storms. (Some passengers may have found *Dreamward's* motions more than a little uncomfortable, though; the dining room had quite a few empty seats at second-seating dinner on Saturday night.)

> Is the storm overblown? I hid me under the dead mooncalf's gaberdine for fear of the storm.
>
> [Shakespeare, *The Tempest* II:2]

Dreamward's stabilizers are finlike devices approximately twenty feet by seven feet in size that are extended outward from the hull below the waterline to counter any side-to-side movement of the hull. The stabilizers are not static, though; they are linked to sensitive gyroscopes and react to actual tendencies of the hull to roll this way or that by generating counterforces in the opposite direction. If the hull begins a roll to starboard, for instance, the starboard fin assumes a lesser angle and the port fin digs in at a deeper angle, thereby countering the roll. The stabilizers are extended or retracted from an appropriately high-tech console on the bridge— colored lights, LED displays, and all the rest. But in a marvelous gesture to "low-tech" communication, there's a small red plastic sign that's kept atop *Dreamward*'s stabilizer control that reads "Fins In" on one side and "Fins Out" on the other. It is appropriately changed—by hand—whenever an officer extends or retracts the stabilizers.

Sunday—our full day at sea en route to Bermuda—began as overcast and windy; by early afternoon the sun was out, and by dinner the wind had moderated considerably. We maintained a heading of 162 degrees for most of the day at a steady speed of 18 knots; by late afternoon we were off Cape Hatteras, 150 nautical miles or so to the west of the normal New York-Bermuda route. *Horizon* was ahead of us and about three or four miles off our port bow. In his noon position announcement, Captain Lindrupsen told us that it was still uncertain if we would be able to enter the port of St. George's the next day because of the wind, but that if we couldn't we would proceed directly to Hamilton.

A word about *Dreamward*'s engines: In an arrangement that is common on contemporary passenger vessels, *Dreamward* is equipped with what are popularly called "father and son" engines. Each of the twin propeller shafts is linked to two diesel engines of different sizes: a larger "father" and a smaller "son." *Dreamward*'s two big engines are eight-cylinder MAN-B&W diesels, and the smaller ones are six-cylinder diesels, also built by MAN-B&W. In addition, a separate pair of eight-cylinder Bergen diesels are used exclusively to generate the electrical current used for all manner of shipboard purposes, from air conditioning, lighting, and cooking to powering the all-important bow thrusters during maneuvering.

(Later, when I asked Staff Captain Kalvoy what was the trickiest kind of docking maneuver to perform, he didn't talk about wind or sea conditions, or mention some particularly difficult harbor; rather, he spoke of a hypothetical hot and humid morning, with the air conditioning drawing heavy electrical current, half the passengers using hair dryers in their cabins, the other half causing further demands for electricity by virtue of their breakfast orders to the kitchen, and he up on the bridge trying to put full power on the bow thrusters.)

The beauty of the "father and son" arrangement is that the two smaller engines linked to each propeller shaft can be disengaged from propulsion work and linked up to generate electricity, either supplementing or replacing the engines normally used for this purpose. The "father" engines are for propulsion only, and the two primary engines used for generating electricity can only generate electricity. But the two "son" engines can be used either for propulsion or for generating electricity, thus giving *Dreamward's* chief engineer considerable flexibility to shut down any of his engines for maintenance or other work without seriously compromising the ship's performance. Both *Horizon* and *Zenith* have similar "father and son" arrangements in their engine rooms.

Finally this: while underway, *Dreamward* consumes a little over 1,100 gallons of diesel fuel per hour—for all purposes, generation of electricity as well as propulsion. Her fuel capacity is 475,561 gallons, and she typically bunkers (i.e., takes on fuel) once every two weeks.

Another important mechanical feature of *Dreamward* is the fact that she is equipped with what are called Becker rudders. This is an unusual kind of rudder that does not merely pivot on a central shaft—there is also a split in the middle of the rudder plate that allows it to effect a compound turn in either direction. When a harbor pilot comes aboard *Dreamward*, the two most critical pieces of information the officer on the bridge passes along are the draft of the vessel—22 feet—and the fact that she's equipped with Becker rudders.

As to *Dreamward's* overall appearance: She is every inch a typical contemporary cruise ship and sports a profile that absolutely nobody will ever confuse with *Ile de France, Mauritania,* or *Monarch of Bermuda.* Many maritime traditionalists tend to speak disparagingly of vessels like *Dreamward* and say they pale in comparison to older ocean liners of a more classic sort. While taking a back seat to no one in my respect for traditional ocean liners—including Celebrity's *Meridian,* to cite a close-at-hand example on the New York–Bermuda run—I think *Dreamward's* profile is just fine and represents an interesting evolution in passenger ship design.

Dreamward's hull lacks a gently tapered bow and has none of the overall sheer associated with older ocean liners. But *Dreamward's* computer-designed hull wasn't built to cross the North Atlantic at 35-knot speed; it was designed to cruise more tranquil waters at 20 knots. Its almost bargelike shape—including a severely squared-off stern—allows maximum standardization in cabin size and layout, and also gives designers more deck space to work with in laying out various public rooms throughout the ship.

Contemporary cruise ships have no cargo holds to speak of; therefore they have no need of cargo booms, nor must any space be reserved for cargo hatches. Consequently, a vessel like *Dreamward* has its pilothouse much further forward than was the case on older passenger ships, which were, in most cases, combination passenger/ cargo ships. *Dreamward's* upper-deck cabinwork begins immediately abaft the pilothouse and extends virtually to the stern, meaning that she has nothing of the "wedding cake" profile of tiered decks associated with more classic vessels.

Another characteristic of contemporary cruise ships is placement of the funnel as far aft as practical; this is nothing but commonsense efficiency. When steam-powered vessels were coal fired, funnels had to be tall and positioned directly over the boilers to ensure proper draft. Today, with diesel engines, naval architects have more flexibility, and the most sensible place to put the exhaust ports is high up and toward the stern so the products of combustion won't waft back onto the ship (not to mention onto its fare-paying passengers). Stories are told from olden days of couples taking a stroll before dinner—he wearing a white dinner jacket and she a light-colored evening gown—and, after but a single turn around the promenade deck, walking into the dining room looking more like coal miners than first-class transatlantic passengers.

Even if contemporary cruise ships have certain basic similarities one with another, that hardly means all vessels look alike today. Celebrity's *Horizon*, for example, has the same general design features as *Dreamward*, but also has a harshness in its lines that makes it a far less attractive vessel. I quickly concede the subjectivity of this assertion—I readily admit that others may find *Horizon* the more attractive vessel—and repeat that I speak only of external appearance, not ranking interior appointments or quality of onboard service. The larger fact, though, is that those who dismiss contemporary cruise ships by measuring them against the standards of older and more traditional ocean liners are missing out on some positively fascinating maritime diversity.

On Monday morning, *Horizon* was still ahead of us, harsh lines and all. Captain Lindrupsen was on the PA early, telling us that the wind in Bermuda had settled down and we should have no difficulty at all making our scheduled visit to the port of St. George's.

And he was right. A Bermuda harbor pilot came out to meet us as we reached Five Fathom Hole and took a fairly sharp turn to starboard. To navigate through Town Cut and into St. George's harbor requires putting the vessel on a very precise course of 264.25 degrees inbound from Five Fathom Hole; deviation is simply not permissible, and as we moved through the coral outcroppings that constitute Town Cut, it became very clear why Captain Lindrupsen would have skipped the stop at St. George's entirely had the wind been any consideration at all. It was a *very* tight fit.

Once inside the sheltered confines of the harbor, it became a matter of using a combination of bow thrusters, twin rudders, and reversible-pitch propellers to turn *Dreamward* around and bring her up against the quay. *Dreamward* would have had no difficulty doing this all by herself, but since regulations issued by the Bermuda government require each passenger vessel to hire a tugboat and have it available during all arrivals and departures, the tug *Faithful*—which had come down from its base near King's Wharf earlier in the morning—gave *Dreamward* a little help during the turning and docking maneuver. "As long as we have to pay for it anyway, we might as well get some use out of it," Captain Lindrupsen told a group of passengers at a cocktail reception later in the day. *Horizon*, meanwhile, had taken a turn to starboard before reaching St. George's and continued on around to Hamilton, her first Bermuda port of call.

Dreamward was secured to the wharf by 1:00 P.M. local time (which is an hour ahead of Eastern Standard Time). It took Bermuda officials another fifteen or twenty minutes to clear the vessel and permit passengers to go ashore. Although we would see a little damage here and there in Bermuda caused by Hurricane Felix's visit the week before, our late arrival in St. George's was the last impact the hurricane would have on our cruise. We were four hours late arriving at St. George's, *Queen of Bermuda* was three hours late into Hamilton on her maiden voyage in 1933, and both delays were weather-related.

While *Dreamward* was docked at St. George's, her crew connected a hose to a standpipe on the quay and pumped waste water into the Bermuda sewage system. Like most contemporary passenger vessels, *Dreamward* is able both to purify sea water for drinking purposes and filter waste water so it can safely be discharged into the open ocean. But because it is expensive to process water on such a relatively small scale, *Dreamward* relies on municipal systems, as appropriate, both for supplementary fresh water and for sewage disposal. As Bermuda is a coral reef, water is a precious commodity, so passenger ships rarely, if ever, take on water there. (In the early Furness, Withy days—before Bermuda's current water systems were in operation—every ship arriving from New York brought with it tanks full of fresh water for the island's residents.)[21] But Bermuda authorities are perfectly willing to let visiting cruise ships pump off waste water—for a fee, of course.

The next morning—Tuesday—we slipped out of St. George's at breakfast time, picked our way through Town Cut, and headed back out to Five Fathom Hole. Here *Dreamward* turned completely around and headed back as if we were returning to St. George's. Before we reached Town Cut, though, we turned sharply to starboard and followed a channel through the coral reefs surrounding the island chain that brought us, within the hour, to the wide expanse of Great Sound and the entrance to Hamilton Harbor. The same pilot who had guided us into St. George's the previous day was on the bridge. A cruise ship materialized on the distant horizon to the northeast as we left St. George's; it was *Meridian*, inbound for King's Wharf. Behind her, someplace, were *Song of America* and *Royal Majesty*.

To reach Hamilton from Great Sound, vessels must proceed through Twin Rocks passage; the tugboat *Powerful*, which was to be on hand for our arrival in Hamilton, moved up immediately astern of *Dreamward* as we navigated through Twin Rocks and was available to assist should we experience any kind of sudden navigational problem. (Photographs in the collection of the Bermuda Maritime Museum show tugboats following *Queen of Bermuda* through Twin Rocks Passage at a similar distance.) Once through the narrow passage and inside Hamilton Harbor, the next task was to turn *Dreamward* around and berth her directly astern of Celebrity's *Horizon* along Front Street. It was accomplished with surgical-like precision and an assist from the tug *Powerful*. "This guy has done this before," one passenger remarked to nobody in particular of Captain Lindrupsen's performance. From casting off at St.

Dreamward is moving through Twin Rocks Passage into Hamilton Harbor. The tubgoat *Powerful* has assumed a position immediately astern in case she's needed.

George's to the gangway being set in Hamilton consumed the better part of two hours.

On Wednesday morning, *Horizon* left her berth ahead of *Dreamward* and headed around to St. George's, while Royal Caribbean's *Song of America* reversed the process and moved from St. George's to Hamilton. Thanks to all of this shifting from one port to another, from Monday through Friday there is at least one cruise ship either arriving or departing from St. George's and Hamilton every single day.

(The forward berth in Hamilton—the one that *Horizon* and *Song of America* both used—is where the motorship *Bermuda* was docked in June of 1931 when she suffered the first of the two fires that ultimately spelled her demise.)

Thursday afternoon we set sail for New York. We passed *Merid-*

Dreamward tied up along Front Street, Hamilton, Bermuda.

ian, expectedly enough, and tied up at King's Wharf, but, somewhat surprisingly, there was another cruise ship riding at anchor in Great Sound; tenders were ferrying her passengers to and from Hamilton. She was the *Regal Empress*, and once *Dreamward* departed, she was scheduled to move into Hamilton proper and tie up at the berth we had used. *Regal Empress* was completing a seven-day cruise out of New York that included stops in Newport, Rhode Island, and Martha's Vineyard. Built in 1953, she was originally the Greek Line's *Olympia*, one of the vessels that ran New York–Bermuda with some regularity after Furness, Withy called it quits in 1966. (See chapter 3 for an unfortunate incident *Regal Empress* experienced in New York the previous year, 1994.)

Outbound, we dropped our Bermuda harbor pilot just off St. George's and before we actually reached Five Fathom Hole. I later learned that he quickly headed back to land aboard the pilot boat and brought *Horizon* out from St. George's for her return to New York. Once clear of Five Fathom Hole we set a course of 307 degrees that would let us intercept the Ambrose-Barnegat traffic lanes at a point south of the pilot station and Ambrose light.

Our final full day at sea—Friday, August 25, 1995—saw *Horizon* maintaining a position ahead of us and to starboard. When he gave his daily position report, Captain Lindrupsen noted that the closest land to *Dreamward* at that very moment was Nantucket Island. It was also on this day that Staff Captain Kalvoy asked me if I'd like to join him on the bridge the next morning when *Dreamward* steamed into the Port of New York.

Despite the fact that my wife and I both stayed up to enjoy the midnight buffet on our last night at sea, I set our two travel alarm clocks for 4:30. I was awake before either of them rang. After a fast shower and a dash up to the twenty-four-hour coffee urn in the Sports Bar, I went to the bridge.

Once my eyes grew accustomed to the darkness, Staff Captain Kalvoy indicated a pair of field glasses I should feel free to use. We had just passed the sea buoy at the end of the Ambrose–Barnegat traffic lanes; up ahead and across the entire horizon were the lights of the world's greatest port. New York assumes different dimensions depending on one's perspective. Approaching from the sea in the darkness before dawn, it was a long, thin, filamentlike band of intense light with subtle differences of color and brightness evident throughout the band. The sky above and the sea below this thin band of light were as black as ebony.

Unlike the long hours at sea when *Dreamward* was on automatic pilot and no crew member had to man the wheel, now a quartermaster was on duty and the vessel was under direct command of the officers on the bridge. Ahead of the quartermaster and just below the ceiling of the wheelhouse, lighted red numerals announced the actual course *Dreamward* was steering. By prearrangement, *Horizon* had fallen behind us during the night and would follow us into port.

Save for the lights of the city, the night sky to the north and west was very dark; to the east, though, the black of night was just ever so slowly starting to give way to the first hints of dawn. Immediately ahead of us and down on the water were some navigation lights, and they were moving about. Red and white mast lights indicated that they were the pilot boats, one the station boat and the other a launch. We slowed as we approached the pilot station; Kalvoy turned on the lifeboat lights along *Dreamward*'s port side to give the boarding pilot as much help as possible. He also retracted the stabilizers. A few minutes later, Captain James F. Haley of the United New York and New Jersey Sandy Hook Pilots Association was on the bridge introducing himself to Kalvoy.

(It was someplace near here, I figured, on September 8, 1934—with Captain Albert R. Francis in command of *Monarch of Bermuda*—that an S.O.S. was picked up and Francis turned his ship around and raced to the rescue of the *Morro Castle*. Had the Sandy Hook pilot already boarded the *Monarch* that morning? Did he stay aboard for the rescue?)

Haley began to give the quartermaster new compass headings as we turned to port and headed for Ambrose Channel. "Three hundred and two degrees," he would say. "Three hundred and two degrees" the quartermaster would answer. As quietly and as silently as one could imagine, a huge container ship passed us outbound on our port side. The stabilizers had been redeployed even before Haley had reached the bridge.

Kalvoy showed me the radar. As with most kinds of electronic gear, the state of the art today is very impressive. One can shift from short range to long range simply by touching appropriate icons on the screen, and, unless I'm mistaken, it was even possible to call for "instant replays" of what the radar was showing five, ten, and fifteen minutes earlier. When the staff captain called for a long-range reading, there on a cathode ray tube emerged a perfect map of Coney Island. The week before, I had been working in the Library of Congress with various period maps of Coney Island in preparing what has since become chapter 4 of this book. I said something absolutely silly, like, "That's a real map of Coney Island."

Captain Haley was the epitome of a classic Sandy Hook pilot. He began as an apprentice, was the son of a Sandy Hook pilot, and had worked his way up through the ranks. He regretted that passenger ships were not as frequent in the port of New York as they once were, and also told me that the number of active pilots was now down to ninety (versus one hundred to one hundred ten some years back). From time to time he would announce over his hand-held radio that *Dreamward* was inbound to North River Pier 90. Haley had worked an outbound vessel the previous afternoon and spent the night on the station ship *New Jersey*. "A container ship?" I asked. "No, the *QE2*," he replied. I then inquired if she handled any differently now that she's a diesel. Haley was unable to say, since he never had a chance to work the big Cunarder in the days when she was steam-powered.

The previous evening Captain Lindrupsen had given this time-table for our arrival: "Five o'clock, board the pilot; six o'clock, Verrazano–Narrows Bridge; seven o'clock, first lines." We picked up Captain Haley right on schedule. As dawn began to paint the clear sky behind us in delicate and ever brighter tints of yellow and orange and purple, and as we were off Norton's Point and drawing a bead on the Verrazano–Narrows Bridge, Haley suggested to Kalvoy that we were running a little fast and should probably slow down, so we did.

Another outbound container ship passed. The sky grew even lighter. We passed under the bridge. The stabilizers were retracted, this time for good. I pointed out to Kalvoy and Haley the erstwhile route of the St. George–69th Street ferry; both agree that their jobs in 1995 are considerably easier thanks to the fact that a fleet of ferryboats aren't continually running back and forth across the channel. This was, I was forced to admit to myself, a perspective on the St. George–69th Street ferry that I had not previously considered.

The municipal ferryboat *John Noble* pulled out of St. George as we continued north. Judging from the way she proceeded away from the slip, I suspected that her captain was first of a mind to pass *Dreamward* to his starboard ("two whistles") but quickly thought better of it, came around our stern, and passed us to his port ("one whistle"). As *John Noble* drew adjacent to *Dreamward*, I reminded Kalvoy that we were saluted by *American Legion* on the outboard voyage because a captain from the municipal ferry fleet was among our passengers. He said it was a little too early in the morning to sound a whistle salute, but he gave *John Noble* a silent greeting with the signal lamp. I wonder what the people in the ferryboat's wheel-house made of it all? They never returned our greeting.

Sunrise caught up with us off Governor's Island, with the Statue of Liberty to port; up ahead, the Hudson was very empty as we continued on toward Pier 90. Off 23rd Street, the tugboat *Amy Moran* was waiting, and when she came alongside *Dreamward*, Captain Kevin Gato, a senior Moran docking pilot, jumped aboard and made his way up to the bridge. By this time, Captain Haley had moved *Dreamward* out of the middle of the river and was proceeding on a course much closer to the Manhattan shoreline. Gato took over from Haley as we were off Circle Line's Pier 83, and he gave the commands that enabled *Dreamward* to pivot sharply at the end of Pier 90 and move into the same berth we had departed from a week earlier. Gato, Kalvoy, and Lindrupsen were all out on the starboard bridge wing. "Thrusters to starboard," Gato said. "Stop thrusters," he said after a few seconds. "Hello *Amy*, go around to the other side" (*Amy Moran* was the sole tugboat assigned to the docking job).

As soon as it was clear that *Dreamward* was secure in her berth, Captain Gato bid the officers on the bridge a quick farewell; he had to rush back down and get aboard *Amy Moran* for a fast trip downriver to board *Horizon* and take charge of her docking. I swapped small talk with Captain Haley back in the interior of the bridge during the final stages of the docking maneuver. He had to get Captain Lindrupsen's signature on some kind of official paper. Then we all said goodbye and headed our separate ways. A tug was moving a fuel barge into the slip on *Dreamward*'s port side. It was an alternate week, and the ship would be fueled before heading out to sea again later that afternoon.

I joined my wife in the Four Seasons dining room to enjoy our final meal aboard *Dreamward* before heading home. The bacon was crisp; the eggs were perfect; the toast was moist. It was just as marvelous as all the meals we enjoyed during our week-long cruise.

In many respects, our arrival in the Port of New York that morning was as routine as anything can possibly be, as ordinary as the bacon and eggs I enjoyed at breakfast. A ship, just another ship, had made its way into the port, something that has happened hundreds of thousands of times over the years.

But isn't that exactly the point?

NCL's *Dreamward* bunkers at New York after a trip to Bermuda.

My grandparents sailed into the Port of New York from the sea, as did so many other grandparents and parents. How many servicemen returning from how many different wars saw the land of their birth for the first time in a long time from the deck of a troopship steaming into Ambrose Channel? How many times over how many years has the shape of Coney Island emerged—either on radar, through binoculars, or to the naked eye—as the first recognizable piece of American geography?

As our chartered bus headed south down the New Jersey Turnpike toward home that afternoon, I tried to calculate how many trips passenger liners must have made over the Hamilton–New York route prior to *Dreamward's* arrival on this August morning. "Let's see, *Queen of Bermuda* made 1,200 trips. . . . I wonder how many the *Monarch* made between 1931 and 1939?" I never finished my calculations, though. Instead, I dozed off to sleep. After all, I had been up since 4:30.

Safely in harbor
Is the king's ship; in the deep nook, where once
Thou calledst me up at midnight to fetch dew

From the still-vexed Bermudas, there she's hid;
The mariners all under hatches stowed,
Who, with a charm joined to their suffered labor,
I have left asleep.

[Shakespeare, *The Tempest* I:2]

Notes

1. For a general treatment of Bermuda's early history, see Wesley Frank Craven, *An Introduction to the History of Bermuda*, 2d ed. (Old Royal Navy Dockyard, Bermuda: Bermuda Maritime Museum Press, 1990); for a more detailed examination of Bermuda's maritime heritage between 1784 and 1901, see Henry C. Wilkinson, *Bermuda from Sail to Steam*, 2 volumes (London: Oxford University Press, 1973); for a general account, see Mary Elizabeth Gray, *A Brief History of Bermuda, 1503–1973* (Hamilton, Bermuda: Gray, 1976).

2. The advent of *Bermudian* also saw the construction of the first berthing facilities in Hamilton Harbor for large, oceangoing passenger vessels, yet another reason why she can be said to represent the start of the modern era in sea transportation between New York and Bermuda.

3. For further details about this company, see David Burrell, *Furness Withy* (Kendal: World Ship Society, 1992); also see Norman L. Middlemiss, *Furness-Houlder Lines* (Newcastle, U.K.: Shield Publications, 1991).

4. Bermuda & West Indies Steamship Company also operated service for Furness, Withy between Canada, New York and Trinidad, as well as other ports in the Caribbean. Some vessels running between New York and Hamilton were owned by the subsidiary, Bermuda & West Indies, others by the parent company, Furness, Withy. See Burrell, *Furness Withy*, pp. 193, 205.

5. *The New York Times*, December 19, 1929, p. 1. There is a brief account of the sinking of *Fort Victoria* in an unexpected place, a four-volume study of the United States Lines passenger steamship *Leviathan*. See Frank O. Braynard, *World's Greatest Ship*, Vol. 4 (Newport News, VA: Mariners' Museum, 1978), pp. 367–69.

6. Even after being declared a total loss in the November 20 fire, *Bermuda*'s bad luck continued. While being towed from Belfast to a scrap dealer in Rosyth, rough weather was encountered, the tow line parted, and the hulk of *Bermuda* grounded on the Sunderland coast.

7. Like *Monarch of Bermuda* and *Queen of Bermuda*, *Morro Castle* was a turbo-electric passenger liner. She and her sister-ship, *Oriente*, were used primarily on the short ocean voyage between New York and Havana, a run not unlike New York–Hamilton. For a detailed account of her ill-fated 1934 trip, see Gordon Thomas and Max Morgan Witts, *Shipwreck: The Strange Fate of the "Morro Castle"* (New York: Stein and Day, 1972); see also "The *Monarch* to the Rescue" and "The Commander of the *Monarch*," *The Bermudian*, October 1934, pp. 8–9, 10, 28, 39.

8. The Bermuda government also arranged for the U.S.-flag *Evangeline*, of Eastern Steamship Lines, to operate between New York and Hamilton for a short period in late 1941.

9. For an account of *Queen of Bermuda*'s wartime exploits, see Elizabeth Downing, "The *Queen* Goes to War," *Bermuda Maritime Museum Quarterly* 3(1) (Spring 1990), 2–5.

10. Piers Plowman, "New York Ships (Part III)," *The Bermudian* 58(7) (July 1988), 13. This article is the third in a three-part series that stands as a thorough and comprehensive treatment of New York-Hamilton steamship service. Parts I and II appeared in the May and June issues of the same publication; the three articles deserve republication for a wider audience.

11. Quoted in *The New York Times*, March 1, 1966, p. 47.

12. For a fine treatment of *Queen of Bermuda* by a distinguished Bermuda

maritime historian, see Stephen J. Card, *"Queen of Bermuda"* (Hamilton: The Bermuda Press, 1985).

13. The differential was—and still is—roughly twenty-four hours by rail to Miami and thirty-six hours by sea to Bermuda.

14. For details about this incident, see "NTSB Issues Warning Following *Royal Majesty* Grounding," *Professional Mariner* 15 (October-November 1995), 65.

15. For information on these various vessels and on cruise ship operators in general, see John Maxtone-Graham, *Crossing and Cruising* (New York: Scribner's, 1992); William H. Miller Jr., *Modern Cruise Ships, 1965–1990* (New York: Dover, 1992); William A. Fox, "*Galileo Galilei*, The Graceful Flagship," *Steamboat Bill* 197 (Spring 1991), 4–15; "Outstanding Cruise Ships of 1992," *Maritime Reporter and Engineering News* 55(3) (March 1993), 43–48, 50, 54; "Cruise Liner *Song of America*," *Marine Engineering/Log* 87(13) (December 1982), 74–75.

16. A report, circa 1970, on the future of Bermuda cruise ship operations spoke of the "assumption that four or five cruise ships in Hamilton Harbour at one time can be handled comfortably" (Government of Bermuda, Marine and Ports Authority, "Bermuda Port Development and Transportation Study; Final Report," 30).

17. Perhaps the most interesting vessel ever assigned to tender duties in Bermuda was the one-time Hudson River Day Line steamer *Chauncey M. Depew*, a) *Rangeley*. She came to Bermuda in 1950 after 37 years of coastal service in the United States for a variety of owners and served until 1969, when she returned to the mainland; she was eventually dismantled in 1987. The name is that of a former U. S. senator from New York and has absolutely no Bermuda relevance, yet it was retained for her full island tenure. She had ample capacity to handle large numbers of cruise ship passengers in a single trip, although the master of the *United States* was unexpectedly critical of her when that superliner anchored in Great Sound because she took too long to load and unload. (See "Report of the Port Facilities Commission" [Bermuda 1965], 25.) For more information on the *Chauncey M. Depew*—both before and after her Bermuda adventure—see Donald C. Ringwald, *The Hudson River Day Line* (New York: Fordham University Press, 1990).

18. Ambrose Channel is named after John W. Ambrose (1838–1899), an Irish-born engineer who spent his professional lifetime improving New York Harbor. The first major passenger liner to use the newly constructed Ambrose Channel is thought to have been the *Lusitania*, when she reached New York on her maiden voyage in September 1907 (on Friday the 13th).

19. For information on harbor pilots in the Port of New York, including the use of station boats, see Greg Walsh, "The Long and Low-Paying Road to Becoming a New York Harbor Pilot," *Professional Mariner* 12 (April/May, 1995), 40–42, 44; for a short historical account, see Jannette Edwards Rattray, *Perils of the Port of New York* (New York: Dodd, Mead, 1973), pp. 29–49.

20. Quoted as "Note C" on Chart No. 12326, published by the National Oceanic and Atmospheric Administration (NOAA), an arm of the U.S. Department of Commerce. The same chart provides a graphic representation of the approaches to New York Harbor from the sea.

21. In bygone years, when the island economy included a substantial agricultural component, steamships sailing out of Hamilton for New York carried quantities of a crop long associated with Bermuda—onions. See Duncan McDowall, "State of the Onion," *Bermuda* 4(1) (Spring 1996), 28–33.

APPENDIX A
Vessel Roster:
Around-Manhattan
Sightseeing Service

Off. No. Hull Type	Name(s)	Dimensions Gross Tons	Built at Year Yard	Disposition Notes
1. Circle Line (1945–current)				
25340 wood st.s.	*Manhattan* a) *Crescent* b) *Ursula* c) *Cora A.*	114 x 28 x 7 186	Albany 1901	abandoned, 1947 [1]
205007 wood ol.s.(+)	*Islander*	80 x 19 x 6 70	E. Boothbay 1909 Adams	out of documentation, 1957 [2]
209870 steel ol.s.(+)	*Visitor* a) *Yantic* b) *Sightseer*	56 x 18 x 5 30	Noank, CT 1912	sold to Savannah interests, 1952; abandoned, 1969
203394 steel ol.s.(+)	*Tourist* a) *Kehtoh* b) *Dixie*	123 x 20 x 10 187	Boston 1906	out of documentation, 1952
206562 steel st.s.	*Traveler* a) *Viking* b) *Falcon* c) *North Star* e) *Harbor Queen*	156 x 23 x 11 295	Wilm., DE 1909 Pusey & Jones	sold to Holiday Outings, 1953 [3]
127649 steel ol.s.(+)	*Circle Line V* a) *Celt* b) *Sachem* c) *Phenakite* *PYc 25* (USN) d) *Sightseer* e) *Circle Line Sightseer*	143 x 23 x 12 235	Wilm., DE 1902 Pusey & Jones	out of service, 1977 [4]

Off. No. Hull Type	Name(s)	Dimensions Gross Tons	Built at Year Yard	Disposition Notes
25544 steel ol.s.	*Circle Line VII* a) *LCI(L) 191* b) *New Yorker* c) *Circle Line Sightseer VII*	151 x 23 x 11 255	Kearny, NJ 1942 Federal	in service (1995)
258367 steel ol.s.	*Circle Line VIII* a) *LCI(L) 179* b) *Vicki* c) *Circle Line* d) *Circle Line Sightseer VIII*	151 x 23 x 11 275	Kearny, NJ 1942 Federal	in service (1995)
229917 steel ol.s.	*Circle Line IX* a) *Stevana* b) *Ace* c) *Circle Line II* d) *Circle Line Sightseer IX* f) *The Diplomat* g) *Bostonian* h) *The Diplomat*	124 x 21 x 11 99	New York 1930	sold to Boston interests, 1958; later ran in Washington (DC); currently running as a charter boat in New York
262270 steel ol.s.	*Circle Line X* a) *LCI(L) 758* b) *Normandy Two* c) *Normandy* d) *Circle Line Sightseer X*	151 x 23 x 11 325	Portland, OR 1944 Commercial Iron	in service (1995) [5]
252719 steel ol.s.	*Circle Line VI* a) *LCI(L) 646* b) *LCI(G) 646* c) *Normandy* d) *Gotham* e) *Knickerbocker II* f) *Day Line II*	152 x 23 x 7 287	Barber, NJ 1944 New Jersey S/B	to exempt status, 1967 [6]
273847 steel ol.s.	*Circle Line IX* a) *LCI(L) 766* b) *LCI(G) 766* c) *Knickerbocker VII* d) *Day Line VII*	152 x 23 x 11 280	Portland, OR 1944	to exempt status, 1971
265404 steel ol.s.	*Circle Line IV* a) *LCI(L) 390* b) *Knickerbocker* c) *Day Line I*	153 x 23 x 11 365	Boston 1943 Lawley	out of documentation, 1977

Off. No. Hull Type	Name(s)	Dimensions Gross Tons	Built at Year Yard	Disposition Notes
273358 steel ol.s.	*Circle Line XI* a) *Calypso* WPC 104 (USCG) b) *Calypso* AG 35 (USN) c) *Calypso* WPC 104 (USCG)	153 x 25 x 11 283	Bath 1932 Bath Iron	in service (1995) [7]
280591 steel ol.s.	*Sightseer XII* a) *Argo* WPC 100 (USCG) b) *Circle Line XII*	156 x 25 x 13 290	Camden, NJ 1933 Mathis	in service (1995) [8, 9]
287848 steelk ol.s.	*Circle Line XV* a) *Perseus* WPC 114 (USCG)	156 x 25 x 13 291	Bath 1932 Bath Iron	in service (1995) [7]
514070 steel ol.s.	*Circle Line XVI* a) *Nike* WPC 112 (USCG)	156 x 25 x 13 298	Point Pleasant, WV 1934	in service (1995) [10]
537690 steel ol.s.	*Circle Line XVII* a) *Triton* WPC 116 (USCG)	156 x 25 x 13 298	Point Pleasant, WV 1934	in service (1995) [9]

2. John P. Roberts (1905–1918)

95530 wood st.s.	*Herman S. Caswell* a) *H.S. Caswell* c) *Marilda II*	82 x 17 x 7 109	Noank, CT 1878	later ran for Goodwin [11]
140095 wood st.s.	*Halcyon* a) Schooner *Lookout* b) U.S. Fish Commission Schooner *Alcyon*	109 x 16 x 8 45	Brooklyn 1875	later ran for Goodwin [12]
76763 wood st.s.	*Observation* a) *Jean* b) *Elsa*	92 x 7 x 9 122	Brooklyn 1888	sold to American Can Co, 1916; see note [13]
116223	*Tourist* a) *Sapphire*	118 x 26 x 10 260	Bath 1888 Bath Iron	later ran for Goodwin [14]

Off. No. Hull Type	Name(s)	Dimensions Gross Tons	Built at Year Yard	Disposition Notes
3. Goodwin Steamboat (1918–1943)				
116223 wood st.s.	*Tourist* a) *Sapphire*	118 x 26 x 10 260	Bath 1888 Bath Iron	out of documentation, 1944 [14]
95530 wood st.s.	*H.S. Caswell* a) *Herman S. Caswell* c) *Marilda II*	82 x 17 x 7 109	Noank, CT 1878	sold, 1931; later ran for Manhattan Yacht Cruises [11]
140095 wood st.s.	*Halcyon* a) Schooner *Lookout* b) U.S. Fish Commission Schooner *Alcyon*	109 x 16 x 8 44	Brooklyn 1875	sold to NJ interests in 1921; see note [12]
205007 wood st.s.	*Islander*	80 x 19 x 6 70	E. Boothbay 1909 Adams	sold to J. Driscoll, 1944; later ran for Circle Line [2]
4. New York Waterways Yacht Cruises (1939–1943)				
229468 steel ol.s.(+)	*Sylph* b) *Sylph* *Py 5* (USN)	136 x 19 x 10 150	Chester 1898	out of documentation, 1943
212433 steel st.s.	*Sylph II* a) *Caroline* b) *Delphine* c) *Stellaris* e) *Lash* *PYc 31* (USN)	166 x 24 x 12 339	New York 1914	out of documentation, 1943 [15]
5. Manhattan Yacht Cruises (1939–1944)				
200639 wood st.s.	*Manhattan* a) *Frank and Helen McAvoy*	72 x 19 x 6 75	Brooklyn 1903	out of documentation, 1944
212510 wood ol.s.	*Marilda*	79 x 16 x 3 49	Greenport, NY 1914	abandoned, 1942

Off. No. Hull Type	Name(s)	Dimensions Gross Tons	Built at Year Yard	Disposition Notes
95530	*Marilda II* a) *Herman S.* *Caswell* b) *H.S. Caswell*	82 x 17 x 7 109	Noank, CT 1878	abandoned, 1944 [11]

6. Battery Sightseeing Boat (1943–1944)

25340 wood st.s.	*Manhattan* a) *Crescent* b) *Ursula* c) *Cora A.*	114 x 28 x 7 186	Albany 1901	sold to Circle Line, 1944 [1]
150652 steel st.s.	*Macom* a) *Patrol*	135 x 23 x 10 235	Sparrows Pt. 1894	out of documentation, 1944 [16]

7. Normandy Sightseeing (1946–1955)

208730 wood st.s.	*Col. Frank H.* *Adams* a) *Southport*	125 x 21 x 8 145	Boston 1911 McKie	dismantled, 1954
252719 steel ol.s.	*Normandy* a) *LCI(L) 646* b) *LCI(G) 646* d) *Gotham* e) *Knickerbocker II* f) *Day Line II* g) *Circle Line VI*	152 23 x 7 287	Barber, NJ 1944 New Jersey S/B	sold to Day Line, 1952; later ran for Circle Line [6]
262270 steel ol.s.	*Normandy* a) *LCI(L) 758* b) *Normandy Two* d) *Cicle Line Sightseer X* e) *Circle Line X*	151 x 23 x 11 302	Portland, OR 1944 Commercial Iron	sold to Circle Line, 1955

8. Sightseeing Around New York Waterways, Inc. (ca. 1946)

219549 wood ga.s.	*Saltaire*	74 x 19 x 6 68	Wareham, MA 1919	reverted to B.B. Wills, ca. 1947 [17]

OFF. NO. HULL TYPE	NAME(S)	DIMENSIONS GROSS TONS	BUILT AT YEAR YARD	DISPOSITION NOTES

9. Panorama Sightseeing (1947–1969)

| 230975 wood ol.s.(+) | *Manhattan* a) *Electronic* b) *North Haven* | 102 x 23 x 9 210 | Portland, ME 1913 Portland S/B | scrapped, 1968 [18] |
| 253076 steel ol.s. | *Manhattan II* a) *LCI(L) ??* b) *Dolphin* c) *San Jacinto* | 151 x 22 x 7 226 | Barber, NJ 1944 New Jersey S/B | sold to Circle Line Statue Ferry 1970; out of docum'ntn, 1972 [19] |

10. Day Line Sightseeing (1953—1962)

252719 steel ol.s.	*Gotham* a) *LCI(L) 646* b) *LCI(G) 646* c) *Normandy* e) *Knickerbocker II* f) *Day Line II* g) *Circle Line VI*	152 x 23 x 7 287	Barber, NJ 1944 New Jersey S/B	sold to Circle Line, 1962 [6]
265404 steel ol.s.	*Knickerbocker* a) *LCI(L) 390* c) *Day Line I* d) *Circle Line IV*	153 x 23 x 11 365	Boston 1943 Lawley	sold to Circle Line, 1962
273847 steel ol.s.	*Knickerbocker VII* a) *LCI(L) 766* b) *LCI(G) 766* d) *Day Line VII* e) *Circle Line IX*	152 x 23 x 11 280	Portland, OR 1944	sold to Circle Line, 1962

11. Holiday Outings (1953–1954)

| 206562 steel st.s. | *Harbor Queen* a) *Viking* b) *Falcon* c) *North Star* d) *Gallant* e) *Traveler* | 156 x 23 x 11 295 | Wilm., DE 1909 Pusey & Jones | dismantled, 1957 [3] |

12. Fairwater Excursions (1964–1965)

| 286092 steel ol.s. | *Dolly Madison* | 59 x 26 x 7 34 | Warren, RI 1961 Blount | see note [20] |

Off. No. Hull Type	Name(s)	Dimensions Gross Tons	Built at Year Yard	Disposition Notes
294423 steel ol.s.	*Fairmaid* b) *Waving Girl*	59 x 21 x 7 77	Warren, RI 1964 Blount	sold to Savannah interests

Explanation of abbreviations:

Type: st.s. = steam engine, screw propeller
      ol.s. = oil engine (*i.e.*, diesel), screw propeller
      ols.(+) = oil engine, screw propeller, originally steam powered
      ga.s. = gasoline engine, screw propeller
Yard: shipyard where vessel was built;
      S/B = ship-building company

Notes:

[1]   Originally owned by Catskill & Albany Steamboat Company; 2-cylinder steam engine (14″, 30″ x 18″); purchased by Joseph A. Moran from William G. Atkins of Albany, NY, in 1942; became part of Moran's contribution to the Circle Line partnership.

[2]   Former Maine coast ferry; later ran in excursion service out of Newark, NJ; purchased by Goodwin in 1943 from Islander Steamboat Company of New Jersey; later sold to J. Driscoll and became part of his contribution to the Circle Line partnership; built as steam-powered, later converted to diesel.

[3]   Final steam-powered vessel to operate in around-Manhattan Island sight-seeing service; last trip made in 1954; 4-cylinder triple expansion engine (14″, 21″, 24″, 24″ x 18″), repurchased by Circle Line after being owned by Holiday Outings, but not returned to service; dismantled, 1957.

[4]   Originally steam powered; re-equipped with 7-cylinder Fairbanks Morse diesel engine in 1936–37 (14″ x 17″); obtained by Circle Line after military service during Second World War; out of service ca. 1977; reportedly sold to midwest interests for historic preservation.

[5]   Gross tonnage recently increased from 305 as a result of structural alterations.

[6]   First LCI(L) to be converted for around-Manhattan Island sightseeing service; all LCI(L)s powered by eight 6-cylinder diesels (4.25″ x 5″).

[7]   Equipped with original twin 6-cylinder Winton diesels from Coast Guard days (14″ x 16″).

[8]   Assigned to sightseeing cruises from South Street Seaport.

[9]   Equipped with surplus LCI(L)-style "twin quad" engines (4.25″ x 5″).

[10]   Equipped with twin V-12 Cummins diesel engines.

[11]   *Possibly* first vessel ever to offer commercial around-Manhattan Island sightseeing service; see text; under Goodwin ownership, used largely for New York Bay sightseeing, not around Manhattan Island; single-cylinder steam engine (16″ x 17″).

[12]   Former schooner, converted to steam power in 1880s; on October 18, 1923, while owned by Frank Winkler of Edgewater, NJ and used as a deep-sea

fishing boat, foundered in a severe storm two miles off Coney Island; 19 people on board, all were rescued except the captain and the engineer, who were lost; 2-cylinder compound steam engine (10″, 20″ x 14″).

[13]   Purchased by Roberts in 1909 from Eloise L. Breese, of New York; powered by two 2-cylinder compound steam engines (17″, 34″ x 26″); not regularly assigned to around Manhattan Island service, although thought to have made occasional trips; on September 9, 1932, while owned by Alexander J. Forsyth of Staten Island, vessel exploded and sank in the East River off East 134 Street; 127 people on board, 72 killed and 31 injured. (See chapter 5 for a full acount of this tragedy.)

[14]   Former yacht with at least five different owners before being purchased by Roberts for sightseeing service in May 1913; 3-cylinder triple-expansion steam engine (11″, 19″, 30″ x 18″.)

[15]   Purchased by Circle Line after World War II service with U.S. Navy, but never operated as sightseeing yacht by Circle Line and never redocumented as a civilian merchant vessel.

[16]   Never operated in around-Manhattan Island sightseeing service; included in roster for interest's sake; see text.

[17]   Vessel was owned by Boat Sales, Inc., one of the marine enterprises of B. B. Wills.

[18]   Purchased by Jeremiah Driscoll from Vinal Haven & Rockland Steamboat Company following government service during Second World War; as *Electronic*, originally worked for Nova Scotian interests; converted to diesel power before beginning sightseeing work at New York in 1947; originally powered by 3-cylinder triple expansion steam engine (12″, 19″, 30″ x 20″).

[19]   No official sources show any identity as an ex-LCI(L), raising possibility vessel was never formally commissioned by U.S. Navy before being sold for civilian use; see text; operated in excursion service in Houston by B. B. Wills before being sold to Jeremiah Driscoll and coming to New York in 1956; earlier ran in excursion service in Pittsburgh.

[20]   Leased from Washington (DC) interests, not owned by Fairwater; later sold to Connecticut interests.

APPENDIX B
Around-Manhattan Island Sightseeing Boats: Selected Incidents from Military Service

VESSEL	DATE	INCIDENT
Argo *WPC-100*	Mar. 15, 1932	keel laid, John H. Mathis Co., Camden, NJ
	Nov. 12, 1932	launched
	Jan. 6, 1933	commissioned
	Jul.–Aug., 1940	cadet practice cruise
	Oct.–Nov., 1940	re-armed by Merrill-Stevens, Jacksonville, FL
	1941–1945	assigned to Eastern Sea Frontier; stationed at Newport, RI
	Jan. 14, 1942	rescued 6 survivors from the 9,755-ton Panamian tanker *MS Norness* that was torpedoed enroute Halifax from New York City
	Jan. 7, 1944	rescued 23 survivors from *USS St. Augustine* (PG-54), which sank after collision with *SS Camas Meadows* enroute Norfolk from New York City; crew of *Argo* decorated.
	Jun. 1945	assigned to air-sea rescue, First District (HQ-Boston)
	Oct. 30, 1948	decommissioned
	Nov. 2, 1955	sold (same day as *Calypso*)
Calypso *WPC 104*	Jan. 21, 1931	keel laid, Bath Iron Works, Bath, ME
	Jan. 1, 1932	launched
	Jan. 16, 1932	commissioned

Vessel	Date	Incident
	Oct.–Nov., 1940	re-armed by Merrill-Steven, Jacksonville, FL
	May 17, 1941	decommissioned and transferrd to U.S. Navy as escort for Presidential yacht *Potomac* (*Potomac* was ex-*Argo*-class Coast Guard cutter *Electra*, WPC-137; has been preserved in San Francisco as *Potomac*)
	Jan. 20, 1942	recommissioned in Coast Guard
	1941–1945	assigned to Eastern Sea Frontier; stationed at Norfolk, VA
	Feb. 15, 1942	rescued 42 survivors from the 5,152-ton Brazilian ship *SS Buarque*, which was torpedoed enroute New York City from Rio de Janeiro
	Mar. 7, 1942	rescued 54 survivors from 7,000-ton Brazilian ship *SS Arabutan* which was torpedoed enroute Trinidad from Norfolk
	May 7, 1942	rescued 13 survivors from the 5,102-ton U.S.-flag *SS Pipestone County* who had been adrift for 17 days off the Virginia Capes after their vessel was torpedoed
	Sept. 15, 1943	rescued 60 survivors from *USS Plymouth* (PG-57)
	Jun. 1945	assigned to air-sea rescue, Fifth District (HQ-Portsmouth)
	Jul. 18, 1947	decommissioned
	Nov. 2, 1955	sold (same day as *Argo*)
Nike *WPC-112*	Nov. 17, 1933	keel laid, Marietta Mfg. Co., Pt. Pleasant, WV
	Jul. 7, 1934	launched (same day as *Triton*)
	Oct. 24, 1934	commissioned
	1941–1945	assigned to Eastern Sea Frontier; stationed at Gulfport, MS
	Feb. 3, 1942	rescued 40 survivors from the 3,627-ton Panamian-flag *SS San Gil*

Vessel	Date	Incident
	Feb. 6, 1942	rescued 37 survivors from the 8,403-ton U.S.-flag tanker *SS China Arrow*, which was torpedoed off Ocean City, MD enroute New York City from Beaumont, TX
	May 5, 1942	attacked surfaced submarine
	May 9, 1942	attacked submarine
	May 14, 1942	rescued 9 survivors from tanker *Portrero Del Llano*
	May 16, 1942	attacked submarine
	Jun. 1945	assigned to air-sea rescue, First District (HQ-Boston)
	Nov. 5, 1964	decommissioned
	May 9, 1966	sold
Perseus *WPC-114*	Jan. 21, 1931	keel laid, Bath Iron Works, Bath, ME
	Apr. 11, 1932	launched
	Apr. 27, 1932	commissioned
	1940	assigned to Bering Sea patrol
	1941–1945	assigned to Western Sea Frontier
	Nov. 1941	stationed at Cordova, AK
	Dec. 1941	stationed at Juneau, AK
	May 1942	stationed at San Diego, CA
	Jun. 26, 1959	decommissioned
	Nov. 4, 1959	sold
Triton *WPC-116*	Apr. 17, 1934	keel laid, Marietta Mfg. Co., Pt. Pleasant, WV
	Jul. 7, 1934	launched (same day as *Nike*)
	Nov. 20, 1934	commissioned; first home port, Gulfport, MS
	Sept. 2, 1937	rescued ten survivors from the *SS Tarpon* which sank the previous day off Panama City, FL

Vessel	Date	Incident
	Mar. 1941	assigned to U.S. Navy's Atlantic Fleet Sound Schol, Key West, FL to serve as training vessel for sonar operators
	Jul. 1, 1941	temporary assignment to U.S. Navy
	July 16, 1941	assigned to Eastern Sea Frontier; stationed at Key West, FL
	Feb. 21, 1942	attacked submarine
	Jun. 1945	assigned to air-sea rescue, Sixth District (HQ-Charleston, SC)
	Nov. 7, 1945	stationed at Corpus Christi, TX
	Jun. 12, 1967	decommissioned; last skipper, Lieut. Harry Smith, USCG; sent to U.S. Navy mothball fleet, Orange, TX
	Jan. 16, 1969	sold
LCI(L) 179	Sept. 10, 1942	keel laid, Federal S/B & Dry Dock Co., Port Newark (Kearny), NJ
	Dec. 7, 1942	launched
	Dec. 16, 1942	delivered to United Kingdom
	Mar. 27, 1946	returned to U.S. Navy at Tompkinsville, NY
	Apr. 26, 1946	out of service
	May 8, 1946	stricken from list of U.S. Naval vessels
	Dec. 4, 1947	accepted for sale and disposition by U.S. Maritime Commission and sold to Edward Harker, Bayonne, NJ
LCI(L) 191	Dec. 7, 1942	keel laid, Federal S/B & Dry Dock Co., Port Neark (Kearny), NJ
	Jan. 25, 1943	launched
	Feb. 3, 1943	commissioned; first commander, Ens. William T. Dom, 3rd, USNR
	Mar. 9, 1943	at Little Creek, VA for training
	Apr. 1, 1943	departed Norfolk with Task Group 68-2 for Algeria, via Bermuda

Vessel	Date	Incident
	Jul. 9–15, 1943	participated in Operation Husky, the invasion of Sicily
	Jan. 22–25, 1944	participated in the landings at Anzio
	Jun. 17, 1944	participated in the landings at Elba and Pianosa
	Aug. 15 thru Sept. 16, 1944	participated in the invasion of Southern France
	Jun. 26, 1945	departed Oran, Algeria, for return to U.S., via Azores and Bermuda
	Jul. 23, 1945	arrived Orange, TX; planned conversion to LCI(R) cancelled when war ended in the Pacific
	Nov. 19, 1945	arrived Little Creek, VA for assignment to Division 22 of LCI(L) Squadron
	Mar. 26, 1946	departed Little Creek for Brooklyn Navy Yard
	Apr. 18, 1946	decommissioned; final commander, Lieut. (jg) James G. Minham, USNR
	Jan. 9, 1948	accepted by Maritime Commission for sale and disposition and delivered to Mill Basin Ship Repair Co., Brooklyn, NY
LCI(L) 390	Nov. 20, 1943	launched, George Lawley & Sons, Neponsit (Boston), MA
	Nov. 30, 1943	commissioned and delivered to representatives of the United Kingdom
	Feb. 15, 1945	Navy Unit Commendation as part of ship salvage, fire fighting, and rescue unit
	Jun. 9, 1946	arrived Norfolk for return to U.S. Navy
	Jun. 19, 1946	accepted by U.S. Navy and decommissioned
	Oct. 8, 1946	stricken from list of U.S. Naval vessels
	May 14, 1947	accepted by Maritime Commission for sale and disposition and delivered to Dave Johnsen, Washington, DC

Vessel	Date	Incident
LCI(L) 646	1944	built, Federal S/B Co., Barber, NJ
	Jul. 10, 1944	commissioned
	Mar. 15, 1945	converted to LCI(R)
	Mar. 26 thru Jun. 30, 1945	participated in assault and occupation of Okinawa; performed fire support duties with 5-inch rockets, plus 22 mm and 40 mm guns
	Mar. 29, 1945	sunk Japanese suicide motor boat with 20 mm guns
	Apr. 1, 1945	two crew members wounded during attack by Japanese torpedo boat
	Sept. 5 thru Oct. 21, 1945	Navy Occupation Service (Asia)
	Jan. 8, 1947	accepted by Maritime Commission for sale and disposition
LCI(L) 758	May 7, 1944	launched; Commercial Iron Works, Portland, OR; sponsor, Mrs. Edward H. James
	May 20, 1944	commissioned
	Nov. 5 thru Nov. 29, 1944	participated in Leyte landings
	Dec. 7, 1944	participated in Ormoc Bay landings; shot down Japanese Zero fighter plane with 20-mm guns
	Dec. 12 thru Dec. 18, 1944	participated in Mindoro landings
	Jan. 4 thru Jan. 18, 1945	participated in Langayen Gulf landings
	Jan. 12, 1945	while 40 miles NW of the Bataan peninsula, attacked by two Japanese suicide dive bombers; shot down one plane with 20-mm guns, the other brought down by fire from other ships in the convoy

Vessel	Date	Incident
	Apr. 17 thru Apr. 23, 1945 May 10 thru May 16, 1945	participated in Mindanao landings
	Sept. 8 thru Dec. 16, 1945	Navy Occupation Service (Asia)
	Feb. 12, 1946	to San Diego for disposition
	May 7, 1946	decommissioned
	Jul. 31, 1947	accepted by Maritime Commission for sale and disposition and sold to Angelo Lomano, Jersey City, NJ
LCI(L) 766	May 15, 1944	keel laid, Commercial Iron Works, Portland, OR
	Jun. 11, 1944	launched
	Jun. 19, 1944	commissioned
	Jun. 24, 1944	arrived Mare Island
	Mar. 15, 1945	converted to LCI(R)
	Mar. 26 thru Jun. 30, 1945	participated in assault and occupation of Okinawa; performed fire support duties with 5-inch rocket, plus 20 mm and 40 mm guns
	Sept. 2 thru Sept. 25, 1945	Navy Occupation Service (Asia)
	Sept. 30 thru Dec. 26, 1945	China service
	Jun. 19, 1946	decommissioned and laid up at Wando River (Charleston), SC
	Jul. 31, 1946	stricken from list of U.S. Naval vessels
	Apr. 16, 1947	accepted by Maritime Commission for sale and disposition and sold to Southeastern Terminal & Steamship Co., Miami
Phenakite *PYc 25*	Feb. 17, 1942	acquired by U.S. Navy
	Jul. 1, 1942	commissioned

Vessel	Date	Incident
—		assigned to Fleet Sonar School Squadron, Key West, FL; fleet flagship, *USS Dahlgren* (DD-187)
	Oct. 18, 1944	rode out hurricane in port

Sources: Naval Historical Center, Ships Histories Branch, Washington, DC; Navy Department, *Ships' Data U.S. Naval Vessels,* Vol. II (Washington: Government Printing Office, 1946); Robert Scheina, *U.S. Coast Guard Cutters and Craft of World War II* (Annapolis: U.S. Naval Institute, 1982); Malcolm F. Willoughby, *The U.S. Coast Guard in World War II* (Annapolis: U.S. Naval Institute, 1957).

APPENDIX C
The North Atlantic Blue Riband
in the Twentieth Century

Year	Winning Vessel	Company	Gross Tonnage	Speed (Knots)
1897	*Kaiser Wilhelm Der Grosse*[1]	North German Lloyd	14,349	22.29
1900	*Deutschland*	H.A.P.A.G.	16,502	22.42
1992	*Kronprinz Wilhelm*	North German Lloyd	19,361	23.09
1994	*Deutschland*	H.A.P.A.G.	16,502	23.15
1906	*Kaiser Wilhelm II*	North German Lloyd	19,361	23.58
1907	*Lusitania*[2]	Cunard	31,550	——
1907	*Mauretania*[2]	Cunard	31,938	23.69
1929	*Bremen*	North German Lloyd	51,656	27.83
1930	*Europa*[3]	North German Lloyd	49,746	27.91
1933	*Rex*	Italian Line	51,062	28.92
1935	*Normandie*[4]	French Line	82,799	30.31
1936	*Queen Mary*	Cunard-White Star	81,235	30.63
1937	*Normandie*	French Line	83,423	31.30
1938	*Queen Mary*	Cunard-White Star	81,235	31.69
1952	*United States*[4]	United States Lines	53,329	35.59

[1]See chapter 3 for an account of a terrible fire involving this vessel in New York Harbor in 1900.

[2]Both *Lusitania* and *Mauritania* subsequently posted even faster crossings than the ones that allowed each to capture the record in 1907, the *Lusitania* becoming the first vessel to cross the North Atlantic in excess of 25 knots, the *Mauritania* the first to cross at better than 26 knots.

[3]After the Second World War, the vessel sailed for French Line as *Liberté*.

[4]Blue Riband captured on maiden voyage.

APPENDIX D
Vessel Roster:
FDNY Fireboats

Off. No. Hull Type	Name(s)	Dimensions Gross Tons	Built at Year Yard	Disposition [Notes]
13176 wood st.s.	John Fuller	78 x 18 x 8	Phila. 1864	see note [1]
80506 wood st.s.	William F. Havenmeyer	106 x 22 x 10	Camden 1875 Wood, Dialogue	retired 1901 [2]
28101 iron st.s.	Zophar Mills	120 x 25 x 12 185	Willm., DE 1882 Pusey & Jones	retired 1934 [3]
116084 wood st.s.	Seth Low	99 x 24 x 9 82	Brooklyn 1885 Trundy & Murphy	retired 1917 [4]
130516 steel st.s.	New Yorker b) The New Yorker	125 x 26 x 12 243	New York 1890 Jonson	retired 1931 [5]
157349 wood st.s.	David A. Boody	105 x 23 x 7 94	Noank, CT 1892 Palmer & Son	retired 19?? [6]
111172 steel st.s.	William L. Strong b) Robert A. Van Wyck c) William L. Strong d) Dutchess e) Ascension	100 x 24 x 12 203	Camden 1898 Dialogue & Sons	sold to Louisiana interests, 1948; converted to diesel; retired ca. 1985 [7]
200103 steel st.s.	Abram S. Hewitt	117 x 25 x 10 223	Camden 1903 New York S/B	retired 1958 [8]

243

Off. No. Hull Type	Name(s)	Dimensions Gross Tons	Built at Year Yard	Disposition [Notes]
200667 steel st.s.	George B. McClelland	117 x 24 x 9 256	Camden 1904 New York S/B	retired 1954 [9]
204998 steel st.s.	James Duane	132 x 22 x 10 326	Newburgh, NY 1908 Marvel	retired 1959 [10]
204989 steel st.s.	Thomas Willett b) Circle Line XIV	132 x 28 x 10 326	Newburgh, NY 1908 Marvel	sold to Circle Line, 1959; see note [11]
205535 steel st.s.	Cornelius W. Lawrence	104 x 23 x 9 172	Newburgh, NY 1908 Marvel	retired 1955 [12]
212224 steel st.s.	William J. Gaynor	118 x 25 x 13 270	E'port., NJ 1914 N.J. Drydock	retired 1961 [13]
221833 steel st.s.	John Purroy Mitchell	132 x 27 x 10 334	Staten Island, NY 1921 Standard S/B	retired 1966 [14]
231225 steel ga.s.	John J. Harvey	130 x 28 x 9 433	Brooklyn, NY 1931 Todd	out of service 1992 [15]
237805 steel ol.s.	Fire Fighter	134 x 32 x 9 324	Staten Island, NY 1938 United	active (1996) [16]
286629 steel ol.s.	John D. McKean	129 x 30 x 9 330	Camden, NJ 1954 Mathis	active (1996) [17]
276460 steel ol.s.	H. Sylvia A.H.G. Wilks b) Ervin S. Cooper	105 x 27 x 9 213	Camden, NJ 1958 Mathis	sold to Dept. of Marine & Aviation, 1972; later sold to Lousiana interests [18]

OFF. NO. HULL TYPE	NAME(S)	DIMENSIONS GROSS TONS	BUILT AT YEAR YARD	DISPOSITION [NOTES]
276938 steel ol.s.	*Harry M.* *Archer, M.D.* b) *Miriam Walmsley* *Cooper*	105 x 27 x 9 213	Camden, NJ 1958 Mathis	sold to Louisiana interests, 1994 [18]
279951 steel ol.s.	*Senator* *Robert F.* *Wagner* b) *Georgia*	105 x 27 x 9 213	Camden, NJ 1959 Mathis	sold to Louisiana interests, 1993 [18]
286653 steel ol.s.	*Governor* *Alfred E.* *Smith*	105 x 27 x 9 213	Camden, NJ 1961 Mathis	active (1996) [18]
289631 steel ol.s.	*John H.* *Glenn, Jr.*	70 x 21 x 5 81	Jacksonville, FL 1962 Diesel S/B	sold to Wash., DC Fire Dept. 1979 [19]
n/a plastic ol.s.	*John F.* *Devaney*	70 x 19 x 5 40	Southhampton, UK 1992 Vosper/Textron	out of service, 1994; see note [20]
n/a plastic ol.s.	*Alfred E.* *Ronaldson*	70 x 19 x 5 40	Southampton, UK 1992 Vosper/Textron	out of service, 1994; see note [20]
987409 aluminum ol.s.	*Kevin C.* *Kane*	52 x 16 x 4 25	Somerset, MA 1992 Gladding-Hearn	active (1996) [21]

Explanation of Abbreviations:
Type: st.s. = steam engine, screw propellor
     l.s. = oil engine (*i.e.*, diesel), screw propeller
     ga.s. = gasoline engine, screw propeller
Yard: shipyard where vessel was built
     S/B = ship-building company

Notes:
[1] Owned by Baxter Wrecking Company, not FDNY; under contract to FDNY, 1866–1875; two Amoskeag pumps (2,000 gpm).
[2] First FDNY-owned fireboat; carried designation of Engine 43 for entire service life; two Amoskeag pumps (6,000 gpm); cost, $23,800.
[3] Single-cyclinder engine (30″ x 30″); twin side-by-side stacks; two Clapp & Jones pumps (6,000 gpm); cost, $57,200.
[4] Originally built for Fire Department of City of Brooklyn; joined FDNY fleet

at time of municipal consolidation in 1898; two screw; twin single-cylinder steam engines; two Clap & Jones pumps (3,500 gpm); cost, $36,850.

[5] Triple-expansion engine (15″, 24″, 39″ x 24″); Clapp & Jones pumps (13,000gpm); cost, $98,250.

[6] Originally built for Fire Department of City of Brooklyn; joined FDNY fleet at time of municipal consolidation in 1898; compound condensing engine; two American Fire pumps (6,500 gpm); cost, $52,000.

[7] Compound engine (16″, 30″ x 22″); two American Fire pumps (6,500 gpm); cost, $56,490; worked as FDNY fireboat for 50 years, then as a Louisiana tow boat for 35 or more years; steam engine replaced with diesel during Louisiana service; longest service life of any FDNY vessel thus far.

[8] Compound engine (17″, 34″ x 24″); 7,000 gpm; cost, $83,750; built as two stack, later converted to single stack; last coal-burning FDNY fireboat in service.

[9] Compound engine (17″, 34″ x 24″); 7,000 gpm; cost, $83,750.

[10] Compound engine (18″, 38″ x 26″); built as coal-burning, later converted to oil; turbine pumps (9,000 gpm); cost, $118,925.

[11] Compund engine (18″, 38″ x 26″); built as coal-burning, later converted to oil; turbine pumps (9,000 gpm); cost, $118,925; sold to Circle Line for use as unpowered barge at the company's maintenance base (not included in Circle Line roster in Chapter One).

[12] Compound engine (14″, 30″ x 22″); two reciprocating pumps (7,000 gpm); smaller vessel designed to pass under Harlem River bridges; cost, $97,800.

[13] Compound engine (18″, 38″ x 26″); built as coal-burning, later converted to oil; burbine pumps (7,000 gpm); cost, $118,749.

[14] Compound engine (18″, 38″ x 26″); only FDNY steam-powered fireboat to be built as oil-burning; turbine pumps (9,000 gpm); cost, $275,000.

[15] Built with five 8-cylinder Sterling-Viking II gasoline engines (8″ x 9″), each driving a separate electric generator; twin screw; in 1957, re-equipped with five 8-cylinder Fairbanks-Morse opposed-piston diesel engines (5.25″ x 7.25″); four centrifugal pumps (16,000 gpm); cost, $605,000.

[16] Two 16-cylinder Winton diesels (8.5″ x 10.5″); twin screw, electric drive; four DeLaval pumps, electrically driven (20,000 gpm); cost, $924,000.

[17] Two eight-cylinder Enterprise diesels (12″ x 15″); twin screw, direct drive; two separate six-cylinder Enterprise diesels linked to four Worthington centrifugal pumps (19,000 gpm); cost, $1,426,000.

[18] Two six-cylinder Enterprise diesels (8″ x 10″); twin screw, direct drive; variable-pitch propellers; two separate six-cylinder Enterprise diesels linked to two Worthington centrifugal pumps (8,000 gpm); costs: *Wilks* and *Archer*, $857,241 each; *Wagner*, $899,000; *Smith*, $907,077; *Wilks, Archer* and *Wagner* all subsequently owned by Crescent Towing and Salvage of Mobile, AL, with New Orleans as home port.

[19] Three 12-cylinder diesels (4.5″ x 5″); triple screw, direct drive; during fire-fighting, center diesel remains a propulsion engine, while two outboard engines are linked to two centrifugal pups (5,000 gpm); cost, $230,000.

[20] Surface-effect ships (SES) with a measured draft of 5′4″ which is reduced to 3′6″ when the vessel is "on air"; two 8-cylinder Detroit diesels (4.8″ x 5″);

single 6-cylinder Detroit diesel drives lifting fans or water pumps only; three Waterous centrifugal pumps (7,075 gpm); hulls constructed by Vosper Hovermarine in England, additional equipment installed by Textron at New Orleans; see text for details on why these two fireboats were retired after but a few months service; cost, $3,500,000 each.

[21]   Two 8-cylinder Detroit diesels for propulsion; two 6-cylinder Detroit diesels for pumping; two Gould centrifugal pumps (5,000 gpm); cost, appx. $850,000.

APPENDIX E
Sources of Fireboat Names

Fireboat	Identify of Namesake
William F. Havemeyer	79th mayor of New York City (1848–1849)
Zophar Mills	19th-century volunteer fireman
Seth Low	23d mayor of Brooklyn (1882–1885) and 92d mayor of New York City (1902–1903)
David L. Boody	26th mayor of Brooklyn (1892–1893)
The New Yorker	—
William L. Strong b) *Robert A. Van Wyck* c) William L. Strong	Strong was the 90th mayor of New York (1895–1897); Van Wyck was the 91st mayor (1898–1901), the first following the 1898 consolidation of Greater New York
Abram S. Hewitt	87th mayor (1887–1888)
George B. McClellan	93d mayor (1904–1909); son of the general
Thomas Willett	first mayor of New York; served two one-year appointed terms, 1665 and 1667
James Duane	44th mayor (1784–1789); elected by vote of the Common Council
Cornelius W. Lawrence	61st mayor (1834–1837); the first to be directly elected by popular vote
William J. Gaynor	94th mayor (1910–1913)
John Purroy Mitchel	95th mayor (1914–1917)
John J. Harvey	member FDNY Marine Division; died in the line of duty
Fire Fighter	memorializes all FDNY members who died in the line of duty
John D. McKean	member FDNY Marine Division; died in the line of duty
Harry M. Archer, MD	late FDNY medical officer
H. Sylvia A.H.G. Wilkes	late benefactor of FDNY

Fireboat	Identify of Namesake
Senator Robert F. Wagner	U.S. Senator (1927–1949)
Governor Alfred E. Smith	Governor of New York (1919–1921; 1923–1929)
John H. Glenn, Jr.	first U.S. astronaut to orbit the earth
Kevin C. Kane	member FDNY; died in the line of duty
John P. Devaney	member FDNY; died in the line of duty
Alfred E. Ronaldson	member FDNY; died in the line of duty

Sources: *The Encyclopedia of New York City* (New Haven: Yale University Press, 1995), pp. 735–744; Clarence E. Meek, "F.D.N.Y. Flotilla," *WNYF* (1969) 1st Issue, pp. 16–21.

APPENDIX F
Selected "Workers" Involving FDNY Fireboats*

Date	Incident	Fireboats Involved
6/30/00	Fire on Hoboken piers used by North German Lloyd spreads to four vessels; *Kaiser Wilheim Der Grosse* saved, but *Bremen, Saale* and *Main* destroyed; FDNY fireboats concentrate on vessel fires, Hoboken FD on piers; $5 million damage; 326 killed [+]	*The New Yorker* *Robert A. Van Wyck* *Zophar Mills*
11/10/02	Fire begins in shack atop Brooklyn tower Williamsburg Bridge (under construction) 300 feet above East River; spreads to temporary wooden catwalk	*David A. Boody* *William L. Strong* *Zophar Mills*
6/15/04	Wooden excursion steamboat *General Slocum* catches fire in the vicinity of Hell Gate; vessel eventually beached on North Brother Island; 1,030 killed [+]	*Zophar Mills* *Abram S. Hewitt* *William L. Strong*
5/27/11	Dreamland Park in Coney Island burns to the ground; fireboats called to supply water for high pressure hydrant system	*Seth Low* *Zophar Mills* *The New Yorker*
7/30/16	Fire in Jersey City rail yard containing munitions enroute to allies in Europe, followed by violent explosions that level 13 warehouses; 5-inch shells hit Statue of Liberty, another shell penetrates wheelhouse of *Strong;* six killed, $20 million property damage; death toll low because incident took place after midnight; known as Black Tom Explosion and later determined to be sabotage	*The New Yorker* *William L. Strong* *Thomas Willett*

Date	Incident	Fireboats Involved
5/6/32	Fire on North River Pier 53, occupied by Cunard Line, but no vessels involved; fire alarms; called worst pier fire in city's history; one fatality[+]	*John J. Harvey* *Thomas Willett* *James Duane*
8/19/41	Fire on Pier 27, Brooklyn; quickly spreads to NY & Cuba Mail Line freighter *Panuco*; fire alarms; damage in excess of $1 million; 34 killed	*William J. Gaynor* *Fire Fighter* *Abram S. Hewitt* *William L. Strong*
2/9/42	*U.S.S. Lafayette*, the former French superliner *Normandie*, catches fire and later capsizes at North River Pier 88; five alarms[+]	*James Duane* *John J. Harvey* *Fire Fighter*
4/24/43	Freighter *El Estro*, loaded with munitions, catches fire in Bayonne, NJ; entire metropolitan area in peril; vessel towed to safe anchorage and sunk	*Fire Fighter* *John J. Harvey*
9/28/47	Fire on Pier 57, North river; occupied by Grace Line, but no vessels involved; over 140 firemen injured; exceeded 5/6/32 fire on Pier 53 in damage and intensity	*George B. McClellan* *Fire Fighter* *Thomas Willett* *Abram S. Hewitt* *William L. Strong*
12/3/56	Fire and explosion on Luckenbach pier, 35 Street, Brooklyn; nine killed; *Fire Fighter* damaged; equivalent of nine alarms	*Fire Fighter* *William J. Gaynor* *John D. McKean* *James Duane*
6/16/66	Tanker *Texaco Massachusetts*, outbound in ballast, collides with inbound tanker *Alva Cape* at point where Newark Bay meets Kill Van Kull; *Alva Cape*, carrying 4.2 million gallons of naptha, explodes and catches fire; 34 killed; 6-28-66: towed to anchorage in Gravesend Bay for off-loading of 122,000 barrels of naptha still aboard, *Cape Alva* suffers a series of explosions; *Smith* damaged; 4 killed on board *Alva Cape*; *Alva Cape* towed to sea on 7/2/66 and sunk 150 miles off Cape May, NJ by gunfire from *USCGC Spencer*[+]	*Alfred E. Smith* *Fire Fighter* *John D. McKean*

Date	Incident	Fireboats Involved
6/2/73	Outbound containership *Sea Witch* collides with tanker *Esso Brussels* while latter at anchor in the Narrows; *Brussels* carrying two million cubic feet of crude oil from Nigeria; as oil flows out of *Brussels*, it catches fire, sending a column of flames 100 feet into the air; five alarms; 16 killed	*Fire Fighter* *John D. McKean* *John J. Harvey* *Harry M. Archr* *Robert F. Wagner*

* = selected for their representational value; no claim that these are the most severe incidents FDNY fireboats have worked

+ = described in greater detail in the text

APPENDIX G
Vessel Roster:
Coney Island Steamboats

Off. No. Hull Type	Name(s)	Dimensions Gross Tons	Built at Year Yard	Disposition Notes
1. Vessels Owned by the Iron Steamboat Company				
125903 iron st.p.	*Cetus* a) *Reliance*	213 x 32 x 10 847	Phila. 1881 Cramp & Sons	abandoned, 1935 [1]
125904 iron st.p.	*Cepheus* b) *Shamrock*	213 x 32 x 11 882	Chester 1881 Roach & Son	abandoned, 1935 [1]
125900 iron st.p.	*Cygnus*	212 x 31 x 11 857	Chester 1881 Roach & Son	abandoned, 1935 [2]
150214 iron st.p.	*Pegasus* b) *America* c) *Mattaponi River* (barge)	211 x 32 x 10 847	Phila. 1881 Cramp & Sons	see note [3]
150213 iron st.p.	*Perseus* b) *Columbia*	211 x 32 x 10 847	Phila. 1881 Cramp & Sons	abandoned, 1935 [1]
115774 iron st.p.	*Sirius* b) *Ambassador* c) *Pamunkey River* (barge)	229 x 32 x 11 993	Chester 1881 Roach & Son	see note [4]
145253 iron st.p.	*Taurus* b) *Commodore*	226 x 32 x 11 916	Phila. 1881 Cramp & Son	abandoned, 1937 [5]
2. Other Steamboats				
125592 wood st.p.	*Columbia* b) *President*	260 x 39 x 12 1468	Greenpoint 1877 Englis	abandoned, 1925 [6]

Off. No. Hull Type	Name(s)	Dimensions Gross Tons	Built at Year Yard	Disposition Notes
85541 wood st.p.	*Grend Republic*	282 x 41 x 13 1760	Brooklyn 1878 Englis	lost (fire), 1924 [7]
116712 steel st.p.	*Empire State* a) *Shinnecock* c) *Town of Hull*	234 x 35 x 14	Wilmington 1896	abandoned, 1944 [8]

Explanation of abbreviations:

Type: st.p. = steam engine, paddle-wheel propulsion

Notes:

[1] Sold to Union Navigation Co., 1933; name changed, 1933; single-cylinder vertical beam engines with the following cylinder dimensions: *Cetus* and *Perseus* (52″ x 132″); *Cepheus* (53″ x 144″).

[2] Sold to James A. Holt, 1933; sold to Anna K. Muller, 1933; single-cylinder vertical beam engine (53″ x 144″).

[3] Sold to Union Navigation, 1933; name changed to 'b', 1933; abandoned, 1935; re-documented as unpowered barge at Newport News under name 'b', 1938; name changed to 'c', 1940; barge dismantled, 1956; single-cylinder vertical beam engine (52″ x 132″).

[4] Sold to Herbert S. Ross, 1933; name changed to 'b', 1933; apparently run for, but not owned by, Union Navigation; abandoned, 1935; re-documented as unpowered barge at Newport News under name 'c', 1940; barge dismantled, 1956; single-cylinder vertical beam engine (53″ x 144″).

[5] Sold to Herbert S. Ross, 1933; sold to Union Navigation Co., 1933; name changed, 1933; re-conveyed to Herbert S. Ross (trustee), ca. 1935; single-cylinder vertical beam engine (52″ x 144″).

[6] Purchased from Baltimore & Ohio R.R., 1910, and used on New York-Long Branch route; earlier owned by R. Cornell White and Knickerbocker Steamboat Company; sold to Delaware River interests, 1902; name changed, 1915. Ran for Iron Steamboat between 1900 and 1902 while owned by New Jersey Navigation Co., a subsidiary of Iron Steamboat; single-cylinder vertical beam engine.

[7] Purchased from Knickerbocker Steamboat Co., 1906, and used primarily on New York-Rockaway Beach route; sold to Highlands Navigation Co., ca. 1917; destroyed by fire in New York at the foot of West 155 Street on April 16, 1924. Ran for Iron Steamboat between 1906 and 1917 while owned by New Jersey Navigation Co., a subsidiary of Iron Steamboat; single-cylinder vertical beam engine (76″ x 144″).

[8] Never ran for Iron Steamboat, merely Union Navigation (see text); owned by Montauk Steamboat Co. (i.e., Long Island R.R.) and Montauk & New London Steamboat Co. under name 'a', 1896 through ca. 1930, and by Nantasket-Boston Steamboat Co. under name 'c'; also ran for Empire State Excursion Steamship Corp. of New Jersey under name 'b'; powered by two-cylinder compound engine.

APPENDIX H
New York-Bermuda Cruise Ships

Name(s)	Dimensions Gross Tons	Built Year Yard	Disposition or Current Operator (Home Port) [Notes]
1. Furness, Withy, Ltd.			
Fort Hamilton a) *Bermudian* b) *Stella D'Italia*	425 x 50 x 25 5,884	Sunderland 1904 Laing & Sons	Sold to Italian interests, 1926; scrapped, 1953 [1]
Fort St. George a) *Wandilla* c) *Cesarea* d) *Arno*	411 x 56 x 34 7,785	Glasgow 1912 Beardmore	Sold to Italian interests, 1935; sunk by British aircraft off Tobruk, 1942 [2]
Fort Victoria a) *Willochra*	411 x 56 x 34 7,784	Glasgow 1912 Beardmore	Lost (collision) at entrance to New York Harbor, 1929 (see text) [2]
Bermuda	525 x 74 x 41 19,086	Belfast 1927 Workman, Clark	Lost (fire), Belfast, 1931 (see text) [3]
Monarch of Bermuda b) *New Australia* c) *Arkadia*	553 x 76 x 39 22,424	Newcastle 1931 Vickers, Armstrong	Sold to British Gov't., 1947; later sold to Greek interests; scrapped, 1966 [4]
Queen of Bermuda	553 x 76 x 39 22, 575	Barrow 1933 Vickers, Armstrong	Scrapped, 1966 [4]
Ocean Monarch b) *Varna*	516 x 73 x 24 13,970	Newcastle 1951 Vickers, Armstrong	Sold to Bulgarian interests, ca. 1966; lost (fire) 1981 [5]

Name(s)	Dimensions Gross Tons	Built Year Yard	Disposition or Current Operator (Home Port)	[Notes]
2. Contemporary Vessels				
Dreamward	624 x 94 x 22 39,217	St. Nazaire 1992 Chantiers	Norwegian Cruise Line (Nassau)	[6]
Zenith	682 x 95 x 24 47,255	Papenburg 1992 Meyer Werft	Celebrity Cruise Line (Monrovia)	[7]
Meridian a) *Galileo* *Galilei* b) *Galileo*	702 x 94 x 28 30,440	Monfalcone 1963 Cantieri Riuniti	Celebrity Cruise Line (Nassau)	[8]
Song of America	703 x 93 x 22 37,584	Helsinki 1982 Wartsila	Royal Caribbean Cruise Line (Oslo)	[9]
Royal Majesty	568 x 91 x 20 32,396	Turku 1992 Kvaerner Masa	Majesty Cruise Line (Panama)	[10]

Notes:

[1] Built for Quebec Steamship Co.; powered by two 3-cylinder triple expansion steam engines (26″, 43″, 71″ x 48″).

[2] Built for Adelaide Steamship Co., of Australia; powered by two 4-cylinder quadruple expansion steam engines (23″, 34″, 50″, 72″ x 54″).

[3] Powered by two 8-cylinder opposed-piston Doxford diesels; quadruple screw.

[4] Powered by two Fraser & Chalmers steam turbines, electric drive; quadruple screw.

[5] Powered by four Vickers-Armstrong steam turbines, direct drive; twin screw.

[6] Powered by two 6-cylinder MAN/B&W diesels (15.7″ x 21.3″), two MAN/B&W 8-cylinder diesels (15.7″ x 21.3″); see text; sister ship of *Windward*.

[7] Powered by two 6-cylinder MAN/B&W diesels (15.7″ x 21.3″), two MAN/B&W 9-cylinder diesels (15.7″ x 21.3″); sister ship of *Horizon*.

[8] Powered by four steam turbines; direct drive.

[9] Powered by four 8-cylinder Sulzer diesels (15.7″ x 18.9″).

[10] Powered by four 6-cylinder Wartsila diesels (15.7″ x 22.8″).

Index of Vessels

Index of Subjects